Philosophical Problems of Classical Film Theory

PHILOSOPHICAL PROBLEMS OF CLASSICAL FILM THEORY

—

NOËL CARROLL

Princeton University Press

Princeton, New Jersey

Published by Princeton University Press,
41 William Street, Princeton, New Jersey 08540
In the United Kingdom: Princeton University Press,
Guildford, Surrey
ISBN 0–691–07321–X
Publication of this book has been aided by the
Whitney Darrow Fund of Princeton University Press
This book has been composed in Bembo

To my parents,
for their unstinting goodwill

Contents

Preface

A great many people have helped in the creation of this book. My mentor in cinema studies, Annette Michelson, introduced me to film theory and warmly encouraged my first essays on André Bazin. Her generosity to me in every way has been inestimable.

P. Adams Sitney, though always skeptical about the prospects for a fully cognitive discipline of film theory, has been indulgent enough to read a number of the essays that have become part of this book, and his astute and articulate criticisms have been extremely useful. Jonathan Buchsbaum, Tony Pipolo, and Stuart Liebman also have discussed my arguments in ways that have forced me to clarify my ideas. And David Bordwell deserves special thanks. My ongoing conversation with him over the last decade has touched every area of my thinking about film. Our exchanges have been of immense profit to me (and to the phone company).

A number of philosophers also have made direct contributions to my work. George Dickie introduced me to the professional study of aesthetics, guided me through the study of each of its major areas, and directed every stage of the first draft of this text. Paul Guyer, Irving Thalberg, Jr., Peter Kivy, Dale Jamieson, and Alan Casebier each read the manuscript in toto, saving me from many embarrassments, both stylistic and substantive. Paul Guyer made particularly constructive suggestions about the reworking of Chapter One, while Dale Jamieson proposed several major structural improvements. Peter Kivy met with me before and after each chapter was composed, and we had long and fruitful discussions about every aspect of the book. He performed the Herculean task of copyediting the first two drafts of the text. I also owe him a major intellectual debt. For it was through his work on music that I learned the value of isolating the philosophical issues of an art form by means of tracing its historically evolving debates. I also am grateful to Paul Ziff and especially to the late Monroe Beardsley for encouraging me to return to philosophy.

Sally Banes has helped me in every way imaginable: she considered my every argument with her characteristic vigor, copyedited the final draft, and, more than once, rescued the footnotes from our omnivorous computer. Without her support, intellectual and emotional, the book could not have been written.

Carole Pipolo produced the final typescript with her typical precision and expertise.

All these people made the book better; none made it worse. For any shortcomings that may remain, I bear sole responsibility.

Noël Carroll
Wesleyan University
1986

Philosophical Problems of Classical Film Theory

Introduction

The Structure

of Film Theory

—

Considering the short history of film—the medium is less than a hundred years old—it is suprising that the field has amassed such a large body of theoretical writing. Proportionally speaking, film theory, which, in all likelihood, only began around 1909, comprises more titles than the theoretical wings of such ancient arts as dance and theater. Perhaps only literature is more theoretically garrulous than film. One reason for this is that film is an art form that was invented not only in living memory but self-consciously. It is a medium that had to prove that it was an art form—as psychology, another recent arrival, had to prove that it was a science. That is, film had to legitimize its place in our culture. And the way that it initially set about getting itself taken seriously was to prove that it was an art—an art on a par with its seven predecessors. This was the first task of film theory. Moreover, such a mission brought film theory in contact with philosophy almost immediately, since proving that film is an art requires making philosophical assumptions about such things as the nature of art and the conditions a medium must meet in order to be regarded as an autonomous art form. As specific film theorists worked out their various theories, they also assumed or set forth additional philosophical theses concerning the nature of representation, expression, photography, aesthetic quality, artistic realism, and the like. Film theory, as a result, is peppered with philosophical assumptions and arguments.

The aim of this study is to isolate some of these philosophical assumptions and arguments in seminal works of three film theorists: Rudolf Arnheim, André Bazin, and V. F. Perkins.[1] In each case, I will isolate the philosophical claims of the theorist in question and examine the cogency of his posi-

1. Rudolf Arnheim, *Film*, translated by L. M. Sieveking and I.F.D. Morrow (London: Faber and Faber, 1933); *Film as Art* (Berkeley: University of California Press, 1957; "On the Nature of Photography," *Critical Inquiry* (Fall 1974). André Bazin, *What Is Cinema?* edited and translated by Hugh Gray (Berkeley: University of California Press, 1967, 1971), two volumes. V. F. Perkins, *Film as Film* (Baltimore: Penguin, 1972).

tion in the argumentative style of analytic philosophy. I have chosen Arnheim and Bazin as subjects for this type of analysis because, though it may be said that their philosophical argumentation leaves much to be desired, they nevertheless represent positions on the nature of photographic recording (indeed, they represent diametrically opposed positions) that are so deeply entrenched in our intellectual culture that these arguments seem always to return whenever discussion of the photographic arts is broached. Therefore, it is philosophically worthwhile to dismantle these influential positions as effectively as possible while also attempting to introduce certain distinctions into the discussion of cinematic representation and realism that will dispose of the kind of perennial, yet misguided debate represented by the rivalry between the likes of Arnheim and Bazin.

Both Arnheim and Bazin are extremely important and exemplary figures in the history of film theory. Consequently, one important task of this study is to exhibit the centrality of these theorists in the history of thinking about film. Although setting the historical stage that makes these theories most intelligible is an abiding concern of mine, it is not my primary one. My major goal will be to subject the theories in question to philosophical analysis. In the cases of Arnheim and Bazin, where the material is somewhat dated, I undertake this because the theories and their guiding tenets and prejudices are still influential.[2] In the case of Perkins, the theory is more or

2. The influence and currency of the Bazinian and Arnheimian positions are especially apparent in recent debates in photographic theory. Bazinian prejudices are represented in, for just two examples, Susan Sontag's *On Photography* (New York: Farrar, Straus and Giroux, 1977) and Roger Scruton's "Photography and Representation," in *Critical Inquiry* (Spring 1981). Joel Snyder attacked this neo-Bazinian line—making explicit references to film theory—in an unpublished paper delivered at the national meetings of the American Society for Aesthetics in Tampa, Florida, in fall of 1982. Snyder adopted an Arnheimian line. Arnheim, himself, has recently developed a theory of photography from his theory of film (see footnote 1 for the reference). Thus, my present study has direct bearing on the recent theoretical-philosophical debate concerning photography. It should also be noted that in terms of film theory the Bazinian theory is not dead; Stanley Cavell

less contemporary. Moreover, from the standpoint of Anglo-American philosophical aesthetics, his is the most intelligibly constructed film theory—that is, the one most comprehensible in light of the concerns of contemporaneous Anglo-American aesthetics—and yet it has not been subjected to any detailed analysis. Thus, it seems worthy of examination.

Film theory is not an area that has been a major topic of concern for analytic philosophers. As might be expected, the available work in this area lacks the rigor of certain other areas of philosophy. By addressing some of the strongest historical and contemporary voices of the field and by confronting some of the most persistently held presumptions about the nature of film, I hope to make a philosophical step in the direction of introducing rigor into the theoretical dicussion of the subject.

This volume is divided into an introduction, three central chapters, and a conclusion. Each of the three central chapters is devoted to the discussion of a single film theorist. Each chapter opens with an exposition of the theory in question, including a detailed discussion of its historical setting that I hope clarifies both the issues and the contextual importance of the theory at hand. I also attempt to expound each theory in its strongest form. The bulk of each chapter, however, is spent in critical discussion of the specific theory under examination.

In Chapter One I examine Rudolf Arnheim's works on film. Though Arnheim wrote on film after the introduction of sound, his work looks back to silent film, which he considers a true candidate for recognition as an art form while heaping disdain on the talkie. Arnheim's original work, *Film als Kunst* (translated as *Film*), was published in the thirties. I will not focus on this book but a shortened edition of it called *Film as Art*, which was published in English in the fifties. My reason for this is that Arnheim rephrased arguments from his earlier work that he no longer found acceptably expressed

---

has designed original defenses for Bazin in his *The World Viewed* (New York: Viking, 1971).

when he edited the shortened English version. Thus, the latter is the authoritative statement of Arnheim's position.

I present Arnheim as the major representative of what might be (loosely) thought of as the "silent-film paradigm" for thinking about cinema. The bias of silent-film theorists—including S. M. Eisenstein, Lev Kuleshov, V. I. Pudovkin, Hugo Munsterberg, Bela Balazs, and the French impressionists[3] as well as Arnheim—is that the most aesthetically significant feature of the film medium is its capacity to manipulate reality, that is, to rearrange and thereby reconstitute the profilmic event (the event that transpires in front of the camera). In this, the silent-film theorists—whether they were writing during or after the period of silent film—were erecting theories that best characterized the actual achievements of the silent film, while also neutralizing the deep prejudices against photographic art that reigned throughout the high culture of the West. I explain how, as a representative of the silent-film paradigm, Arnheim shapes his theory to refute arguments against the possibility of film art based on the claim that *the mechanical* and *the artistic* are unalterably opposed.

The specific philosophical issues discussed include Arnheim's commitment to Lessing-type arguments for medium specificity (an essay in *Film as Art* is entitled "A New *Laocoön*: Artistic Composites and the Talking Film"), his espousal of an expression theory of art, his account of expressive qualities

3. S. M. Eisenstein, *Film Essays and a Lecture,* edited and translated by Jay Leyda (New York: Praeger, 1970); *Film Form,* edited and translated by Jay Leyda (New York: Harcourt, Brace and World, 1949); *Film Sense,* edited and translated by Jay Leyda (New York: Harcourt, Brace and World, 1942); *Notes of a Film Director,* translated by X. Danko (New York: Dover, 1970). Lev Kuleshov, *Kuleshov on Film,* translated by R. Levaco (Berkeley: University of California Press, 1974). V. I. Pudovkin, *Film Technique and Film Acting,* translated by I. Montague (London: Vision Press, 1954). Hugo Munsterberg, *The Film: A Psychological Study* (New York: Dover, 1969). Bela Belazs, *Theory of Film: Character and Growth of a New Art* (New York: Dover, 1970). For information on the French impressionists in film see David Bordwell's *French Impressionist Cinema: Film Culture, Film Theory, Film Style,* doctoral dissertation, University of Iowa, 1974.

in art in terms of physiognomic properties and his (and most other theorists') rather ill-defined notion of film-as-merely-mechanical-reproduction-of-reality as the central contrast to film-as-art. At times in this chapter, I will refer to Arnheim's *Art and Visual Perception* in order to establish the theoretical foundations for his claims about film.[4] I also will argue against each of Arnheim's philosophical tenets.

André Bazin is the subject of Chapter Two. Bazin is probably the most influential theorist and critic in the history of film. He directly encouraged the emergence of the generation of critic/filmmakers that includes Truffaut, Godard, Chabrol, Rohmer, and many others. His defense of depth-of-field photography and the long take largely shaped the evaluative standards of many film critics until the mid-seventies. Even today when his theories appear to have been rejected by film academics, those theories live on in a perverse way. The most fashionable academic theories reject what they castigate as the "illusionism" of the commercial, narrative cinema, and, in this, they reject some of the things that Bazin stood for. Yet, when these theorists give an account of the false beliefs that they think the narrative "representational" cinema engenders, they rely on a Bazinian account of the way in which cinema is perceived by audiences. That is, many of Bazin's opponents disagree not so much with Bazin's account of the effect of film on spectators but with the moral evaluation they attribute to that effect.

Historically, Bazin represents what might be thought of as the "sound-film paradigm" of cinema theory. This position arose in explicit opposition to the silent-film paradigm; indeed, some might regard it as simply a reaction formation. Given the cultural context of pre–World War II aesthetics, silent-film theorists denigrated the recording/photographic element of cinema. Sound-film theorists—including Kracauer and Cavell as well as Bazin—celebrate what the silent-film theorist represses. And in the case of Bazin, of course,

4. Rudolf Arnheim, *Art and Visual Perception: A Psychology of the Creative Eye* (Berkeley: University of California Press, 1967).

this is partially motivated by a contextually rooted concern for finding a way to defend the achievements of the emerging styles of sound cinema from the prohibitions of silent-film theory.

Bazin was not only a film theorist; he was first and foremost a film critic, but I will not attempt to canvas the totality of his writings on film. I will dwell only on those articles that are generally regarded as the core of his film theory. It is often pointed out that in his criticism Bazin relaxed the strictures of his theoretical articles. It may be further argued that since Bazin reversed himself or was willing to contradict his theory when confronted with a great film, that it is unfair to belabor the inadequacies of his theory. I do not wish to be unfair to Bazin, yet for the purposes of a consideration of film theory, I am not primarily concerned with Bazin's criticism, which, admittedly, was often brilliant. Thus, I will not consider the arguments, based on the criticism, that Bazin didn't really believe his own theory. For I am concerned with the theory— the theory that has influenced so many succeeding theorists (for example, Cavell)—rather than with the presentation of Bazin's total intellectual life.

The primary philosophical issues discussed are Bazin's account of the nature of cinematic representation and his characterization of film realism. I also will examine some of Stanley Cavell's recent arguments in support of a Bazinian position on the ontological status of film. Though Cavell falls into the chronological span of contemporary film theory, his position is actually that of a sound-film realist like Bazin. Cavell, perhaps, could be called the last of the sound-film realists. I will also suggest some distinctions about different types of representation in cinema that I believe will help to clarify and finally dispell the conflict between silent-and sound-film theorists by showing that there need not be a single account of cinematic representation. This recognition, I believe, enables us to see that silent-film theorists have a good account of certain types of cinematic representation while sound-film theorists have an equally insightful account of other forms of cinematic representation. Both theories of cin-

ematic representation are useful for the relevant cases but neither succeeds as an exclusive account of representation in
film.

In Chapter Three I examine V. F. Perkins's *Film as Film*.
Perkins rejects previous attempts at film theory on the basis
of an argument much like those that are associated, in philosophical aesthetics, with the open-concept theory of art. Perkins holds that the aim of film theory is not the discovery of
the essence of film but, rather, metacriticism. He believes that
film theory should construct general premises that film critics
can use in their work; the aim of film theory is to enable film
criticism to conduct itself rationally. To this end, Perkins develops a theory of film evaluation the purpose of which is to
rationally ground film criticism. I will question whether Perkins succeeds in escaping the essentialist bias of classical film
theory, and discuss specific philosophical questions about (1)
the idea that the task of film theory is metacriticism and (2)
the adequacy of a formalist (film qua film) system of aesthetic
evaluation.

In my opinion, Perkins represents an attempt to reconcile
the kind of oppositions that one finds between proponents of
the silent-film paradigm (exemplified here by Arnheim) and
proponents of the sound-film paradigm (exemplified by Bazin). Perkins's attempt to combine aspects of these two trends
in classical film theory might be seen as analogous to (but not
identical with) the project of Jean Mitry. In this respect, Perkins is a significant figure because he represents a moment of
dialectical synthesis within the species of film theorizing that
has come to be called classical film theory.

Roughly, classical film theory refers to the conduct and
conversation of film theory prior to the advent of semiotic
and poststructural theories of film. These latter theories came
to dominate academic film literature in the seventies. Moreover, these latter theories explicitly disavow the tendencies—
particularly toward essentialism—found in classical film theory. Thus, the reader may well ask for my reasons for devot-
ing so much attention to a conversation within film studies
that many experts believe is obsolete.

My first defense of this project is that, although it is true that many contemporary film theorists do not concern themselves with the classical tradition, it seems to me that this is often done without proper consideration of the arguments proposed within that tradition. Like film buffs, film theorists are frequently fickle, opting for what is new and fashionable without carefully examining the intellectual issues involved. Classical film theory may be riddled with error. Yet, the meticulous assessment of those errors, rarely rigorously undertaken in the past, will be beneficial—if only to demonstrate the dangers inherent in certain strategies of theorizing. Furthermore, outside the narrow confines of academic film theory, the types of prejudices and presuppositions found in classical film theory—about such things as the nature of photographic representation—are still influential and, therefore, warrant detailed criticism. Moreover, as the contemporary paradigm in film theory can be—as it already has been—questioned, researchers must again ask what, if anything, of value is salvageable from the classical tradition.

One major, *ostensible* difference between contemporary film theory and classical film theory is that the latter gravitates towards essentialism.[5] That is, the classical film theorists proceed by means of isolating and explicating cinema-specific characteristics and goals of the film medium in general or, in particular, of film expression, film representation, filmed fiction, and film criticism. Throughout the body of the text, and in the conclusion, I resist this tendency in classical film theory. In this, I am at least superficially in agreement with the stated bias of contemporary film theory. However, despite this correspondence, I should not be identified with the reign-

5. The reason for the italicized "ostensible" above is that though certain contemporary film theorists claim they are anti-essentialist, they nevertheless adopt essentialist analyses. This is apparent in Christian Metz's "The Imaginary Signifier," in his *Imaginary Signifier* (Bloomington: University of Indiana Press, 1981). I attack Metzian methodological essentialism in my review of his book in the *Journal of Aesthetics and Art Criticism* (Winter 1985) 211–16. Metz's essentialist approach is followed unabashedly in John Ellis's *Visible Fictions* (London: Routledge and Kegan Paul, 1983).

ing program in film theory. I have written against this project at length; and I am now preparing a book about the fads and fallacies that possess contemporary, as opposed to classical, film theory.[6] The arguments propounded herein against classical film theory should not be taken as implicitly endorsing the extravagances of contemporary film theory. Classical film theory is wrongheaded, but the answer is not poststructural film theory, a claim that I hope to redeem in subsequent writings. Moreover, the failures of classical film theorizing can be instructive for anyone who wishes to think theoretically about film. That is, we can begin to increase our understanding of film in the very process of correcting the errors of classical theory.

Before engaging each of the three theories individually and in detail, it will be worthwhile to consider the kind of film theory that is exemplified across the work of Arnheim, Bazin, and Perkins. These three theories share a similar structure, indeed a structure that appears common to the work of most classical film theorists.[7] Conceiving of film theories as a series of answers to abstract questions, we can describe the structure of theories under consideration by noting that they all both address the *same central questions and expect the answers to these questions to be related logically in the same way*.

The first question that these theories ask is "What is the determinant or crucial feature of film?" Bazin, for instance, answered this question by emphasizing film's capacity to record profilmic reality.

Often this question has been answered by invoking the notion of an essence, that is, in the idiom of an attribute that an object must have if it is to be identified as a film. The idea of the "cinematic," for example, as it is generally used, falls back

6. Noël Carroll, "Address to the Heathen," *October*, no. 23 (Winter 1982, 89–163; "Reply to Heath," *October*, no. 27 (Winter 1983), 81–102; and *Mystifying Movies: Fads and Fallacies in Contemporary Film Theory* (New York: Columbia University Press, forthcoming).
7. This structure is also discussed in my "Film History and Film Theory: An Outline for an Institutional Theory of Film," *The Film Reader*, no. 4 (1979), 81–96.

on some idea of the essential nature of cinema. But the question is broader, I believe, than the essentialist-type answers it has often received. A film theorist need not presuppose that there are such things as essences. Framing the question in terms of "determinant characteristics" leaves open the possibilities that film may have no essential feature, that it may have more than one essential feature, and that even if it has one or more essential feature(s), it may not be that this feature (or features) should be determinant in our thinking about cinematic processes. A case in point: Perkins *ostensibly* argues that film has no essence.

The question can be answered in either the singular or the plural. For example, the theory defended in Perkin's *Film as Film* fundamentally argues that cinema has two determinant characteristics: the capacities both to reproduce and to reconstitute profilmic reality. Also, though the history of film theory leads us to expect a positive answer to this question, a theorist could resolve it by denying that film has any determinant characteristic whatsoever. For Arnheim, Bazin, and Perkins, however, it is possible to identify a determinant characteristic for each of them. And, moreover, classical film theory does appear biased towards essentialism.

Another question answered either explicitly or implicitly in the major film theories is "What is the value or role of cinema?" Arnheim, along with such historical figures as Munsterberg and Balazs, overtly gives "art" as the answer to this question, while Perkins presupposes a similar commitment. The theorist's answer to the question of the role or value of cinema is especially important because it places the theorist in a particularly enabling conceptual position for discussing the determinant feature of film. If one takes art as the value of cinema, then one's characterization of the nature of art can be used to pick out the determinant feature of the medium.

There is a strong relation between the answers to the first and second questions stated above—namely, the items listed as determinant features will generally be items that are instrumental in realizing or actualizing the value or role the theorist names for cinema. For example, Bazin claims that the role of film is to immortalize the past; this commitment enables him to zero-in on recording as the determinant factor because it is the most plausible means to the end that he adduces for cinema. Of course, a theoretician may hold that film has more than one value or role. Indeed, it is logically possible to deny that film has any role, though it does seem very unlikely that such a large social institution doesn't have at least some function, even it if is a thoroughly venal or pernicious one. And, in any case, Arnheim, Bazin, and Perkins each assign clear-cut roles to cinema.

The last question asked by most film theories is really a brace of questions iterated again and again so that they occupy the bulk of the text of most theories. It is "What are the processes of articulation in film in relation to the previous two answers?" Dealing with this question usually involves drawing up lists of articulatory processes and relating each process back to the determinant characteristic and the value of cinema. A given theory may include accounts of types of montage or types of spatial disjunctions or types of camera angles or all of these. Though a theory may not be complete in this regard, the question could be exhaustively answered by considering each dimension of cinematic articulation (composition, editing, sound, and so on) and by charting the basic variables or structures open to manipulation in each of these dimensions (the close-up, the long take, parallel editing, jump-cuts, and so forth). The elaboration of these taxonomies can consume the largest amount of space in the exposition of a theory; this is certainly the case with Arnheim and Perkins.

Film theories are full of available schemas for the presentation of material cinematically; however, film theories are not simply lists. They differ from filmmaking guides or manuals, which also contain lists of structures, because film theories attempt to elucidate each process or structure of articulation in terms of its commitment to a particular determinant feature and to the value of film.

Most classical film theories—including those of Arnheim, Bazin, and Perkins—relate answers to the three basic questions in the following way: the determinant characteristic stands to the role of cinema as a means to an end, while the articulatory processes are assessed as instances of the determinant characteristic of cinema. This structure can be briefly illustrated by the theory of Hugo Munsterberg. Munsterberg holds that film is art, that art is freedom, and that the determinant characteristic of film is its capacity to mime certain mental processes that free us from mere physical existence. In treating parallel editing, Munsterberg analyzes it in terms of the way in which it frees us from an experience of sheer spatiotemporal succession. Munsterberg's theory may ultimately be incoherent but its form is instructive and can be generalized; the cinematic variables he itemizes are not only described but analyzed as instances of his proposed determinant characteristic, which, in turn, is a means by which film art realizes its goal.[8]

Film handbooks and film guides tell us some of the structures that are available to filmmakers. They may even offer practical advice like "use flat lighting for comedy."[9] But these lists and suggestions are not theoretical insofar as the items are not related to larger questions such as film's determinant characteristic and value. Film theorists, of course, have aspired to answer more abstract questions about film than the three I have enumerated. But I think that the classical texts that we now consider film theory—as opposed to artistic manifestoes and critical jeremiads—have interrelated answers to, at least, these three questions.

8. See Munsterberg, *The Film*.
9. For an example of a handbook, see Karel Reisz, *The Technique of Film Editing* (New York: Hastings House, 1968).

Chapter One

Cinematic Expression: Rudolf Arnheim and the Aesthetics of Silent Film

—

Arnheim in Perspective

"Film as Art": a note about sources

The authoritative statement of Rudolf Arnheim's theory of film is contained in *Film as Art*. This volume was published in 1957 and is the focus of the present chapter.[1] Yet despite the late date of its publication, this particular volume is my chief representative of silent-film theory. This choice requires some explanation.

Though *Film as Art* was issued in 1957, the core of the book (pages 8–160) is adapted from an earlier work, *Film als Kunst*, which was translated into English in 1933 under the title *Film*.[2] Of the relation of *Film as Art* to *Film*, Arnheim has written that

> The first part of *Film*, which develops the thesis, has worn reasonably well and is reproduced here [in *Film as Art*] practically complete under the headings "Film and Reality" and "The Making of a Film." I have omitted much of the rest: some of the chapters tangled with tasks for which respectable techniques are now available, such as my sketchy "content analysis" of the standard movie ideology; others dealt with temporary questions—for example, the early fumblings of the sound film—now mercifully forgotten. The translation of what is left has been revised sentence by sentence, and many a puzzling statement attributed to me in the earlier edition is now restored to its intended meaning. (*FAA*, 3–4)

Moreover, the remaining major essays in *Film as Art* were written in the thirties. Thus, *Film as Art* is a curious book—a work essentially of the early thirties, rewritten and adapted for the fifties. Arnheim never recanted the extremism of the

1. Rudolf Arnheim, *Film as Art* (Berkeley: University of California Press, 1957). Henceforth I will abbreviate references to this book as *FAA*.
2. Rudolf Arnheim, *Film*, translated by L. M. Sieveking and I.F.D. Morrow (London: Faber and Faber, 1933).

earlier edition. If anything, the passage of time radicalized Arnheim's position as a silent-film advocate during a period when that species was—and is—effectively extinct. This introductory remark shows that Arnheim stood by his improbable guns.

> As to my own position . . . I find that my predictions have been borne out. The talking film is still a hybrid medium, which lives from whatever fragments are salvageable from the beauty of the creatures, things, and thoughts it reproduces; the color film, incapable of controlling its multidimensional instrument, has never gone beyond tasteful "color schemes"; the stereoscopic film is still unrealizable technically, and in its recent substitutes has increased the realism of the performance to the extent of requiring first-aid stations in the theaters without exploiting the new resources artistically; the wide screen, finally, has gone a long way toward destroying the last pretenses of a meaningfully organized image. The critics, to be sure, still find occasion for the highest praise, but then, as a matter of survival, their standards shift with the times. In the meantime, television viewers are noticing that live performances are better than "canned" ones. This sounds like the knell of justice for the illusionists: he who vies with nature deserves to lose! (*FAA*, 5)

Furthermore, even as recently as the mid-seventies, Arnheim has reaffirmed his endorsement of the view he formed of the film in the twenties.[3] In short, the condensed version of Arnheim's 1933 book, *Film as Art*, though published in the fifties, remains the clearest reflection of the aesthetic principles of the silent film—an art form that disappeared during the transition from the twenties to the thirties. This means, among other things, that the book responds polemically to some of the earliest debates that centered on the film medium in its attempt to legitimize itself as an art form.

3. Rudolf Arnheim, "On the Nature of Photography," *Critical Inquiry* 1 (September 1974), 149-61.

The context of Arnheim's theory of film

The lateness of the publication of *Film as Art*—Arnheim's considered statement of his argument for silent film—certainly confirms Hegel's dictum that "The owl Minerva spreads her wings at dusk." *Film as Art* is essentially a work of silent film theory and as such must be viewed in the context of the debate over whether film could be art—a debate that lasted from the turn of the century into the thirties. This debate, in turn, has its origin in the belief that photography—of which cinema was regarded to be a simple extension—could not be art. Historically, the task of silent-film theory was to overcome certain prejudices against cinema, prejudices based on the premise that it could not be an art because it was nothing but mere mechanical reproduction.

The prejudice against cinema derived from the fact that a major constituent of the new medium was photography. Many theorists and critics of the nineteenth and early twentieth centuries held that photography could not be an art form because it was nothing but a copying process. Charles Blanc wrote: "What is drawing? Is it a pure imitation of form? If it were that, the most faithful of drawings would be the best, and consequently no other copy would be preferable to the image fixed on the daguerreotype plate or traced mechanically or drawn by means of a diagraph. However, neither the diagraph nor tracing nor the camera will give you a drawing comparable to that by Leonardo, Raphael, or Michelangelo."[4] Emile Zola repeated the same sentiments: "The individual element, man, is infinitely variable; as much as in his creation as in his temperaments. If temperament had not existed, all paintings would have of necessity to be simple photos."[5] The question of whether photography was an art became the subject of a law-suit in nineteenth-century Paris, and artists including Ingres and Puvis de Chavannes presented the following position to the court:

4. Quoted in Aaron Scharf, *Art and Photography* (Baltimore: Penguin, 1975), 149.
5. Ibid.

Whereas in recent proceedings, the court was obliged to deal with the question of whether photography should be counted as fine art, and its products be given the same protection as the work of artists.

Whereas photography consists of a series of completely manual operations which no doubt require some skill in the manipulation involved, but never resulting in works which could *in any circumstances* ever be compared with those works which are the fruits of the study of art—on these grounds the undersigned artists protest against any comparison which might be made between photography and art.[6]

Photography, and by extension film, was problematic because its mechanical process aspect was said to make it impossible for the temperament and intelligence of the artist to be expressed; that is, to shine through the representation.

Diatribes against photography also flowed from what might be thought of as the growing anti-mimetic perspective that increasingly dominated vanguard fine art sensibilities in the late nineteenth and early twentieth centuries. If the slavish imitation of nature was inimicable to true fine art, then it could be argued that photography, which did its slavish copying mechanically, could not be art. Baudelaire says in the *Curiosities aesthetiques* that

In these lamentable days a new industry has arisen, which contributes not a little to confirming the stupidity in its faith and to ruining what might have remained of the divine in the French genius. The idolatrous crowd postulates an ideal worthy of itself and appropriate to its nature, that is perfectly understandable. As far as painting and sculpture are concerned, the current credo of the sophisticate public, above all in France . . . is this: "I believe in nature and I believe only in nature . . . I believe that art is and cannot be other than the exact reproduction of nature (a timid and dissenting sect wishes that re-

6. Ibid., 153.

pugnant natural objects should be excluded, things like chamber pots or skeletons). Thus, the industry that could give us a result identical with nature would be the absolute form of art." A vengeful God has granted the wishes of this multitude. Daguerre was his messiah. And now the public says to itself: "Since photography gives us all the guarantees of exactitude that we could wish (they believe that, the idiots!), then photography and art are the same thing." From that moment squalid society, like a single Narcissus, hurled itself upon the metal, to contemplate its trivial image.[7]

Baudelaire's point, in advance of twentieth-century abstractionism, is that art is not to be identified with the imitation of nature, let alone with the imitation of the beautiful in nature. Those who believe otherwise make a Philistine mistake. Misconceiving photography to be an art can only be the consequence of such Philistinism. Croce echoes this contempt of slavish mimesis in a passage somewhat more civil than Baudelaire's:

. . . if by imitation of nature be understood that art gives mechanical reproduction, more or less perfect duplicates of natural objects, in the presence of which is renewed the same tumult of impressions as that caused by natural objects, then the proposition [that art is the imitation of nature] is evidently false. The colored waxen effigies that imitate the life, before which we stand astonished in the museums where such things are shown, do not give aesthetic intuitions. Illusion and hallucination have nothing to do with the calm domain of artistic intuition. But on the other hand if an artist paint the interior of a wax-work museum, or if an actor give a burlesque portrait of a man-statue on the stage, we have the work of the spirit and artistic intuition. Finally, if photography have in it anything artistic, it will be to the extent that it transmits the intuition of the photographer, his point of view, the

7. Ibid., 145.

pose and grouping which he has striven to attain. And if photography be not quite art, that is precisely because the element of nature in it remains more or less unconquered and ineradicable. Do we ever, indeed, feel complete satisfaction before even the best of photographs? Would not an artist vary and touch up much or little, remove or add something to all of them?[8]

Like Baudelaire, Croce holds that slavish illusionism or mimesis is not enough for something to be art. Like Blanc and Zola, Croce seems to fear that the mechanical aspect of photography stands in the way of true expression.

The low esteem in which photography and film were held by turn-of-the-century connoisseurs of fine art can be exemplified by the opinions of Clive Bell, who denied that William Powell Frith's painting *Paddington Station* was art exactly because he found it to be functionally equivalent to a film.

Paddington Station is not a work of art; it is an interesting and amusing document. In it line and color are used to recount anecdotes, suggest ideas, and indicate the manners and customs of an age; they are not used to provoke aesthetic emotion. Forms and relations of forms were for Frith not objects of emotion, but means of suggesting emotion and conveying ideas.

The ideas and information conveyed by *Paddington Station* are so amusing and so well presented that the picture had considerable value and is well worth preserving. But, with the perfection of photographic processes and of the *cinematographic* [emphasis added], pictures of this sort are becoming otiose. Who doubts that one of those *Daily Mirror* photographers in collaboration with a *Daily Mail* reporter can tell us far more about "London day by day" than any Royal Academician?[9]

8. Benedetto Croce, *Aesthetic* (Boston: Nonpareil Books, 1978), 16–17. Parenthetical material has been interpolated from the opening sentence of this paragraph.
9. Clive Bell, *Art* (New York: Capricorn Books, 1958), 23.

Bell thinks that *Paddington Station* is not art because it simply documents in the manner of film. This obviously presupposes that film is not art. Indeed, photography and film are regarded as the dull underworkers of true art. With the advent of these media, fine art has been freed from the bothersome and burdensome work of representation. For example, Auguste Renoir thought that artists should thank Daguerre for freeing them from the boring task of portraiture.[10] And, we can see in Bell's stated position the foreshadowing of the idea that photography and film relieved painting from the drudgery of mimesis in such a way that painting could explore the more glorious avenues of abstraction and nonobjective imagery. Implicit in this account, of course, is the notion that film and photography are inferior media.

The authority of imitation theories of art deteriorated apace with the prestige of mimetic painting and sculpture. Various new theories of art—including formalism, reflexive modernism, and expressionism—arose to replace the defunct imitation theories. These newer theories differed in many respects from each other, but they also had one thing in common—a shared avowal that a work of art was not essentially a copy, a duplicate, or a reproduction of reality. There had to be a discernible difference between the artwork and the brute real thing it might portray—a difference marked by the addition of form or expressiveness. In short, the artwork must in some detectable way—specified by the theory in question—diverge from the real thing (where there is some such thing from which the artwork was derived). Because of this requirement—that art palpably diverge or depart from what it represents—film was disparaged by observers who said they could see no difference between what films showed and those profilmic events that caused the images in question. Film's dominant feature was its capacity to reproduce reality. But this capacity was said to be inessential to art and could even interfere with the higher effects of art—for example, the clarification of emotion or intuition or form. Insofar as film's

10. J. Renoir, *Renoir* (Paris: Hachette, 1960), 172.

only claim to fame—its only relevant feature—was said to be the mechanical reproduction of reality, film could not be an art because mechanical reproduction, automatic copying, slavish imitation, etc. was the one thing that everyone could agree was nonartistic.

The preceding arguments against film art might be thought of as coming from the direction of fine art. The argument basically asserts that film mechanically records nature—a menial, nonartistic vocation that the modern painter has foresworn. But there is another argument against film art—one that also involves the charge of mechanical recording. This charge, however, comes from the direction of theater rather than fine art, and it does not complain about mechanical recording of brute reality. The argument begins by noting that many films are in fact dramatizations. A great number of these are films of inferior plays, memorialized on celluloid. But, it is contended, where these films excel, it is because they are of superior plays, not because of the artistry of filmmaking. Superior dramatizations may be considered to be art. But when such a dramatization is embodied in celluloid, it is not the film—that is, the filmed play—that gives the object whatever art it possesses. Here it is important to recall that the kind of movie the proponent of this argument had in mind was the early *Film d'Art*—unflinching recordings of great performers, like Bernhardt and Duse, with stationary cameras stolidly cranking away from a centered position roughly the distance from the middle of the orchestra ring to the theater stage. And the assault against these pretentious films was that the films themselves were not art at all. All the artistry—where there was some—was in the various aspects of the profilmic event—the acting, blocking, writing, lighting, costuming, setting, and so on. All the film did was to record—indeed, mechanically record—the art that was in front of (not inside) the camera. The act of filming was simply the recording of a work of art, not a work of art on its own terms. The intuition here is that just as a postcard of Manet's *The Execution of the Emperor Maximilian* is not art even though the original canvas is, so a film of *Hamlet* is not art even though the performance that the film records is. The postcard and the film merely reproduce and memorialize antecedently existing artworks. They are special types of containers—in the case of film, the container is a time capsule. But one should not confuse the container with what it contains—the cookie box with the cookies. Even if the acting, plotting, blocking, and directing recorded in the film *drama* are artistic, the film is not. Film merely reproduces and mechanically preserves art rather than makes art itself.

We have all seen the type of film-documents the proponents of the preceding argument have in mind: Olivier's *Othello*, Burton's *Hamlet*, Ernie Gehr's record of Richard Foreman's *Sophia = Wisdom*. The claim of the preceding argument is that all films—all enacted fiction films—are of this sort. Most civilized people will probably now agree that this is just empirically false. At the turn of the century, however, the evidence was not so clear-cut, especially prior to the popularization of the basic conventions of film editing and narration by, first and foremost, D. W. Griffith. Many of the "prestige" films of early primitive cinema, however, might seem to run afoul of this argument. And, of course, the argument challenged defenders of film to show that film diverged or departed from the mere mechanical recording of theater and to show exactly how and where the differences between film and theater arose and operated.

These two charges—that film is but a mechanical recording either of reality or else of theater—form the fundamental problematic with which most major silent-film theorists concern themselves. And the major silent-film theorists seem to respond to these charges in pretty much the same way: they want to deny that film is mere recording of anything. But by taking this route, they seem to accept the premise that if film were mere mechanical recording, then film would not be art. It is in this way that silent-film theorists like Arnheim differ from sound-film theorists like Bazin and Kracauer (who find the art of film precisely in its capacity to mechanically record). The tendency of silent-film theorists is to attempt to meet the mere reproduction/non-art argument head-on. That is, they postulated that the relevant role or value of film is to make art. However, they buy into the notions of art espoused by the critics of film and photography. They agree that if film is to be an art it cannot be the mere mechanical recording of either realities or dramas but must in some sense depart from mere mechanical recording. Indeed, most silent-film theorists uphold the necessity of "departure" (from mere recording) as a condition for a representation to be art. This commitment more or less determines how silent-film theorists must answer their critics. They must show the skeptics that they have overlooked the many ways in which the devices and conventions of cinema diverge from mere recording in such a fashion as to allow the emergence of expressive or formal qualities.

Silent-film theorists examine at length the processes of cinematic articulation to show how these diverge from the mere recording or duplication of normal perceptual experience. Each characterizes the processes differently, but all the major silent-film theorists—such as Munsterberg, Balazs, Kuleshov, Eisenstein, Pudovkin, and Rotha—tend to resemble each other in two respects: 1) they generally—with the possible exception of those like Vertov—see the role or value of film to be its capacity to make art, and (2) their different theories of art—with the possible exception of those like Victor Freeberg—are generally anti-mimetic in their fundamental bias, that is, they all demand divergence between artworks and represented real things as a criterion of art. This leads each silent-film theorist to scrutinize the processes of cinematic articulation and to show that they are more productive than reproductive—a means for creating rather than merely copying; a means of manipulating reality rather than merely recording it. This ethos, which may be called *creationist*, is very obvious in Arnheim, but is equally apparent in the montagists in their championing of editing above the photographic element of the medium.

The arguments against film—those that charge that film is but mere mechanical recording—issue from two sources: fine art and theater. Of the two sources, the theatrical one seems more vexing to silent-film theorists. Thus, they spent reams in exposition of the ways in which film added to dramatic spectacles rather than simply copying them, as well as showing the many things that film could do that theater could not. Perhaps the reason that the theatrical variant of the recording argument caused such consternation for film theorists was that film and theater were in direct economic competition for the same type of audience, whereas film and painting were not.

In order to deal with the two "mechanical recording" arguments, film theorists had to demonstrate how film could differ both from a mechanical duplication of our normal perceptual experience of reality and from a mere recording of a theatrical performance. In the course of argumentation, some theorists, notably Munsterberg, seem to lose track of the fact that they are confronting two logically distinct arguments and behave as though a single mechanical reproduction argument were at issue. Thus, Munsterberg at times stresses the difference between film and theater in contexts that seem to assume that this difference has something to do with film's divergence from reality. The confusion, though not justifiable, is at least understandable, since in one sense the silent-film theorist was confronted by one argument that had two variations, such that each required an independent refutation. And the strategy for answering both variations was the same. Through close scrutiny of the processes of cinematic articulation and with examples, the silent-film theorist argues that cinema manipulates, amplifies, and transforms whatever stands before the camera.

In emphasizing the manipulative dimensions of film, silent-film theorists were reflecting the ethos of the film-historical period in which and about which they theorized. Not only theorists but ambitious filmmakers like D. W. Griffith wished to legitimize film's place in Western culture by establishing that the medium was an art in its own right. They wanted the medium taken seriously; and it seemed this could be done by establishing that the medium was an art. At times, makers of silent films pursued this end by miming established arts outright—for example, the pictorialism of C. B. de-

Mille's "Rembrandt lighting" in *The Cheat*. But they not only aped particular effects of the established artistic media; they also strove to achieve what, at the turn of the century, were taken to be the ends of art: the manipulation of reality for formal or expressive purposes. The most memorable movements of silent cinema—German expressionism, French avant-gardism, Soviet montage, and the International style of the late twenties—all evince a highly interventionist attitude on the part of the filmmaker. This is no more apparent than with the Soviet montagists who, perhaps, believed that Marxist theory demanded that they not copy reality but change it. Even American silent-film comedy can be seen in this light, for its central structural gambit—the sight gag, perfected by the late twenties—denies that film is a simple recording insofar as its basic donnée is always that reality can be seen in more than one way. In *The Gold Rush*, for example, a boot can be a turkey; a nail, a bone; and a shoelace, spaghetti. Film, in showing that there is more than one way to see reality, transcends the single viewpoint that simple recording implies.

Given this context, the silent-film theorist can be seen as motivated by and in concert with the historical practice of the makers of silent film, who developed their medium—emphasizing manipulation—so that it would be regarded seriously as art. In the Western art world of the first half of the twentieth century, this required that film be made to exhibit how the medium could reconstitute reality rather than merely copy it. Silent-film theory then, can be seen as a reflection and a codification of the principles underlying the ambitious and aspiring society of filmmakers who were seeking to turn their medium into an art on the terms set by the culture and the art world of their day. Thus, even if the silent-film theorists were wrong in their assertion of the proposition that the primary role or value of film was art, these theoreticians would still be interesting historically for the way in which they express abstractly and clearly the deep-seated assumptions of the silent-film world.

An outline of Arnheim's theory

In the Introduction I claimed that classical film theories traditionally ask three interrelated kinds of questions: (1) What is the role or value of film? (2) What is the determinant characteristic of film (the feature of the medium that enables it to implement—as a means or instrument—the role or value designated in answering the previous question)? and 3) What are the various processes of articulation in film—editing, lighting, camera movement, and so on—and how do they each function as instances of the determinant characteristics of film? Using these three questions as a guide, I will begin outlining the structure and theory of *Film as Art*. In summary, Arnheim holds that one role of filmmaking—the one that concerns him—is art. He also contends that the determinant characteristics of the medium—those relevant to the purpose of art making—are the various ways that the medium diverges from the mechanical duplication of reality; and finally, Arnheim spends the bulk of *Film as Art* on lengthy examinations of the various modes of cinematic articulation, in order to demonstrate how they diverge from mechanical recording. Arnheim, moreover, is concerned with this divergence to establish that the medium can be expressive. It is the potential expressiveness of the medium that convinces Arnheim that film can be art. And, for him, it is the difference between normal perception and the cinematic image that yields the means of promoting expression. If for no other reason, *Film as Art* is useful as a handbook giving examples of how each process of articulation can be used expressively. For Arnheim, the key to the production of expression is the isolation of the way in which representation by the device in question—say, a close-up—will diverge from the normal close-up view of an object in nature. Thus, there is a kind of double-approach in *Film as Art*. The opening section, "Film and Reality," shows how various devices diverge from mechanical recordings. Then the same devices are discussed again under the heading "The Making of Film," which shows how these divergences supply the basis for expressive uses of film.

Arnheim opens *Film as Art* by acknowledging that the film medium can perform a multiplicity of roles. Not all of these roles are necessarily artistic. Arnheim's point is not that all films are art, but only that film, some films, can be art. He draws an analogy with dance. Not all dance is art, stripteases for example. The dance medium, however, can make art— Balanchine's *Serenade* is surely art. To show that film can be art means "to refute thoroughly and systematically the charge that photography and film are only mechanical reproductions."

Arnheim pursues this rebuttal by means of examples. In reference to these examples it pays to note that Arnheim is not always consistent in what he takes his *bête noir*—mechanical recording—to be. Some of them are aimed at very different concepts of mechanical recording than others. Arnheim's opening example, for instance, shows that photography is not simply mechanical, where "mechanical" means something like automatic, that is, not requiring imagination and skill to achieve proper results.

> Let us consider the visual reality of some definite object such as a cube. If this cube is standing on a table in front of me, its position determines whether I can realize its shape properly. If I see, for example, merely the four sides of a square, I have no means of knowing that a cube is before me, I see only a square surface. The human eye, equally the photographic lens, acts from a particular position and from there can take in only such portions of the field of vision as are not hidden by things in front. As the cube is now placed, five of its faces are screened by the sixth, and therefore this last only is visible. But since this face might be the base of a pyramid or one side of a sheet of paper, for instance—our view of the cube has not been selected characteristically.
>
> We have, therefore, already established one important principle: If I wish to photograph a cube, it is not enough for me to bring the object within the range of my camera. It is rather a question of my position relative to the

> object, or of where I place it . . .—the reproduction of
> even a perfectly simple object is not a mechanical process
> but can be set about well or badly.
>   . . . There is no formula to help one choose the most
> characteristic aspect; it is a question of feeling. (*FAA*, 9–
> 10)

From the above we see that Arnheim rejects the claim that film is simply mechanical because the production of recognizable images can *succeed or fail*. Recognizable images are not produced automatically, and it takes wit, skill, and imagination to make an object appear in its most characteristic, most recognizable aspect. Discovering an object's most characteristic aspect is not reducible to a mechanical formula nor is it a machine procedure.

Elsewhere in *Film as Art*, however, Arnheim has other things in mind when he says that film is not a mere mechanical recording. Sometimes he means that film diverges from the way reality is and cannot, therefore, be a mechanical— here, read "perfectly replicating"—recording of reality. Arnheim notes, for example, the lack of color in film (many films, at least) and he counts this as a "divergence from nature" (*FAA*, 14).

But most often when Arnheim says that film diverges from a mere mechanical recording, he means that the film image (or series of film images) differs in salient ways from the way we normally experience or perceive the world. Consider, for example, his discussion of the lack of three-dimensional effects—Arnheim says film is experienced as neither 2-D nor 3-D (*FAA*, 12)—and the loss of the constancy of size phenomenon; here, it is clear that Arnheim believes that the film image is not a mechanical recording because it is not a replica of normal vision—it diverges from normal vision.

> . . . when the three-dimensional impression is lost, other
> phenomena, known to psychologists as the constancies
> of size and shape, disappear. Physically, the image
> thrown onto the retina of the eye by any object in the
> field of vision diminishes in proportion to the square of

the distance. If an object a yard distant is moved away another yard, the area of the image on the retina is diminished to one-quarter of that of the first image. Every photographic plate reacts similarly. Hence in a photograph of someone sitting with his feet stretched far in front of him the subject comes out with enormous feet and much too small a head. Seriously enough, however, we do not in real life get impressions to accord with the images on the retina. If a man is standing three feet away and another equally tall six feet away, the area of the image of the second does not appear to be only a quarter of that of the first. Nor if a man stretches out his hand toward one does it look disproportionately large. One sees the two men as equal in size and the hand as normal. This phenomenon is known as constancy of size. It is impossible for most people—excepting those accustomed to drawing and painting, that is, artifically trained—to see according to the image on the retina. This fact, incidentally, is one of the reasons the average person has trouble copying things "correctly." Now an essential for the functioning of the constancy of size is a clear three-dimensional impression; it works excellently in a stereoscope with an ordinary photograph, not hardly at all in a film picture. Thus, in a film picture, if one man is twice as far from the camera as another, the one in front looks very considerably the taller and the broader. (*FAA*, 13–14)

That is, in normal (binocular) vision we perceive an object to be the same size even though it casts retinal images of quite varying proportions when it is far and when it is near—we don't, for instance, believe that an automobile mysteriously grows in size as it comes toward us, though its retinal image is growing. In film, however, the image *is* growing, like the retinal image, when the car approaches us *and*, further, it appears to be enlarging, phenomenally speaking, to the film spectator. Film, in other words, can make an object appear, phenomenally, large or even gigantic by placing a camera near it, likewise, a camera can make a man seem small or even shrinking by drawing away from him. This is a way the film image differs from normal perception; and Arnheim counts this as evidence that film is not necessarily mechanical recording.

Arnheim also refers to editing in this regard. Editing involves the absence of the space-time continuum of normal experience.

> In real life every experience or chain of experiences is enacted for every observer in an uninterrupted spatial and temporal sequence. I may, for example, see two people talking together in a room. I am standing fifteen feet away from them. I can alter the distance between us; but this alteration is not made abruptly. I cannot suddenly be only five feet away; I must move through the intervening space. I can leave the room; but I cannot suddenly be in the street. In order to reach the street I must go out of the room, through the door, down the stairs. And similarly with time. I cannot suddenly see what these two people will be doing ten minutes later. These ten minutes must first pass in their entirety. There are no jerks in time or space in real space in real life. Time and space are continuous.
>
> Not so in film. The period of time that is being photographed may be interrupted at any point. One scene may be immediately followed by another that takes place at a totally different time. And the continuity of space may be broken in the same manner. A moment ago I may have been standing a hundred yards away from a house. Suddenly I am close in front of it. I may have been in Sydney a few moments ago. Immediately afterward I can be in Boston. I have only to join two strips together. (*FAA*, 20–21)

In normal experience, we are locked into the space-time continuum. But in film abrupt transitions—leaps over the space-time continuum—are possible. Thus, film again can be said to differ from normal experience and can in this regard (vis à vis editing) be touted as not merely a mechanical recording.

For different reasons—though the differences in the reasons do not always appear apparent to him—Arnheim believes that features of film such as the absence of color (roughly pre–*Becky Sharp*), dialogue and sound (roughly pre–*The Jazz Singer*), smell, the space-time continuum, and guaranteed, automatic characteric-aspect viewpoints (see Arnheim's discussion of the cube for an example), and the presence of the phenomena Arnheim calls "delimitation of the image and distance from the object" (*FAA*, 18–20), all mark the cinematic image as something other than mere mechanical recording. Two things are especially important for Arnheim about every one of these phenomena. First, each is a result of the peculiar nature of the cinematic medium. Arnheim calls his theory of film a *Materialtheorie*, which means it is a theory designed to "show that artistic and scientific descriptions of reality are cast in molds that derive not so much from the subject matter itself as from properties of the medium—or *Material*—employed" (*FAA*, 2). Thus, all the aforesaid differences between cinematic representations and their objects or their perceptual representations are the result of the specific properties of the film medium. It is no accident, therefore, that one of the articles in the book is entitled "A New Laocoön," since Arnheim is clearly a descendent of Lessing (*FAA*, 199–230). Arnheim thinks that it is the task of the aesthetic theorist to chart the permissible avenues in a medium by examining the formal potentials and physical structures of its basic sign patterns. Arnheim, however, differs from Lessing and many of Lessing's followers—such as Panofsky and Kracauer—in that rather than asking "What does the film medium, given its material structure, represent [imitate] most perfectly?" Arnheim asks "Where does the film medium fall short of perfect reproduction?" Arnheim argues that the special creativity of the medium must flourish not where the medium best captures reality but where its material properties block perfect imitation.

The second point to note about Arnheim's list of cinematic

divergences is that he is concerned with film's departing from the duplication of reality or normal perception not because divergence is valuable for its own sake but because it makes expression possible. In the section "Film and Reality," Arnheim enumerates the various differences between film and perfect recordings and then goes on, in "The Making of a Film," to show how each of these medium-specific limitations on perfect duplication can be used to an expressive end. These differences, moreover, are the consequence of the peculiar—that is, specific—material structures of the cinematic medium. And Arnheim asserts that it is in exploiting these peculiarities that film art is made. But Arnheim is not interested in the peculiarities of the medium in the way that a modernist/formalist might be. That is, he has no particular commitment to the reflexive program of revealing the basic nature, materials, peculiarities, and so forth of the medium as such. Rather, Arnheim urges the filmmaker to exploit the limitations of the medium because by doing so, expression can (not *will*, but only *can*) result.

> In order that the film artist may create a work of art it is important that he consciously stress the peculiarities of his medium. This, however, should be done in such a manner that the character of the objects represented should not thereby be destroyed but rather strengthened, concentrated, and *interpreted*. (*FAA*, 35, italics added)

Arnheim, reflecting on his film theory in 1974, summed up his original intent:

> I am thinking back to my own way of dealing with the psychology and aesthetics of film in *Film als Kunst*. In that early book I attempted to refute the accusation that photography was nothing but a mechanical copy of nature. Such an approach was suggested as a reaction to the narrow notion that had prevailed ever since Baudelaire in his famous statement of 1859 predicted the value of photography for the faithful documentation of sights and scientific facts, but also denounced it as an act of a revengeful god who, by sending Daguerre as his messiah,

granted the prayer of a vulgar multitude that wanted art to be an exact imitation of nature. In those early days, the mechanical procedure of photography was doubly suspect as an attempt by industry to replace the manual work of the artist with a mass production of cheap pictures. Such critical voices, although less eloquent, were still influential when I decided upon my own apologia for the cinema. The strategy was therefore to describe the differences between the images we obtain when we look at the physical world and the images perceived on the motion picture screen. *The differences could then be shown to be a source of artistic expression.*[11]

Thus, we see that the differences between the film images that Arnheim calls art and mere mechanical recordings are important because they afford the possibility of expression.

Arnheim supplies his reader with a wealth of illustrations of the relation between the limitations of the medium and artistic expression. For example, due partly to the absence of constancy of size common in film, a shot taken from a low angle can make a person appear enormous, and this can be done for expressive purposes. This technique was exploited often in silent film, for example, in *The Last Laugh* and *The General Line*. Arnheim comments on the inner workings of this device, noting that "In the Russian films—other people have copied the idea—the *domineering forcefulness* of a character is often expressed by taking a shot from a worm's-eye view. An iron captain of industry or a general—the camera looks up at him as at a mountain. Here again the fact that the actor has to be taken from some particular point of view is not handled perfunctorily but is consciously exploited: the perspective angle acquires meaning." (*FAA*, 38-39, italics added). Later, returning to the subject of camera angulation, Arnheim says:

> An unusual camera angle . . . has still another result apart from characterizing the object in a particular sense and introducing an attractive element of surprise. Pu-

11. Arnheim, "On the Nature of Photography," 155.

dovkin has said film strives to lead the spectator beyond the sphere of ordinary human conceptions. For the ordinary person in everyday life, sight is merely a means of finding his bearings in the natural world. Roughly speaking, he sees only so much of the objects surrounding him as is necessary for his purpose. If a man is standing at the counter of a haberdasher's shop, the salesman will presumably pay less attention to the customer's facial expression than to the kind of tie he is wearing (so as to guess his taste) and to the quality of his clothes (so as to know what his requirements are likely to be). . . .

In order to understand a work of art, however, it is essential that the spectator's attention should be guided to such qualities of form, that is, that he should abandon himself to a mental attitude which is to some extent unnatural. For example, it is no longer merely a matter of realizing that "there stands a policeman" but rather a realizing "how he is standing" and to what extent this picture is characteristic of policemen in general. Notice how well the man is selected; what a characteristic movement that one is in comparison with another, more obvious movement; and how the *forcefulness* of the figure is brought out by the shot being taken from below. (*FAA*, 42–43, italics added)

Implicit in this passage is the notion that by exploiting a peculiarity of the medium—the tendency of low angle shots to monumentalize objects—a qualitative feature of characters, in this case their forcefulness, can be made salient. The peculiarity of the medium is, when analyzed, its inability to sustain the constancy of size effect. Thus, this expressive quality is being made vivid by exploiting a limitation of the medium, that is, by creatively using the fact that the medium falls short of a perfect duplication of normal perception. And by diverging from normal perception, the cinematic representation enables the spectator to see the object afresh, replete with expressive qualities like "forcefulness" that would go unremarked in normal practical perception and that would not emerge in the mechanical recording correlative of practical perception.

Arnheim performs similar analyses for other of the medium-specific divergences that he inventories. With each he shows how it is the difference between representation by the device and normal perceptual representation that gives rise to expression. In "Film and Reality," Arnheim discusses a phenomenon dubbed "delimitation of the object": in normal perception our eyes can move freely in any direction and our field of vision is potentially without limit, whereas the film image is strictly bounded by the frame (*FAA*, 73). Furthermore, control of the frame in film can be a source of artistic and expressive effects.

> Sternberg's *The Docks of New York* has a scene in which a suicide jumps off a boat. Nothing is shown in the shot except the quivering surface of the water in which is seen the reflection of the boat with the woman standing up and then jumping overboard. The woman is shown indirectly by her reflection in the water. The next moment, however, the woman herself is seen falling into the water, at the very spot where her reflection has been. This unexpected sequence of the direct upon the indirect view is most impressive. The effect is achieved by a careful choice of what is to be photographed. The camera is so placed that the most important part of the shot, namely, the boat with the woman on board, does not come in at all—a position which is quite absurd from the standpoint of ordinary representation of an object. The important part of the event, the only reason for which the shot has been taken, only throws its reflection into the picture. But the spectator, who perhaps might have watched a direct shot of the event with merely passing interest, is caught and thrilled by the unusualness of the presentation. (*FAA*, 78)

Though Arnheim does not name the expressive quality that this shot from *The Docks of New York* instills—referring only to the pleasurable surprise it imparts—viewers familiar with the scene undoubtedly will recall the special feeling of consternation evoked in the transition from the placid reflecting surface to the chaotic splash. Of course, Arnheim's point about the expressive power of the frame line could be made with other examples. Often in horror films, the monster, who is excruciatingly close to his victim, is kept off screen—the invisibility caused by the framing functions to heighten the creature's fearsomeness. If such a scene were perceived normally (!), viewers could turn their heads and catch sight of the beast. But in film the frame line, under the control of the filmmaker, can generate powerful feelings of anxiety that are due to the effectively invisible presence of off-screen denizens. Thus, a difference between how we would normally see a scene in everyday experience and how we see the scene under the peculiar conditions of cinema can become an occasion for the expression of feeling.[12]

Arnheim considers the close-up under the heading of the delimited image (*FAA*, 79). One example he proposes of its expressive potential comes from Soviet cinema.

> In Pudovkin's *Mother* the scenes taking place in the law courts are ushered in by rapidly successive close-ups of the cold gray ashlars of the building, and in one case a huge shot of the boot of one of the soldiers on guard, a dark uncanny apparition, which is an excellent introduction to the mood of the following scenes. The Russians, indeed, have created an entirely new technique of close-ups. (*FAA*, 81)

This example involves not only an analysis of close-ups but also of editing, because Arnheim is speaking of a string of close shots. And, for Arnheim, editing represents one of the greatest differences between the cinematic image and normal perception.

> Unlike real life, film permits of jumps in time and space. Montage means joining together shots of situations that occur at different times and in different places. . . .

12. For a discussion of the systematic, artistic use of off-screen space, see my "Lang, Pabst and Sound," *Ciné-tracts*, no. 5 (Fall 1978), 15–23.

It can be easily seen . . . why montage might be thought of as the royal road to film art. The single image, after all, arises from a recording process, which is controlled by man but which, regarded superficially, does no more than reproduce nature. But when it comes to montage man takes a hand in the process—time is broken up, things that are disconnected in time and space are joined together. This looks much more like a tangibly creative and formative process . . .

It was a much bolder stroke to intervene in one unitary scene, to split up an event, to change the position of the camera in midstream, to bring it nearer, move it farther away, to alter the selection of the subject matter shown. This has up to the present been the most vigorous and stimulating move toward the emancipation of the camera.

In montage the film artist has a first-class formative instrument, which helps him emphasize and give greater significance to the actual events that he portrays. From the time continuum of a scene he takes only the parts that interest him, and of the spatial totality of objects and events he picks out only what is relevant. Some details he stresses, others he omits altogether. (*FAA*, 87–89)

Though Arnheim esteems the importance of editing, he does part company with Soviet montagists over certain issues. He believes that the montagists are too extreme in their deprecation of the single shot. As his examples purport to show, the single shot—for instance, a low-angle shot of a policeman—can be self-sufficiently expressive. That is, Arnheim does not hold that expression in film only accrues through editing. Having made that qualification, however, Arnheim does believe that editing is a major expressive means in film, and he spends five pages literally charting the different categories of cutting (*FAA*, 94-98). In this section he is primarily expanding upon the classificatory schemes of montage devices proposed by Pudovkin and Timoshenko. Included are lists of temporal editing conventions, such as parallel editing (cutting back and forth between two or more simultaneously occurring events), as well as conventions for proposing conceptual relations between shots—for example, a playground swing in motion is cut against the swinging pendulum of a clock, thereby suggesting that the movement of the swing is similar to that of the clock.

The above examples, from camera angulation to editing, and similar examples throughout *Film as Art*, are meant by Arnheim to show that the film image is not a mechanical recording because it is not a duplicate of normal perception. There is a difference between what we see on screen and the manner in which we normally perceive things. Moreover, this difference—really a series of differences—provides the film artist with a basis upon which to build expression. Just because the film image diverges from normal experience does not entail that it is expressive. That deviation from normal experience, however, can be worked up into expression, as Arnheim's examples are supposed to show. Nevertheless, it is important to note that Arnheim's examples are not always examples of exactly the same thing. What some of his devices evoke are expressive qualities—the *forcefulness* of the policeman. On the other hand, some of the devices seem to suggest propositions—"the swing is like the pendulum." Moreover, the devices, like parallel editing, seem better thought of as elements of narrative representation rather than as examples of expression or expressiveness narrowly conceived; that is, they are structures of denotation rather than of connotation (as that distinction is used in literary and film studies rather than in philosophy). Arnheim himself speaks of these various devices as a means that the director has of *interpreting* his material (*FAA*, 35). And this seems to encompass a multitude of phenomena including not merely the foregrounding of expressive qualities but also the statement of themes—for example, the shot of an unemployed, starving man juxtaposed against a shot of a shop window full of delicious food (*FAA*, 98). Thus, the operative extent of the types of expression that Arnheim has in mind, at least in *Film as Art* (as opposed to

Art and Visual Perception),[13] is very broad; perhaps it is coextensive with the idea of communication.

The general outline of Arnheim's theory is clear. The relevant role of film is artmaking. The determinant characteristic of film—the features of the medium that enable it to make art—are all the peculiar ways that the medium departs or diverges from duplicating the matter-of-fact experience of reality. These divergences thereby afford film an expressive potential, a capacity to manifest the connotative (expressively qualitative) dimension of the world and to communicate and interpret).

As summarized in the preceding paragraph, Arnheim's theory is logically incomplete. Arnheim says, for example, that the relevant role of film is artmaking and that the determinant characteristics of the medium are embodied in its capacity for expressive divergence from mechanical recording. But what is the connection between art and expressive divergence from mechanical recording? That is, the theory should show explicitly how and why expressive divergence can serve as a means to the goal of art. Furthermore, Arnheim appears to hold that the filmmaker must exploit only those expressive divergences from mechanical recording that result from material or formal peculiarities of the cinema; for instance, a recording of a Kabuki play—say, *The Girl at Dojo Temple*—is not likely to be film art because all the expressive stylization therein derives from the medium of theater, not film. But why is it that only medium-specific expressiveness can implement the purpose of artmaking in cinema? To fill in these gaps in Arnheim's theory so as to complete it requires some speculation, as well as reference to Arnheim's other writings, especially *Art and Visual Perception*.

Some of these questions can partially be answered by noting that Arnheim holds an expression theory of art. Thus, the logical connection between his designation of the artmaking role of film and the reference to expression in his characteri-

13. Rudolf Arnheim, *Art and Visual Perception: A Psychology of the Creative Eye* (Berkeley: University of California Press, 1967). Henceforth I will abbreviate references to this book as *AVP*.

zation of the determinant characteristic of the medium is grounded logically in his presupposition that art is, first and foremost, expressive. In *Art and Visual Perception*, Arnheim claims that "Every work of art must express something" (*AVP*, 425). And, at another point, he attempts to capture the same insight—perhaps misleadingly—by saying that "All art is symbolic" (*AVP*, 440). I say this is *perhaps* misleading because, as Arnheim himself notes, "symbolic" is popularly taken to signal a relation between a sign and an idea where one infers the latter from the presentation of the former. But this is not the notion of "symbolic" that Arnheim has in mind. Rather, he believes that all art is symbolic in the sense that it enables us to see (rather than to infer) general qualities of objects (individually) and experiences (collectively). Art, for Arnheim, is symbolic because it promotes perceptual understanding (Arnheim believes in what he calls "visual thinking"), which is something he distinguishes from inferential reasoning. Thus, when Arnheim says all art is symbolic, he means that it enables us to perceive general qualities of individual things, thereby enhancing our sensuous understanding of the concrete individual by highlighting some general property in the thing.

In *Art and Visual Perception*, Arnheim claims that his concept of expression is not coextensive with the idea of communication (*AVP*, 425). And this is generally true in that book insofar as most of his examples seem restricted to instances of expressive qualities in particular artworks. Even in *Art and Visual Perception*, however, Arnheim seems to be dealing with the expression of themes (*AVP*, 432) and not merely with the expression of qualities. And in *Film as Art* Arnheim deals not only with expressive qualities but with communication per se. Thus, the critical evaluation of Arnheim's theory must test the validity of Arnheim's expression theory as it (1) narrowly claims that art must project expressive qualities and (2) broadly claims that art must communicate.

Here it should be noted not only that Arnheim is an expression theorist of art but also that he holds a special theory of expressive qualities. According to Arnheim, human beings *directly* perceive anthropomorphic qualities—sadness, strength, forcefulness—in artworks and real things. The distinguishing point of Arnheim's theory is that the perception of these qualities is direct—it is not a matter of either convention or association (*AVP*, 427). Expression is embedded in the structure of artworks and real things; we see the "sadness" in the weeping willow tree not because we associate the shape of the tree with the disposition of our body when we are unhappy but because we see sadness *in* the visual pattern the tree projects. How can this be? Purportedly, the pattern of the tree *resembles* the pattern or structure of the feeling of sadness. Arnheim writes:

> Wertheimer asserted that the perception of expression is too immediate and compelling to be explainable merely as a product of learning. When we watch a dancer, the sadness or happiness of the mood seems to be directly inherent in the movements themselves. Wertheimer concluded that this was true because *formal factors of the dance reproduced identical factors of the mood*. The meaning of this theory may be illustrated by reference to an experiment by Binney in which members of a college dance group were asked individually to give improvisations of such subjects as sadness, strength, or night. The performances of the dancers showed much agreement. For example, in the representation of sadness the movement was slow and confined to a narrow range. It was mostly curved in shape and showed little tension. The direction was indefinite, changing, wavering, and the body seemed to yield passively to the force of gravitation rather than being propelled by its own initiative. It will be admitted that the *psychical mood of sadness has a similar pattern*. In a depressed person the mental processes are slow and rarely go beyond matters closely related to immediate experiences and interests of the moment. In all his thinking and striving are softness and a lack of energy. There is little determination, and activity is often controlled by outside forces.

Naturally there is a traditional way of representing sadness in a dance, and the performances of the students may have been influenced by it. What counts, however, is that the movements, whether spontaneously invented or copied from other dancers, exhibited *a formal structure so strikingly similar to that of the intended mood*. And since such visual qualities as speed, shape or direction are immediately accessible to the eye, it seems legitimate to assume that they are carriers of an expression directly comprehensible to the eye. (*AVP*, 428, italics added)

Thus, along with holding an expression theory of art, Arnheim holds a special, independent theory about the nature of expressive qualities—as those are found both in artworks and in real things. This theory of expressive qualities can be called an analogy theory of expression because it holds that objects—either natural or artistic—have expressive qualities just because they are structurally similar or analogous to the moods and anthropomorphic states they project. We pick up these structural correspondences or analogies immediately in perception, and as a result we perceive the expressive quality directly. Here one recalls Langer's notion of Forms of Feeling. Arnheim goes so far as to suggest that this pattern triggers a recognition mechanism in *the nervous system of the spectator* (*AVP*, 429)—as a gestalt psychologist Arnheim is prone to physiological reductionism.

Arnheim, then—though not all his examples and analyses support this—believes that all art should project expressive qualities, qualities that (1) resemble the structures of moods and (2) "are not reserved to . . . [the object represented] but common to many or all other things" (*AVP*, 440). This second condition enables art to engender understanding, because understanding requires generality of some sort. The objects represented in a Cezanne still life for example, though each is unique, are able to express "stability," a quality common to many or all other things, thereby proposing to the understanding a conception of reality (*AVP*, 440–42).

Given Arnheim's commitment to an expression theory of

art, it is clear why his advocacy of the role of art making for film leads him to see the expressive potential of the medium as a component of film's determinant characteristic. But the medium's potential for expression is only part of its determinant characteristic. The determinant characteristic as fully conceived includes the peculiar *way or ways the medium diverges from mechanical recording* such that the result is expression. But why is divergence from mechanical recording part of the determinant characteristic? What is its connection with art and with expression?

In *Art and Visual Perception* Arnheim writes, "If art could do nothing better than reproduce the things of nature, either directly or by analogy, or to delight the senses, there would be little justification for the honorable place reserved to it in every society" (*AVP*, 440). This sentence provides a purely negative reason why anything that is art avoids mechanical reproduction and, therefore, diverges from it. Perhaps this reason is best summed up by a witticism that Nelson Goodman attributes to Virginia Woolf: "Art is not a copy of the real world. One of the damn things is enough."[14] The idea is that little purpose would be served by the brute mechanical reproduction of something we've already got. Thus, a characteristic of anything that is art is that it diverges from mechanical recording. If a medium cannot diverge from mechanical recording it cannot be art, nor can it serve much of a purpose in society because it redundantly replicates what we've got enough of already. Therefore, the capacity to diverge from mechanical recording is a requisite feature for determining whether a medium can be art.

But Arnheim assigns no artistic credit to a representation just because it diverges from reality. Art must not only avoid boorishly duplicating what is; art, positively characterized, must promote understanding (*AVP*, 440), which it does by way of expression. What, then, is the connection between di-

14. Nelson Goodman, *Languages of Art* (Indianapolis: Bobbs-Merrill, 1968), 3.

vergence from mechanical reproduction and dissemination of understanding through expression?

Arnheim does not answer this question directly, but the answer is clear enough. The relation between expression and divergence from mechanical recording is causal—divergence from mechanical imitation is *a* causal condition for bringing about expression and its recognition by spectators. Discussing drawing rather than filmmaking, Arnheim writes.

> . . . the training of art students should be expected to consist basically in sharpening their sense of these [expressive] qualities and in teaching them to look to expression as the guiding criterium [*sic*] for every stroke of the pencil, brush, or chisel. In fact many good art teachers do precisely this. But there are also plenty of times when the spontaneous sensitivity of the student to expression is not only developed further, but is even disturbed and suppressed. There is, for example, an old-fashioned but not extinct way of teaching students to draw from the model by asking them to establish the exact length and direction of contour lines, the relative positions of points, the shape of masses. In other words, students are to concentrate on the geometric-technical qualities of what they see. In its modern version this method consists in urging the young artist to think of the model or of a freely invented design as a configuration of masses, planes, directions. Again interest is focussed on geometric-technical qualities.
>
> Such teaching follows principles of description often employed in mathematics or physical science rather than those of spontaneous vision. There are, however, other teachers who will proceed differently. With a model sitting on the floor in a hunched-up position, they will not begin by making the students notice that the whole figure can be inscribed in a triangle. Instead they will ask about the expression of the figure; they may be told, for example, that the person on the floor looks tense, tied together, full of potential energy. They will suggest then

that the student try to render this quality. In doing so the student will watch proportions and directions, but not as geometric properties in themselves. These formal properties will be perceived as being functionally dependent upon the primarily observed expression, and the correctness and incorrectness of each stroke will be judged on the basis of whether or not it captures the dynamic "mood" of the subject. Equally in a lesson of design, it will be made clear that to the artist, just as to any unspoiled human being, a circle is not a line of constant curvature, whose points are all equally distant from a center, but first of all a compact, hard, restful thing. Once the student has understood that roundness is not identical with circularity, he may try for a design whose structured logic will be controlled by the primary concept of something to be expressed. For whereas the artificial concentration on formal qualities will leave the student at a loss as to which pattern to select among innumerable and equally acceptable ones, an expressive theme will serve as a natural guide to forms that fit the purpose. (*AVP*, 431–32)

Here, though the discussion is of drawing rather than filmmaking, the idea is advanced that mechanical reproduction—concentrating on what are here called geometric-technical qualities—gets in the way of expression. The word "mechanical" is not being used literally in the sense of a machine-produced copy, but instead is employed metaphorically—meaning "without imagination and without feeling for connotations." In Arnheim's writing the concept of the mechanical seems to rely on an ambiguity such that at times its reference is to literally mechanical copying, whereas at other moments "mechanical" suggests without wit, ingenuity and feeling. Thus, what Arnheim says of the mechanical style of drawing, where there is no question of a literal machine at play, can supply some inkling of what he feels is the problem with photographic recording, which is both machine produced and also uninspired. That is, we regard mechanical reproduction as primarily the copying of only geometric-technical qualities.

Arnheim opposes any sort of mechanical reproduction basically because he feels it interferes with or blocks the emergence of the expressive properties of the objects, persons, and events that are the subjects of the representations in question. Reproduction of the geometric-technical properties of objects obstructs the emergence of expressive patterns in representations. An accurate geometric-technical representation does not provide enough information—in terms of foregrounding and salience—for a single expressive pattern to dominate the visual array. In mechanical reproductions there is not a determinate expressive pattern but a bland multiplicity of possibilities for unrealized patterns. Thus, divergence from mechanical reproduction apparently is justified as a means to avert the anti-expressive and therefore anti-artistic tendencies inherent in mechanical reproduction. Mechanical reproduction tends to swamp expression; divergence from mechanical reproduction short-circuits this effect. That is, the function of diverging from mechanical reproduction in artmaking is at least prophylactic—it checks the expression-neutralizing tendencies of geometric-technical copying. Thus, diverging from mechanical reproduction secures a necessary causal condition for expression.

Though the preceding explication is derived from Arnheim's description of a type of "mechanical" copying in drawing, it is clear that he is committed to something similar in regard to filmmaking. Recall Arnheim's discussion of the low-angle shot of the policeman. Arnheim noted that though we normally perceive things pragmatically, in artistic perception the spectator should be brought to attend to qualities: "it is no longer a matter of realizing that 'there stands a policeman,' but rather of realizing 'how he is standing' " (*FAA*, 42–43). The low-angle shot can project a view of the policeman standing *forcefully*. The unusual angle, which delivers a distorted variation of the geometric-technical information in the array, enables us to see the particular quality of forcefulness just because the image diverges from a mechanical—that is, an accurate geometric-technical—copy.

> If an ordinary picture of some men in a rowing boat appears on the screen, the spectator will perhaps perceive that here is a boat, and nothing further. But if, for example, the camera is suspended high up, so that the spectator sees the boat and the men from above, the result is a view very seldom seen in real life. The interest is thereby diverted from the subject to the form. The spectator notices how strikingly spindle-shaped is the boat and how curiously the bodies of the men swing to and fro. Things that previously remained unnoticed are the more striking because the object itself appears strange and unusual. The spectator is thus brought to see something familiar as something new. At this moment, he becomes capable of true observation. For it is not only that he is now stimulated to notice whether the natural objects have been rendered characteristically or colorlessly, with originality or obviously, but by stimulating the interest through the unusualness of the aspect the objects themselves become more vivid and therefore more capable of effect. In watching a good shot of a horse I shall have a much stronger feeling that "here is an actual horse—a big beast with satiny skin and with such a smell. . . ." That is to say, therefore, not only form but objective qualities will impose themselves more compellingly. (*FAA*, 43–44)

Here, the function of the departure from mechanical recording—the departure from the reproduction of normal perception—is not only prophylactic, but constitutive of the emergence of the qualitative aspect of the array. The unusual angle that makes us see the qualities in the array is a sufficient causal condition for the expressive effect.

At times, divergence from mechanical recording is a necessary causal condition for cinematic expression and at other times, a sufficient condition. In either case, however, it is clear that Arnheim rests his positive case for the requirement that the artistic film diverge from mechanical recording on the grounds that this is some kind of causal condition for the realization of expression. In and of itself divergence from mechanical reproduction has no intrinsic value. It is only valuable instrumentally as a means—a causal means—of bringing expression about. It is included in Arnheim's account of the determinant characteristic of the medium because it is the relevant causal factor in the creation of cinematic expression—which, in turn, is the feature that enables cinema to fulfill the goal of making art.

In *Art and Visual Perception* the animus against mechanical recording is also connected with a complicated psycho-historical thesis. Arnheim asserts that in the natural order of things normal perception includes perception of expressive qualities. In fact, "natural" perception attends first of all to expressive qualities. Arnheim refers to this phenomenon as the "priority of expression" (*AVP*, 430). But, due to various historical forces, we of Western culture have become alienated from the content of our own natural perception.

> We have been trained to think of the perception as the recording of shapes, distances, hues, motions. The awareness of these measurable characteristics is really a fairly late accomplisment of the human mind. Even in the Western man of the twentieth century it presupposes special conditions. It is the attitude of the scientist and the engineer or of a salesman who estimates the size of a customer's waist, the shade of lipstick, the weight of a suitcase. But if I sit in front of a fireplace and watch the flames, I do not normally register certain shades of red, various degrees of brightness, geometrically defined shapes moving at such and such a speed. I see the graceful play of aggressive tongues, flexible striving, lively color. The face of a person is more readily perceived and remembered as being alert, tense, concentrated rather than as being triangularly shaped, having slanted eyebrows, straight lips, and so on. This priority of expression, although somewhat modified in adults by a scientifically

oriented education, is striking in children and primitives.
. . . (*AVP*, 430)

. . . our kind of scientific and economic thinking makes
us define things by measurements rather than by the dy-
namics of their appearance. Our criteria for what is useful or useless, friendly or hostile, have tended to sever the
connections with outer expression, which they possess
in the minds of children or primitives. If a house or a
chair suits our practical purposes, we may not stop to
find out whether its appearance expresses our style of living. In business relations we define a man by his census
data, his income, age, position, nationality, or race—that
is, by categories that ignore the nature of the man as it is
manifest in his outer expression. (*AVP*, 435)

In these passages Arnheim contrasts the scientific-pragmatic
mode of perception with another kind of perception—one
that sounds like what is sometimes called "aesthetic" perception—that is directed at expressive patterns. The latter is said
to be more normal, though the former has been inculcated
into adults in our culture. One function of art, then, is to re-
vive this perceptual sensitivity to expressive pattern. To do
this art cannot rely on the mechanical reproduction of geometric-technical properties because that is the very thing that
stands in the way of the apprehension of expressive patterns.
Rather, things must be represented in ways that distort geometric-technical accuracy so that expressive patterns become
perceptible.

   The notion from *Art and Visual Perception* that natural/nor-
mal perception attends to expressive qualities, superficially
contradicts the rhetoric of *Film as Art*. In *Film as Art* the filmmaker is urged to depart from mechanical reproduction,
which most often seems to allude to normal perception. But
why would Arnheim urge the filmmaker to subvert normal
perception for the sake of foregrounding expressivity if normal perception is in fact naturally attuned to expression? Indeed, in *Film as Art* Arnheim says that the perceptual mode
that attends to expressive patterns is "to some extent unnat-

ural" (*FAA*, 43) whereas in *Art and Visual Perception* attentiveness to expressive patterns is natural. Clearly, a shift in reference has occurred in Arnheim's notion of "normal" perception between *Film as Art* and *Art and Visual Perception*. Specifically, in the earlier book normal perception is perception of geometric-technical properties, the things that are accurately reproduced by mechanical recordings. But in *Art and Visual Perception* this sort of scientific-pragmatic perception opposes normal perception, the perception of expressive patterns. Despite the surface contradictions, it is easy to summarize their mutually compatible points in a consistent way. Both books hold a variously named dichotomy between the perception/reproduction of geometrical-technical properties for pragmatic, utilitarian, or scientific purposes and the perception/projection of expressive qualities. In both books, art eschews the mechanical reproduction of geometric-technical properties because this stands in the way of the aim of art—the foregrounding of expressive qualities. In the language of *Art and Visual Perception*, film art, by transcending mechanical recording, shows objects in such a way that spectators jaded by the quantitative way of seeing can once again perceive "normally" and naturally as children do—that is, the expressive dimension of things once again shines forth.

Thus far I have explained the connection that Arnheim presupposes between the goal of film (to make art) and his inclusion of both film's capacity for expression and film's capacity to diverge from mechanical reproduction in what he assumes to be the determinant characteristic of the medium. It remains now to be seen what connection there is between exploiting film's *medium-specific* deviations from mechanical recording and cinema's role as an art form.

I have already quoted several passages in which Arnheim urges that the filmmaker stress the peculiarities of his medium. Given Arnheim's exposition in *Film as Art*, this injunction initially appears to entail that the filmmaker should exploit film's limitations in the perfect replication of normal perception. Undoubtedly, Arnheim thinks that unless the limitations are specifically cinematic, the art in question would not be film. Arnheim, however, also goes on to make medium-specificity arguments at a Lessing-like level of generality. That is, he names a definite type of representation that film is said to be best suited for. The peculiar characteristics of film, it is held, make it the art of the animated image (*FAA*, 224), in contradistinction to theater, which is the art of speech (*FAA*, 210). As one might imagine, these points are made during discussions of the sound film. Arnheim opposes sound, particularly dialogue—of the 100 percent all-talking variety—because he believes that truly artistic dialogue—dialogue of Shakespearean complexity—perforce paralyzes action (*FAA*, 228–29) as the camera focuses on stationary actors delivering intensively ornate speeches. The result is theater rather than film art: "The pure talkie differs from the theater only technically" (*FAA*, 228). For Arnheim, the media of theater and film have different natural subject matter. In theater, the visual action merely serves the dialogue (*FAA*, 218), whereas in film, the animated image is impeded by dialogue. As a result, the talking picture is problematic.

> The average talking film today endeavors to combine visually poor scenes full of dialogue with the completely different style of rich silent action. In comparison with the epoch of the silent film there is also an impressive decline of artistic excellence, in the average films as well as in the peak productions—a trend that cannot be due entirely to the ever increasing industrialization. (*FAA*, 230)

Underlying this evaluation is the belief that in the dialogue film the purposes of theater have come to dominate at the expense of the ends of film art. Arnheim presupposes that for a medium to be used artistically it must pursue its natural purposes, which, in the case of film, is the portrayal of animated action.

Arnheim offers no argument that explains why different artistic media cannot pursue the same generic subject matter. He presumes this Lessingesque axiom without comment. Perhaps the only justification for the claim that artistic media have distinct and not permissibly mixable central domains.[15] was offered by Bosanquet, who appears to support this idea with a rhetorical question that may be framed as: "Why else would there be distinct media were it not the case that each has its own goal?"[16] Part of what it is to be a distinct art form, for Arnheim, will be the commitment to the peculiar—that is, not perfectly mimetic—features of the symbol system of the medium. Thus, reference must be made to the *peculiar* mimetic limitations of the medium to specify its determinant characteristic and to clarify how the medium can perform the role of artmaking.

A full statement of Arnheim's theory of the relation between the role of film-as-art and the determinant characteristic of the film medium takes the following form:

1. One function of film is art. (premise)
   a. Art is necessarily expressive. (premise)
   b. Art is divergence from matter-of-fact, mechanical recording.
      This is supported by two considerations:

15. I have employed the term "central" in stating the preceding case because in *Film* Arnheim allows the ideals and aims of one art form to be mixed with work done at the periphery of an art form—his example is relief-painting—but he does not allow mixing at the center. He writes, "It is not the boundaries of a sphere of art that are important but its center. At its edges it may encroach upon other domains" (*Film*, 209). This distinction between the center of an art form and its periphery, however, seems to offer very little aid in marking off the legitimate mixing of media from the illegitimate, since I see slight prospect for Arnheim's distinguishing the "central" from the "peripheral" concerns of an art form in a non-question-begging way. To see how this problem erupts for Arnheim, consider the following passage: "Great artists strive toward the center of their subject. Their greatness consists in the fact that they work in perfectly clean media. What is the situation as between the theater and the sound film? We have seen that the possibility of merging the peripheries of two arts implies no identity—and, moreover, it is clear that while the methods of sound film are accessible to the theater, they are not its purest media, and therefore will be no particular credit to it" (*Film*, 209). But this quotation, strictly applied, rules Jean Renoir from the ranks of great *cinéastes* by definition!
16. Bernard Bosanquet, "The Esthetic Attitude in Its Embodiments," in *A Modern Book of Esthetics*, edited by M. Rader (New York: Holt, Rinehart, and Winston, 1966), 222–27.

i. What justification would there be for art if it only du-
plicated what we already have—call it reality or normal
perception?

ii. Diverting from duplication is a means of bringing
expression about. (That is, a mechanical duplication
stands in the way of or obscures the bodying forth of
the expressive, connotative aspect of the world, over-
whelming or otherwise masking the connotative dimension of the world and/or experience with the denotative. Demanding divergence from mechanical
recording is at least a prophylactic maneuver calculated
to contrive a situation where the expressive can emerge.
Emphasizing divergences from recording is a straightforward way of implementing the commitment to
expression presupposed in 1*a*.)

c. Each art form must depart from mechanical reproduction of the matter-of-fact in terms of its peculiar limitations in reproducing reality or normal perception. (This
premise appears to be meant to support the Lessing-type
prejudice that each art form has its own specific concern
and subject; the art in question would not be *film* art
unless the specific features of cinema are exploited)

2. The determinant characteristic of film comprises the multiplicity of peculiar ways it diverges from duplicating the
matter-of-fact experience of reality, thereby affording an
expressive potential by emphasizing the connotative dimension of the world over the matter-of-fact. (This follows from 1 through 1*c* along with the principle that determinant characteristics are those that implement the
function of film.)[17]

Critical Analysis of Arnheim's Film Theory

The central aesthetic tenets of Arnheim's film theory include:
(1) art is expression, (2) art diverges from mechanical record-

17. This outline rests on the analysis of the structure of classical film theory
presented in the Introduction. The material under (1) answers what was
previously identified as the first question of film theory and (2) answers the
second question of film theory.

ing, and (3) each art form must diverge from mechanical re-cording *in terms of the peculiar limitation of its medium*. They may be called, respectively, the expression thesis, the divergence thesis, and the specificity thesis. Because Arnheim believes that film can be art and because he holds these theses about what it is to be an art, it is understandable that he takes the determinant characteristic of film art to be the *peculiar* ways it *diverges* from duplicating the matter-of-fact experience of reality, thereby affording an *expressive* potential by emphasiz-ing the connotative dimension of the world over the matter-of-fact. I do not wish to disagree with Arnheim's assertion that film can be art. Indeed, at this point in history, such a claim hardly seems open to question; almost everyone can think of a cinematic masterpiece that could serve as a para-digm case of a work of art—*Rules of the Game* would be one of my candidates.

Certainly expression is a central aspect of film art. And Arnheim's analyses of the particular cinematic devices he ex-amines most often seem correct for the species of expression he considers. But no one could mistake Arnheim's review of the articulatory processes of film as comprehensive. There are more cinematic techniques than those Arnheim canvasses. I am sure Arnheim would admit this, where the preceding sen-tence is read as saying there are more expressive devices than those Arnheim explores. My claim however, is that Arn-heim's theory is not comprehensive because there are other than expressive techniques that are part of the art of cinema. These, Arnheim's theory ignores. Here the lack of compre-hensiveness is traceable to his view of film's determinant characteristic, which in turn is traceable to his conception of art. There is a problem with the expression thesis as Arnheim applies it both in his conception of art and in his conception of the determinant characteristic of film.

The expression thesis

Arnheim's thesis is that expression *or* expressiveness is a de-fining characteristic of film. The disjunction here is meant to capture a certain slipperiness in Arnheim's theorizing. Most of the time Arnheim says his idea of expression is quite broad; indeed, to this reader it seems as broad as the concept of communication. There are times, however, when Arnheim, evidence to the contrary, says his theory is restricted to covering phenomena that we would customarily group under the label of expressive qualities, such as "sadness." When I say Arnheim believes art is fundamentally involved with expression or the projection of expressive qualities, the "or" is inclusive rather than exclusive. That is, art proper for Arnheim seems to include both message-like themes, expressions in the propositional sense (say, the moral contrasts of Soviet montage), *and* the projection of expressive qualities.

Given that Arnheim has both broad categories in mind when discussing expression, one wonders whether when he claims that art is expression he means us to take this as a declarative statement, a sort of factual generalization, or as an imperative.

Taken as a factual generalization, the claim that art is defined by expression is false. For if expression entails the communication of proposition-like messages, then many works of art are bereft of expression. Can it be that every Haydn quartet implies some proposition(s)? (My point is not that music cannot entail or, at least, suggest statements; my query is, rather, does all music in fact do so?) Or, to take a more contentious example, does the very expressive (quality-wise) American Regency couch by Duncan Phyfe in the New York Metropolitan Museum collection have anything to say to us (I mean generally)? Weston was able to imbue raw vegetables with the aura of hardness and monumentality. But he did not thereby state anything we could put into a sentence or an article.

Perhaps the more plausible line to take is to assert that every work of art is expressive, where this means that every work of art has or projects some expressive quality. Whether this thesis proves true depends in large part on what is to count as an expressive quality. Arnheim is very liberal on this matter—in fact, too liberal. He includes things such as "night" and "stability." But surely these are not expressive qualities if we are referring to qualities named by terms relating to human feelings.

Predictably, Arnheim rejects such a narrow view of expression.

> To define visual expression as a reflection of human feelings would be misleading on two counts: first, because it makes us ignore the fact that expression has its origin in the perceived pattern and in the interaction of the brain field of vision to this pattern; second . . . such a description unduly limits the range of what is being expressed. (*AVP*, 434)

Without contesting Arnheim's psychological points, one can note that his fear of restricting the compass of what can be expressed, in effect, leads him to include many things—such as stability—that we might ordinarily consider to be qualities, though not expressive qualities. This enables Arnheim's expression theory to cover a lot of ground we might have thought such a theory incapable of covering. Arnheim's theory does so, however, by vitiating the concept of expression, loosening its connection to the root concept of anthropomorphic projection. Yet even if this extension of the concept were acceptable, it is still doubtful that the expression thesis succeeds as an empirical generalization. For even if we read "expression" as broadly as "projection of an (aesthetic?) quality," some works of art, especially bad ones, lack any qualities of the relevant kind. Nor can the day be ingeniously saved by claiming that such works have negative qualities, formlessness for example. For even if they have such negative qualities, they cannot be said to project them; they merely have them. Clearly something can be amorphous and a work of art as well as not being internally structured in a way that projects *amorphousness*. Such a work is just amorphous. Indeed projecting amorphousness, as opposed to being amorphous, would in many cases be a redeeming quality. Part of expression in art is *projection* (specifically, expression is the projection of anthropomorphic qualities). By "projection," moreover, I am referring to internal structures of presentation and focus. A work of art can have a quality but fail to project it. So even if it were true that every art object has some quality, it does not follow that every art object expresses that quality, because not every art object successfully projects the qualities it has.

There is an argument, which Arnheim does not use, that attempts to show that all art is expressive. It takes as its major premise the proposition that all human artifacts are expressive. That is, in making something a human necessarily leaves in it a trace of his or her attitude, personality, concerns, and point of view. We cannot, it is held, produce anything that fails to point back at us—like the telltale clue in a murder mystery. As we move through the world everything we touch or handle becomes a Peircean index of our passing. Therefore all art has, so to speak, the artist's expressive fingerprints all over it.

Some film theorists, like Balazs, rely on such arguments.[18] But this argument is usable only by the theorist who champions a self-expression concept of art, that is, the notion that all art is the expression of artist's inner thoughts and feelings. It is not viable for a theorist like Arnheim, who holds that expressive qualities are in the patterns of things—that they inhere in the surface structures of objects rather than being the outward sign of something inner and deep, usually a feeling welling up. The self-expression theorist explains expression in terms of the outer imprint of the authentic inner emotion of the artist.[19] The self-expression theory easily segues with the "telltale trace" or "fingerprint" argument. But Arnheim cannot mobilize the "telltale trace" argument since traces need not have anything to do with expression as Arnheim conceives it—that is, as a function of patterns.

Of course, Arnheim does not attempt to use anything like

18. Bela Balazs, *Theory of Film: Character and Growth of a New Art* (New York: Dover, 1970), 89–90.

19. This framework is, of course, badly adapted to account for the undeniable expressivity of commissioned works—for example, the heavy, brooding quality of *film noir* by a jovial contract-director who knows what structures will deliver the expressive effects the script (not his inner life) calls for. Arnheim's locating expression in the structure of the work of art is better calculated to handle such cases.

the "telltale trace" argument. Nor should he, since the argument is unconvincing. First, the argument seems to conflate the idea of a symptom with expression. It holds that a work of art is always somehow symptomatic of something about its maker—but is what it is symptomatic of the same as what it is expressive of? One difference between the two concepts is that what a work expresses is internally focused (or is the focus of the work), whereas a symptom is a telltale clue that surfaces somewhere in the work and may be focal or not. Indeed, a symptom may be almost completely peripheral or virtually imperceptible, whereas an example of artistic expression will have noteworthy salience. As a chosen bit of local detail, the popcorn machine in the amusement park in *Strangers on a Train* may be a clue to or a symptom of Alfred Hitchcock's deep-seated preferences in junk food, but this is not something the film could be said to express. The point is similar to the one brought against the idea that every work of art can be said to be expressive because every work of art has some quality. If a work of art bears a symptom of an artist's inner life that does not entail expression because symptom-bearing does not imply projection.

Nor is the self-expression/symptom argument true in its assertion that objects always bear the trace of their maker. First, there is no reason in principle why an artist cannot efface all the indices of self in a work; it is only as an article of faith that the self-expression theorist believes in the inevitability of the artist's personality surfacing. What of all the techniques employed by twentieth century artists to denude their work of personality? To cite but a few examples: Tristan Tzara's poems composed by randomly drawing cut-out words from a hat; the Surrealists' Exquisite Corpses; the use of chance phrasing in Merce Cunningham's choreography. Have all these impersonalizing strategies failed, and if they have (which I doubt), have they failed as a matter of principle?[20]

20. Another problem that the self-expression theorist has are artworks such that one is hard put to say what emotion or inner impulse the work could be expressing. Two avant-garde candidates for non-expressivity are Walter

But in any case, we need not pursue the "telltale trace" argument any further, because it is basically an argument employed by self-expression theorists, a line from which Arnheim explicitly disassociates himself (*AVP*, 432). Since the "telltale trace" argument seems to be the only available defense for the thesis that all art is expression, however, we must assume that Arnheim does not espouse this tenet on the grounds that it is a factual generalization or empirical summary of the facts. Instead, Arnheim must hold that "art is expression" should be understood as an injunction.

Taking Arnheim's expressionism injunctively, squares with certain aspects of his writings. First, Arnheim believes that certain artistic procedures (like teaching drawing as the replication of geometric-technical properties), though considered artistic in the classificatory sense are not really sensitive to the goals of true art. That is, Arnheim is clearly advocating certain sets of what in the classificatory sense are regarded as artistic practices, while excluding other practices even though he knows that they are normally classified as artistic. This indicates that Arnheim does not believe everything that is called art in our culture *is* expressive, but believes instead that all art *should* be expressive. He begins the chapter called "Expression" in *Art and Visual Perception* by stating that "Every work of art must express something." Since this is not

de Maria's *High Energy Bar*, a length of steel with a certificate attached saying the bar is a work of art only when the certificate is present and E. T. Cone's *Poeme symphonique*, in which a hundred metronomes are turned on and allowed to unwind at their own pace. Neither of these works express any isolatable feeling. Some self-expression theorists attempt to deal with counterexamples by claiming that indeed an inner emotion is expressed but it is one we don't have a name for. It is the emotion that the artist had while creating the work. Call this reflexive self-expression. It is an unlikely hypothesis, however, for its very statement makes it sound like it is being rigged in such a way that it is unfalsifiable. Nevertheless, it does run afoul of certain facts. With nameable emotions there need be no necessary correlation between what the artist is feeling while creating and what is expressed in the finished product. None of the composer's anxiety need show up in the serene sonata. Why, then, is it the case that only unnameable emotive expressions must necessarily be identified with what was felt during the creation of the artwork?

a true generalization, we must presume that the "must" in this sentence is imperatival. It means "ought to." The sentence should not be construed as "Every work of art necessarily does in fact express something" but as "Every work of art ought to express something." On what grounds does Arnheim ask us to accept this commandment?

Arnheim seems to have two basic arguments to support his preference for expressive art. The first is the argument against redundancy: Why should art duplicate the things of nature? Why take snapshots of roses when we already have roses? What purpose is served? Slavish imitation is redundant. Therefore, art should pursue expression. This argument, of course, has a suppressed premise, which is "Art must be either slavish imitation or expression." The premise, moreover, is clearly false insofar as it does not enumerate all the alternative things art could be—for example, formal invention and play.

Furthermore, the second step in Arnheim's argument is also problematic. He holds that art cannot be slavish imitation because slavish imitation serves no purpose. But the purported lack of purpose has not really been defended. For Arnheim has not examined any of the possible purposes that imitation and recording might serve. André Bazin, for example, believed that human beings have a psychological need to immortalize the past.[21] This need was satisfied imperfectly by painting and then ideally by the invention of photography. Thus, when confronted by the ostensibly unanswerable rhetorical question—what purpose could slavish imitation and redundant recording serve?—Bazin had an answer: they serve the purpose of satisfying the human need to immortalize the past, to preserve things (or their appearances) from the corruption of time. I am not here endorsing Bazin's theory. Rather, I refer to it only to make a logical point, namely, that Arnheim's redundancy argument will not succeed unless he eliminates all the plausible answers to his rhetorical question.

21. The next chapter is devoted to Bazin. The psychological theory mentioned above is discussed there at greater length.

He has not done this, so the argument is at least incomplete. Bazinian-type motivations for slavish imitation shift the burden of proof to Arnheim. The argument is probably wrong, as well, because legitimate purposes can probably be found for slavish imitation. It may not be that all imitation serves a single noble purpose, as Bazin has it, but rather that some imitations have diverse purposes. Perhaps some works of art have value because they preserve the past in the sense that they provide us with information about how things looked two hundred years ago. Or possibly some artistic representations are valuable because, though slavish, they show us how something is done, how it hangs together, or how it works. Insofar as slavish imitation may serve various purposes, often cognitive, Arnheim cannot use the redundancy argument.

Arnheim might respond by saying that the purposes I have adduced for slavish imitations do not defeat his argument, for they are not artistic purposes. Two problems, however, would confront Arnheim were he to make this move. First, he attributes a cognitive purpose to expression—it is said to aid our understanding. Thus, if the purposes Arnheim designates for expression is admissable, then the cognitive purposes I advanced above are admissable. Secondly, Arnheim cannot demand that the supporting purposes that warrant expression or imitation be artistic in nature, for this very argument is supposed to establish what is artistic. If Arnheim argues at this point in his theory that art must satisfy artistic purposes, then he will be trapped in a circle.

Arnheim's second argument that art should be expressive is connected to the first: art should serve a purpose or there would be little justification for the place of honor it is given in every known society. Arnheim's previous discussion putatively shows that slavish imitation and mechanical copying serve no purpose. Expression, on the other hand, aids the understanding, because for Arnheim expressiveness is the foregrounding of the characteristic aspects or common properties of things. Thus, in showing us the *forcefulness* of a policeman, we learn something of the police in general. But slavish imitation, mired as it is in the particular, cannot aid the imagination in this way. Therefore, expression rather than imitation should be pursued in art.

I have already questioned Arnheim's implicit assumption that slavish imitation can serve no purpose. But is it true that slavish copying can serve no cognitive purpose, can be of no aid or assistance to the understanding? Clearly with any neutral conception of the understanding, the idea that imitation cannot serve the understanding is false. One can learn a great deal, come to understand much, by perusing mechanical copies. To take a banal example, haven't most of us learned how milk is bottled from mere mechanical recordings of automated assembly lines in dairy plants? Mechanical recordings seem often adequate to the task of showing "so that's how it's done," which indicates that such recordings can be of service to the understanding.

Arnheim appears to believe that slavish imitation cannot aid the understanding because understanding requires relating the object of understanding to other things. Often these are similar things. Understanding subsumes numerically distinct things under common aspects. Art that serves the understanding does so by presenting an object in order to make salient the general qualities the object shares with like objects. One wonders why mere imitation cannot achieve this. Trivially, the artist could copy more than one thing of a kind—for example, paint two locomotives—so viewers could see for themselves what the objects have in common. But more importantly, it does not seem plausible to believe that there is any style of imitation or recording—the supposed geometric-technical procedure notwithstanding—that causes the spectator to see objects absolutely uniquely (that is, not in terms of any general categories or connections with other things).[22] The charge of being so locked to the particular is a red her-

22. Ironically, if there were forms of representation so rooted in the particular and the unique, then aestheticians of a rationalist or German idealist stripe would be prone to declare that this very particularity is what makes representations of this sort the highest form of art—indeed, perhaps the only art.

ring, since people must and do see the objects of imitations in terms of categories.

Another problem with Arnheim's argument is the concept of expression he employs. According to Arnheim, generality is a component of artistic expression. A work of art is expressive of qualities that are common features of things.

> . . . anything can be understood only because it is made up of ingredients not reserved to itself but common to many or all other things. In science, greatest knowledge is achieved when all existing phenomena are reduced to common law. This is true for art also. The mature work of art succeeds in subjecting everything to a dominant law of structure. In doing so, it does not distort the variety of existing things into uniformity. On the contrary, it clarifies their differences by making them all comparable. Braque has said: "By putting a lemon next to an orange they cease to be a lemon and an orange and become fruit. The mathematicians follow this law. So de we." He fails to remember that the virtue of such correlation is twofold. It shows the way in which things are similar and, by doing so, defines their individuality. By establishing a common "style" for all objects, the artist creates a whole in which the place and function of every one of them are lucidly defined. Goethe said: "The beautiful is a manifestation of secret laws of nature, which would have remained hidden to us forever without its appearance." (*AVP*, 440–41)

Artistic expression is the projection of such common qualities. Art serves the understanding by presenting such shared qualities to us.

What is perhaps the most unsettling aspect of this account is its bizarre characterization of artistic expression (which Arnheim treats under the rubric of symbolism in the section of *Art and Visual Perception* from which I drew the preceding quotation). Artistic expression or artistic symbolism is not generally thought of as essentially involved in making us see common properties among things, even among members of the same class of things. An expressive quality is not essentially a quality that an object shares with others of it kind—though it may share such a quality. Rather, an expressive quality is ordinarily an anthropomorphic quality. It is not anthropomorphic quality that a represented object shares with other members of its class. The *dizziness* of a Van Gogh cornfield is not something that his cornfield shares with the cornfields that flank Vermont highways. Thus, at the very least, Arnheim's argument in favor of art-as-expression doesn't support an expressionism that resembles any of the types we are familiar with. Rather, it is an argument for some other sort of art, since expression does not normally involve underlining common features. Arnheim has a new idea of expression in mind that has been articulated in a way that makes it a handmaiden to the understanding.

This may, of course, be dismissed as a quibble. It may be argued that even if the kind of art Arnheimesque expressionism recommends is not ordinary expressions, Arnheim has established its value as the sort of art we ought to make and seek out because of its contribution to the understanding. But the kind of art that Arnheim valorizes has little in common with much art that we count as paradigmatic. And my suspicions here are based on the heavy cognitive burden Arnheim assigns art when he drafts it into the service of the understanding. Through the analogies he draws between art and science, Arnheim seems to be committing the artist to making discoveries about the world and its objects. This would entail that the general properties the artist presents truly apply to the members of the class objects he represents. But this is at odds with what we know of much art. Weston's peppers look impenetrable and Pat O'Neill's waterfalls look metallic. But neither is impenetrability ordinarily a property of peppers nor are cascades usually metallic. Both impenetrability and metallicness here are undeniable instances of aesthetic qualities. But it is difficult to see what service they perform for the understanding. For the understanding is concerned with generalizing from particulars to the common properties of classes. Yet, it is hoped that impenetrability is not a property of the class of green peppers and that waterfalls are not metallic. The expressive and aesthetic qualities of much art are of this sort. The *tortured* folds in the robes in El Greco's *The Vision of St. John the Divine* do not project a general quality of clothing, not even of the garments of the very holy. Thus, the kind of art that Arnheim is urging for adoption is quite different from much of the art we are familiar with. Why should we opt exclusively for this new type of art? Because of the service it promises to perform for the understanding, Arnheim seems to say. But doesn't science do well enough by us as far as the understanding is concerned? It is not my intention to deny that art—some art—might be cognitively valuable and might serve the understanding in the way Arnheim suggests. What I am questioning is Arnheim's argument, which seems to rely on the doubtful premise that *all* art must be cognitively valuable.

If it is false that all art must be expressive, then the concept of art upon which Arnheim builds his film theory is suspect. Art need not be expressive of anything—not of ideas, feelings, or qualities. This, of course, has immediate repercussions for Arnheim's proposed candidate for the determinant characteristic of film. For at the center of that proposal is the notion that the capacity for expression is the key for isolating what features of the medium are essential to film art. The attack on Arnheim's assertion that art is expression, then, reveals that Arnheim's account of cinema's determinant characteristic is too narrow because the expression thesis is not defensible. Art may pursue ends other than expression. Formal invention and representation—to choose two traditional contrasts to expression—are not foreclosed as viable alternatives. This finding, of course, can be run *down* the flagpole. What applies to art in general applies to film art in particular. If other than expressive effects can be explored in art in general, then the same is true of film. Arnheim's determinant characteristic is not compendious enough. It speaks only of the medium's potential for expression although it should also include, for example, reference to its capacity for formal play.

Oscar Fischinger's *ballets mécanique* in cigarette advertisements and David Haxton's complicated cinematic *tromp l'oeils* (and their subversions)—works by formalists, not expressionists—cannot be ruled out of the canon of art or film. Arnheim's account of the determinant characteristic of film needs to be expanded to cover a case like Haxton.

A brief digression: the analogy theory of expression

Arnheim not only holds an expression theory of art, he also has a special theory of expression that I call an "analogy theory of expression." The theory has two components. First, expression in art is said structurally to resemble patterns of feelings. If a work of art has the expressive quality of "sadness," that is because the artwork imitates the structure of sadness. The second component is the requirement of generality, that is, the requirement that the expressive quality the work projects be a quality common to objects of its class. I have already challenged the generality condition as it is applied to expression in the previous section. Now I wish to consider the analogy requirement.

Arnheim explains how objects come to express the qualities they do by claiming that they structurally resemble the moods or feelings that are used to label them. A painting is *joyful* or a shot of a policeman is *forceful* because the pattern of the image resembles the actual feeling-qualities the image is said (perhaps metaphorically?) to possess. The low-angle shot of the policeman makes him appear *large* and *towering*. These are then construed as formal constituents of the feeling of forcefulness. The shot structurally imitates these elements of forcefulness, and thereby projects that quality.

The first thing to note about this theory is that there appear to be certain expressive qualities that cannot be easily captured by this theory, because some anthropomorphic qualities do not have the kind of constituents that lend themselves to structural imitation. Consider Jasper Johns's *Painted Bronzes*, a life-size replica of two Ballantine Ale cans. Looking at the sculpture, I would say that it has a very matter-of-fact quality about it. Now what about the matter-of-fact attitude or mood that is being imitated by these two beer cans? That is, what is there about a matter-of-fact state of mind that can be structurally imitated by a sculpture—that can be distilled into lines and volumes and masses?

I could say that the beer cans are ordinary and that *ordinariness* is part of the matter-of-fact attitude. But is this true? The mind and manner of a Robert McNamara are matter-of-fact but hardly ordinary. Indeed, the way that these beer cans get called matter-of-fact has more to do with homology than with simple resemblance or analogy. That is, when I say that the beer cans are matter-of-fact, I have in mind something like "Baroque statues of princes are to sculptures of beer cans as romantic grandiosity is to matter-of-factness." I perceive the beer cans as matter-of-fact because I identify the choice of subject matter as contrasting with the traditional subject matter of sculpture and as thus projecting quality opposite to the grandiosity associated with the traditional choice. My own opinion is that expression—that is, the projection of expressive qualities—is more often a matter of homology than it is a matter of imitation. This is not the place to develop this theory. Suffice it to say that I have challenged Arnheim's analogy theory by showing there are some cases where imitation is not the appropriate explanation of the basis of some artistic expressive qualities.

Arnheim's theory could also be contested by noting that if the connection between the sculpture and the anthropomorphic quality were based on ordinariness, it is not the case that the ordinariness of the sculpture is part of its formal design or pattern. Arnheim claims, speaking of dance, that "since such visual qualities as speed, shape, or direction are immediately accessible to the eye, it seems legitimate to assume that they are carriers of an expression directly comprehensible to the eye." But the ordinariness of *Painted Bronzes* is not comprehensible to the eye as a concomitant of the visual pattern of the beer cans. Rather the ordinariness is an association appended to the subject matter of the sculpture. The look of the beer cans is not ordinary (nor is it extraordinary);

instead, the beer cans are mundane and ordinary in the socio-economic scheme of things where there is Rothschild Bordeaux. Indeed, Arnheim often tends to confuse various types of associations—including verbal literalizations[23] and homologies—with structural imitations of moods.

The entire process of imitation that Arnheim believes obtains in expression is murky. Speaking of a dance whose movements are said to be expressive of sadness, Arnheim writes:

> The direction was indefinite, changing, wavering, and the body seemed to yield passively to the force of gravitation rather than being propelled by its own initiative. It will be admitted that *the psychical mood of sadness has a similar pattern*. In a depressed person the mental processes are slow and rarely go beyond matters closely related to immediate experiences and interests of the moment. In all his thinking are a softness and a lack of energy. There is little determination, and activity is often controlled by outside forces. (*AVP*, 428, italics added)

The linchpin in this analysis is Arnheim's request that we admit that the mood of sadness possesses a pattern similar to that ascribed to the dance. But should we grant this?

One reason to deny the assertion is that there does not seem to be a single pattern of sadness. In contrast to Arnheim's account, we can easily imagine sadnesses where there is no softness, but hard, pressing pain; where memories pass not slowly but hurriedly and implacably; and where the source of sadness pulses or throbs from the inside and does not control us from the outside. Aren't these sadnesses too? But if they are, can't dances with movements opposite those described by Arnheim also express sadness?

This, then, poses a problem. If sometimes fast movements will be dolorous and at other times slow movements will be, how do spectators recognize sadness in movement? Arn-

---

23. See my "Language and Cinema: Preliminary Notes toward a Theory of Verbal Images," *Millennium Film Journal*, nos. 7/8/9 (1980), 186–217.

heim's theory presupposes a set of invariant features for given moods, which can then be imitated, resulting in expression in artistic media. But if there are no invariant features of moods—if every aspect of a mood can vary—then how do spectators recognize imitations of a single mood?

This objection might be waved aside on the grounds that it raises a question that will be answered in the fullness of time by empirical psychology. When more research is completed we will discover the deep invariant structural elements at play in sadness recognition.

But whether this retort succeeds or is merely a bluff, Arnheim's analogy theory of expression faces the threat of an even deeper sort of skepticism, namely, whether it is appropriate at all to speak of moods and attitudes as having patterns. This is a deeper challenge than claiming that moods have more than one pattern. That at least leaves the artist who expresses sadness with a plethora of things to imitate—even if it fails to tell the artist what is best to imitate. If moods do not have patterns, however, the analogy theory is left completely in the lurch, with nothing to imitate.

Why would anyone doubt that moods have patterns or forms? Reconsider what Arnheim says about the pattern of sadness. Sad people think slowly and respond only to the interests of the moment. They feel lethargic and sense a softness to their thought. Their actions are controlled from the outside. Here are five putative constituents of sadness taken from three different perspectives: two are cognitive features, two are phenomenological features, and one is behavioral. So this is a multidimensional portrait of sadness. Does it propose a pattern? I think it does not. It is a conjunction or a conglomerate or a composite of features, but it is not a pattern. For it makes no sense to speak of *the arrangement* of these features in relation to each other. They suggest no internal design, no formal structure or configuration. True, these elements may compose a regularly recurring conjunction over time. Thus, they are elements of a recurring pattern. But in isolation, viewed from outside of time so to speak, these five features do not hang together as a coherent pattern, that is, as a pattern in the sense of a design—specifically, as a design capable of imitation.

When we speak of patterns in the sense of a design or configuration, we are talking about something that it is easy to imagine being copied or mirrored by the perceptible media of lines, masses, speeds of objects, and so forth. That is, where the phenomenon has a discernible arrangement, we can conceive of that arrangement being mapped in another medium with a correlatable range or field of relations. But the five constituents of sadness do not propose a pattern of interrelations that can in any straightforward way be copied. The dance does not imitate the pattern of sadness. At best it imitates the constituents—and those individually, so to speak, not as an ensemble.

Even this may be admitting too much. For one must wonder whether "imitation" best characterizes the nature of the correlation between these dance elements and the mood to which they putatively correspond. For example, sad thinking, we are told, barely stretches beyond immediate circumstances and interests. The dance movement embodies this constituent of sadness through many changes in the movement. Is changing one's direction often an imitation or copy of thought that is rooted in the here and now? Clearly not—there is a much more complicated story to be told about how this changing movement comes to symbolize sad thought. One important idea behind this choreographic choice is the notion that thought tied to immediate circumstances is *liable* to change a great deal, as circumstances change. But, of course, the circumstances need not change a great deal. The sad person may lead a sad but uneventful existence. Thus, to portray sad thought via changing directions is not to copy the inevitable circumstances of sad thinkers but to abstract one possible scenario of sad thought and to make it ideally exemplify sadness.

Also, the dancer does not mimetically enact the wavering behavior of sad thinkers. No reference is made to concrete surroundings or circumstances. The dancer is not portraying a realistic walk with many twists and turns. Rather, the behavior of the wavering sad thinker is being transposed into wavering, non-naturalistic dance movement. That is, in the abstract, atmospheric sort of piece Arnheim describes, the dancer does not look like any sad person anyone has ever seen or is likely to see. Sadness is expressed through a complex process of transpositions, in which a train of thought is correlated to continuous lines of movement so that breaks and changes in thought are signaled by breaks and changes in the line of movement. This complex symbolic structure is not reducible to a simple matter of imitation. It is more like a charade than a mimetic, naturalistic enactment. Indeed, the success of the changing line of movement probably relies more on linguistic associations than upon mimesis. That is, we see the line of movement as standing for a train of thinking because in our language we speak of *lines of thought*. The choreography exploits a commonplace metaphor to make its point. Thus, the concept of imitation scarcely comprehends the symbolic complexity in this partial example of expressing sadness. Abstraction, transposition, and literalization are all primary devices in this case. Similar demonstrations can be given for many of Arnheim's other examples—for instance, passivity standing for lack of determination. I would not go so far as to claim that imitation plays no role in expression. But it cannot explain the whole of expression as Arnheim's analogy theory purports.

Moods, like sadness, are not objects or things that can be copied. Nor do they have patterns whose structures can be imitated. Moods may have constituents, however, and these may be translated into and evoked by artistic media. But there is not one process of translation (or perhaps more aptly—association at play here, such as imitation, but many, including abstraction, transposition, literalization, homology, metonymic association, and so on.

The divergence thesis

Arnheim holds that an art form must diverge from mechanical recording. The first problem in evaluating this imperative is to identify what Arnheim could mean by "mechanical recording" and what exactly Arnheim counts as divergence from mechanical recording. Sometimes Arnheim seems to call for divergence from the mechanical recording of *reality*. But this construal does not readily cover all his cases. For example, he counts editing as a divergence from mechanical recording, but editing is not necessarily a divergence from reality. Suppose there is a brush fire and it is put out by three firemen. I take a shot of the fire, a shot of the three firemen stepping off their tanker truck, and a shot of them dousing the flame. Then I splice the shots together. The result is a sequence of film that shows "The brush fire was put out by the three firemen." It does not make sense to say that this edited array diverges from reality, because the event just described is what really happened. Thus "reality" cannot always explicate what Arnheim means by mechanical recording.

Of course, Arnheim does not have reality as his foil for art. Rather, he wants art to diverge from normal perception. But it is difficult to grasp the relation between mechanical recording and normal perception. Arnheim cannot mean that art must diverge from the mechanical recording of normal perception—no one can mimetically copy my perceptions. My percepts, for example, make no imprint on celluloid.

To understand the connection between mechanical recording and normal perception we must grant two things. First, that "mechanical" is being used metaphorically as well as literally. Mechanical recording is rote, pragmatic, utilitarian, quantitative, scientific, unimaginative. In this metaphoric sense, it can be executed by a person—a painter—as well as by a machine (though it must be added that Arnheim seems to assume that this is a kind of recording that a machine like a camera will deliver if used in terms of its standard, minimum capacity). Moreover, "normal," in the concept of normal perception does not only mean "sights we can see in ordinary experience," but also "sights seen in a certain attitude," in what might be thought of as the proper, pragmatically correct way of seeing. That is, the normal perception that Arnheim wants films and other works of art to diverge from is normative in nature. He wants artworks to diverge from attention to only the quantitative, pragmatic, geometric-technical representation of things that is the standard that has been inculcated in our normal habits of perception. Thus, the call for art to diverge from mechanical reproduction is really the call for art to focus attention on the other-than-geometric-technical qualities of things. Arnheim fears that, given its basic design, film tends (if used without imagination) to reproduce only the geometric-technical properties of its referents.

One consideration that Arnheim uses to endorse the divergence thesis seems to be the redundancy argument: "Why copy reality, when the original is already enough?" As I have shown earlier, this is a weak point. Reasons for copying what we already have can be supplied. Bazin said that by recording the past, film satisfies psychic needs humans have to counter the corruptions of time. Kracauer felt that by using the furniture of the universe as its vocabulary, the film medium redeems physical reality; it acquaints us again with the particulars in all their uniqueness at a point in our cultural history when the scientific-generalizing tendency reigns supreme. Or, more modest motivations can be offered, at least for some copying—as a means of disseminating information and coming to know something through simulation. There need not be a single answer to the question, "Why bother to copy the world?" There may be many answers, pertaining to specific cases of copying. And once this is admitted, the rhetorical force of the redundancy question dissolves into thin air.

Arnheim's major reason for upholding the divergence thesis, however, is that he believes that when the normal appearances of things are subverted, their expressive properties will become perceptible. Arnheim seems to say at some points that divergence affects the object, by casting it in a new light; but at other times he seems to say that divergence affects the spectators, thrusting them into a special attitude. In either case, divergence is not valued for its own sake, as it might be for a nineteenth-century Parisian aesthete like Huysmans. Rather, divergence is upheld as a means to the end of making expression perceptible.

Since Arnheim justifies divergence in terms of what it does, one way to refute Arnheim's theory is to show that in certain cases divergence may stand in the way of the effect that supposedly justifies it. In fact, there are some cases where divergence from mechanical recording would result in sacrificing the expressive qualities an artist is after. The reason for this is that certain expressive qualities actually accrue to mechanical recordings. One such quality has already been discussed: matter-of-factness. I can imagine a filmmaker opting for mere mechanical recording because of the feelings it projects. Though I never saw Warhol's legendary film *Empire*—surely a paragon of mere mechanical recording from all accounts—I imagine that it delivered an intended, cool, detached feeling exemplifying the icy, deceptively vacant stare of its director. Moreover, Arnheim seems to take any nonquantitative property that an object vividly possesses to be an expressive quality. Given this broad extension, it is clear that there are a great many qualities that mechanical recording can be used to project. Often fiction filmmakers opt for the simple recording technique of documentaries to give their films a "raw" or "authentic" feel. And, of course, a filmmaker might adopt the mechanical look of an earlier period of filmmaking—for example, the look of the forties home movie, as in *Raging Bull*—to evoke the feeling of a certain period. I might make a comedy in a turn-of-the-century format to invoke the feeling of that supposed age of innocence. Likewise, a director might choose to emphasize the geometric-technical qualities in his materials to promote a feeling of "objectivity."

Earlier I noted that arguments against film-as-art are made on the basis of objections not only to the mere recording of reality, but also to the mere recording of theater. Arnheim, of course, wants film to diverge from both. I have already shown, however, that in certain cases the mechanical recording of reality may be justified. Likewise, the mechanical recording of theater may be artistically warranted. To see this in terms of film, one need only note the conventions in many American films that have certain characters portrayed in a very theatrical style while other characters are played more naturalistically. This is often done to portray the theatrically enacted character in terms of some quality expressible by or connected to stage, theater, or acting metaphors—for example, so and so is playing a role. In the film *Becky Sharp*, the eponymous leading character, played by Miriam Hopkins, shifts from naturalistic acting to stage acting almost every time she becomes involved in deceiving people.[24] This technique appropriately underlines her deceitfulness by invoking such notions related to stage acting as artifice, illusion, fiction, pretense, and so on. Now, what is true of parts of films, I take it, can be true of whole films as well. Thus, someone might make a film that is a mere mechanical recording of a theater piece for the purpose of mining metaphors of theatricality. Perhaps the director wishes to show that all the world is a stage and all the people are role-players. Some such point seems to accrue to the film of Genet's *The Balcony*. Or perhaps a related point might be made—for example, everything is false. In retrospect, the theatricality of *The Cabinet of Dr. Caligari* might be felt by some to have this connotation. Theater and acting are deep and rich metaphors in our culture. I see no reason why a filmmaker cannot attempt to exploit them for expressive effects by presenting what appear as mere mechanical recordings of theater.

Arnheim's primary defense of the divergence thesis is that it makes expression possible. But this overlooks cases where mechanical recording itself can be used to project expressive qualities. Thus, there are some cases where divergence from recording stands in the way of expression. But since divergence is only important in terms of the production of expression, in such cases where it blocks expression, divergence is not warranted. Therefore, divergence from recording is not a necessary condition for either art or film art. The divergence theory is false.

24. A more detailed description of the theatrical acting in this film is contained in my "Becky Sharp Takes Over," in *The English Novel and the Movies*, edited by Michael Klein and Gillian Parker (New York: Frederick Ungar Publishing Co., 1981).

The specificity thesis

The notion that each art form has its own special subject matter that it of all the arts is best suited to represent is an eighteenth-century idea. The idea grew in reaction to an earlier style of art theorizing, represented by works such as Abbé Charles Batteux's 1746 treatise called *The Fine Arts Reduced to the Same Principle.*[25] For Batteux, all the arts were similar because they all had the same subject—the imitation of the beautiful in nature. This tendency to reduce the arts to their common denominator was the dominant trend in pre-Enlightenment art theory. During the eighteenth-century, however, thinkers began to oppose this type of theorizing. They began to focus on what differentiated the arts from one another. An important work in this new tendency was Abbé Jean Baptiste Dubos's *Critical Reflections on Painting and Poetry.*[26] Dubos claimed that poetry and painting differ, in that painting imitates the single moment whereas poetry imitates process. Similar analyses were offered in the works of James Harris and Moses Mendelsohn.[27] The best known work of this revisionist sort, entitled *Laocoön*, was published in 1766 by Gotthold Ephraim Lessing. That book contains several important presumptions of Arnheim's *Materialtheorie*: that the arts (1) differ from each other in terms of (2) what each represents (imitates) best, due to (3) the peculiar (specific) structure of its formal/physical medium.

Comparing painting and poetry, Lessing writes:

> I argue thus. If it be true that painting employs wholly different signs or means of imitation from poetry—the one using forms and colors in space and the other articulate sounds in time—and if signs must unquestionably stand in convenient relation with the thing signified, then signs arranged side by side can represent only ob-

25. In Monroe Beardsley, *Aesthetics: From Classical Greece to the Present* (New York: Macmillan, 1966; Alabama: University of Alabama Press, 1975), 160.
26. Ibid.
27. Ibid.

jects existing side by side, or whose parts so exist, while consecutive signs can express only objects which succeed each other in time.

Objects which exist side by side, or whose parts so exist, are called bodies. Consequently, bodies with their visible properties are the peculiar subjects of painting.

Objects which succeed each other, or whose parts succeed each other in time, are actions. Consequently, actions are the peculiar subjects of painting.[28]

Here we see Lessing attempting to extrapolate from the structure of the medium—the structure of what, in advance of semiotics, he calls "signs"—to the appropriate subject matter of the medium. Arnheim, as well, attempts to move from the structural peculiarities of the medium to injunctions about the proper direction of filmmaking.

Before examining the specificity thesis in terms of truth or falsity, I would like to note that although for many reasons the thesis no longer seems acceptable, in its day it performed a useful service. The specificity thesis served as a corrective to the vagueness of the tendency to reduce all the arts to a common denominator. As a result, theorists began to look more closely at the various art forms. The gain was one of rigor. This does not, of course, entail that the specificity thesis is true. However, theorists like Arnheim who adopt it do tend to give very close, precise accounts of artistic structures. Thus, even if the specificity thesis is false, it has beneficial side effects.

One difference between Lessing and Arnheim is that Lessing focuses on the physical medium, of painting for example, and teases out of that an analysis of what the medium can represent at its best—what is most convenient for its signs to depict—whereas Arnheim, in *Film as Art*, examines cinematic devices to find where they fall short of successful representation. Lessing is concerned to find where a medium excels in representation, whereas Arnheim is most interested in where

28. Gotthold Ephraim Lessing, *Laocoön* (New York: Noonday Press, 1969), 91.

a medium falters in terms of perfect representation. In and of itself, this contrast does not present a problem for Arnheim. Arnheim, like Lessing, wants to establish a special domain for each medium. Film, he tells us, is the realm of the animated image. But there is a lacuna in this New Laocoön. For how do the various peculiarities that Arnheim points to—the lack of constancy of size and of the spatio-temporal continuum, and so forth—ever add up to or imply that film is concerned with the animated image? The peculiarities or specificities of the medium that Arnheim points to constitute a list of things that cinematic representations do not have. How do these amount to a positive commitment to the animated image? If the peculiar structures of the medium are what entail the medium's commitment to the animated image, it is not clear how Arnheim's examples show this.

Another problem with the specificity thesis is that Arnheim seems to believe that, as a matter of fact, every medium diverges from the referents it represents because of its own peculiar formal/physical structure. Arnheim says "Representation never produces a replica of the object but its structural equivalent in a *given* medium" (*AVP*, 162). But if each medium automatically, so to speak, diverges not only from each referent but also from the depiction of such referents in other media, then what point is there to the specificity thesis stated as an injunction? That is, why urge artists to make certain that they exploit the peculiarities of their medium if this is unavoidable and bound to happen anyway? Moreover, how can Arnheim rail against sound films? Sound films will automatically be differentiated from theater because the media are physically different. If one believes that every medium is automatically unique in terms of the structure of its symbols, then why fear that media will illegitimately spill over each others' boundaries? It will be impossible.

Arnheim's specificity thesis is not a description; it is a recommendation. Were the specificity thesis a description, there could be no problems involving the trespassing of the sound film in the domain of theater. It would make no sense to use the specificity thesis to attempt to chide filmmakers if the

specificity thesis were a description—filmmakers would necessarily employ the peculiar (specific) characteristics of their
medium.

As a recommendation, the specificity thesis appears to have
two components. One component is the idea that there is
something that each medium does best. The other is that each
of the arts should do what differentiates it from the other arts.
These two components can be called the excellence requirement and the differentiation requirement. The two can be
combined in the imperative that each art form should explore
only those avenues of development in which it exclusively excels above all other arts. The incorporation of "exclusively"
in this formula sounds the differentiation requirement while
the rest of the formula states the excellence requirement. Applied to Arnheim's film theory, the specificity thesis states
that filmmakers should stress the differentiating features (the
limitations) that enable the medium to portray animated action (what cinema does best).

Some of the problems with the specificity thesis are the result of the combination of the differentiation and excellence
requirements. The assumption is that what a medium does
best will coincide with what differentiates it. But why should
this be so? For example, many media narrate. Film, drama,
prose, and epic poetry all tell stories. For argument's sake, let
us say narration is what each does best—that is, best of all the
things each of them does. However, this does not differentiate
these artforms. What does the specificity thesis require in
such a situation? If film and the novel both excel in narration,
should (1) neither art form narrate since narration fails to differentiate them? or (2) should film not narrate since narration
will fail to differentiate it from the novel and the novel
claimed the domain of narration first? or (3) should the novel
give up narration and let the newcomer have its chance?

The first alternative is simply absurd; it would sacrifice a
magnificent cultural invention—narration—for whatever bizarre satisfaction that could be derived from adherence to the
differentiation requirement. I am assuming that excellence is
more important to us than differentiation.

The second alternative is also unattractive. In this case the specificity thesis would seem to confuse history with ontology. That is, film is to forswear narrating just because literature already has that turf staked out. But surely this is only an accident of history. What if movies had arisen before writing? Then would literature have to find some other occupation? Clearly such accidents of history should not preclude a medium from pursuing an area in which it excels. Nor should accidents of history be palmed off as ontological necessities—another proclivity of the specificity thesis. The special subject matter of each medium supposedly follows from its nature. But the story is more complicated, since a medium specializes in what it excels in only if that area of special achievement differentiates it from other media. The question of differentiation is not simply a question about the nature of the medium; it is a question about the comparison of arts. And it is quite possible that a new art may be invented that excels in an area where an older art already excels. Awarding the domain to the older art just because it is already established seems arbitrary, as does the third alternative—awarding the domain to the younger art just because it is younger. If two arts both excel in domain, it seems natural to allow them both to explore it. That will enrich the culture by multiplying the number of excellent things. This is surely the case with narrative. The world is far richer for having novels *and* fiction films *and* epic poems *and* dramas *and* comic books *and* narrative paintings *and* operas, though the differentiation component of the specificity thesis would block this.

One point should be emphasized in the preceding discussion: narration does seem to be one instance where many arts do share the same pursuit. And yet specificity theorists, especially the major film theorists who champion the specificity thesis, rarely seem to be ruffled by this fact. It seems as though they are so concerned to differentiate film from theater that they fail to notice that film is similar to other narrative arts, such as the short story and the novel. These latter similarities or overlaps seem to be tolerable. Why? The only way I can account for this anomaly is that historical circumstances were such that only the canned theater argument against film vividly presented itself as so threatening that it had to be dealt with. For, of course, in the days when these arguments raged, theater and film could be thought of as directly competing for the same audience. They were locked in economic conflict as well as aesthetic struggle, which meant that more was at issue in the battle between them than in the relation between film and the other narrative arts. Thus, many film theorists who upheld the specificity thesis never noticed that they should have been exercised by the overlap with the other narrative arts, even though such an overlap should call into question the specificity thesis.

The specificity thesis has both an excellence component and a differentiation conponent. Perhaps one interpretation of the theory is that each art form should pursue those projects that fall in the area of intersection between what the art form excels in and what differentiates it from other art forms. But this does not seem to be an acceptable principle because, among other things, it entails that the reason an art form might not be employed to do what it does best is that some other art form also does it well. *The specificity thesis seems to urge us to sacrifice excellence on principle.* But excellence is, in fact, always the overriding consideration in deciding whether a particular practice or development is acceptable in art.

Indeed, I believe that what could be called the priority of excellence is the central telling point against the specificity thesis. To dramatize this, let us imagine that for some reason the only way that G. B. Shaw could get backing for *Pygmalion* was to make it as a talking picture—since in our possible world Shaw was known only as a successful screen writer. Let us also suppose that in some sense it is true that theater is a better showcase for aesthetically crafted language. Would we decide that *Pygmalion* should not be made? I think our answer is "no," because our intuitions are that the specificity thesis should not be allowed to stand between us and excellence.

Nor need the excellence in question be a matter of the highest excellence achievable in a given medium. The specificity thesis seems to urge that a medium pursue only what it does best. But if a medium does something well and the occasion arises to do it, why should it be inhibited because there is something it does better? Certain magical transformations—turning weaklings into werewolves for example—can be most vividly executed in cinema. But they can also be done quite efficiently on stage. Should this minor excellence be foregone in a stage adaptation of *Dr. Jekyll and Mr. Hyde*, either because transformation is not what theater does best or because film can do it better?

Another disturbing feature of the specificity thesis is that it appears to envision each art form on the model of a highly specialized tool with a range of determinate functions. A film, play, poem, or painting is thought of, it seems, analogous to something like a Phillips screwdriver. If you wish to turn a screw with a cross-shaped groove on top, use a Phillips screwdriver. If you wish to explore the potentials of aesthetically crafted language, use theater. If your topic is animated action, use film. Likewise, just as you should not use a Phillips screwdriver as a church key (though it can open a beer can), you should not, all things being equal, use cinema to perform theater's task, and vice versa. But I think it is incumbent on us to question whether this underlying metaphor has any applicability when it comes to art forms. Are artforms highly specialized tools? I think not. If art forms are like tools at all, then they are more like sticks than like Phillips screwdrivers. That is, they can be used to do many things; they have not been designed to perform a specific task. In most cases art forms are not designed—that is, they are not invented with a specific task in mind. Moreover, even with self-consciously invented arts like film, it is soon discovered that the form can perform many more tasks than the one it was originally designed for. Indeed, interest in art forms is to a large measure interest in how artists learn or discover new ways of using their medium. The idea of the artist discovering new ways of using the medium would make no sense if the medium were designed for a single purpose.

An artistic medium, including a self-consciously invented one, is such that many of its potentials remain to be discovered. But discovery would not be a relevant expectation to have of artists nor would an interest in it be relevant to an art form, if the task of the art form were as fixed as that of a Phillips screwdriver. A correlative fact against the idea of the fixedness of function of artforms is the fact that they very often continue to exist over time, obviously because they are periodically reinvented and new uses are found for them. But if art forms were as determinately set in their functions as are Phillips screwdrivers, one would expect them, or at least many of them, to pass away as their function becomes archaic. That they are readapted, reinvented, and redirected bodes ill for the metaphor of the art form as specialized tool— a view that seems strongly suggested by the specificity thesis.

One consideration offered in favor of the specificity thesis proceeds by asking why else there would be *different* media unless they were supposed to pursue different ends? That is, the specificity thesis is, in this light, an inference to the best explanation. Given the fact that we have a number of arts, we ask "Why?" The answer that seems most reasonable is that each art has, or should have, a different function.

This particular line of thought presupposes that it is legitimate to ask why we have different arts. It also supposes that it is legitimate to expect as an answer to this question something like a rational principle. Perhaps for idealists it is reasonable to expect a rationale or a rationalization here. But for others the issue appears to be a matter of historical accident. I believe that it was Wittgenstein who said that where there is no question, there is no answer. We can use this principle, I think, to rid ourselves of the preceding argument. For its question, when stated nonelliptically, is not "Why are there diverse arts?" but "What is the rationale that explains why we have exactly the diverse arts that we have?" Now there may be no single answer to this question. Rather we may have to settle for a series of answers to the former question—answers of a historical and anthropological variety. For example, we have film because Edison invented it to supplement the phonograph; we have painting because one day a Cro-Magnon splashed some adhesive victuals on a cave wall and it looked strikingly like a bison; and so on. But there is no answer to the second question: "What is the rationale for having exactly the several arts we do have?" Rather, each art arose due to a chain of events that led to its discovery or invention and to its popularization. The result is the *collection* of arts we have, which we only honorifically refer to as a *system*. There is no rationale for the system, for in truth it is only a collection. Thus, we have no need for the specificity thesis, for the question it answers—"Why is there a system of different arts?"—is really not an admissible question at all.[29]

Before concluding this section, some discussion of Arnheim's application of the specificity thesis to sound film is appropriate, for Arnheim's maledictions against the talking picture are undoubtedly the most notorious part of his film theory. Arnheim holds that if there is a truly composite art form, then none of the constituent media can be anything but fully developed. That is, in a truly composite art form none of the media combined would be subservient, nor would any be redundant, that is, merely repetitive of what is already conveyed by another, more dominant, medium. Each must function equally and be fully articulated on its own terms. For Arnheim, opera is not really a composite because music is the dominant constituent medium to which the language and the scenography are subservient. Nor are laconic talking films with functional dialogue acceptable composites, because such dialogue is subservient to the visuals and, for the most part, is redundant to the action. On the other hand, more fully developed dialogue tends to make the film medium subservient to speech, paralyzing the action and thwarting the medium's commitment to animated movement. Dialogue cannot be artistically expanded upon and articulated without interfering with the depiction of action, which will transform the work

29. For expanded and amplified arguments against the specificity thesis, see my "The Specificity of Media in the Arts," *The Journal of Aesthetic Education* 19 (Winter 1984), 5–20; and my "Medium Specificity Arguments and the Self-consciously Invented Arts: Film, Photography and Video," *Millennium Film Journal*, nos. 14/15 (1984–1985), 127–53.

into a piece of theater, denying the camera the opportunity to represent what it alone portrays best (*FAA*, 288–30).

There are two sides to this argument. Either dialogue is made to facilitate action, in which case the medium of speech is short-changed, or dialogue is developed artistically, in which case the action of the film is paralyzed. In neither case is the art truly composite. Instead, the sound film is a mongrel.

Of course, one wonders whether Arnheim's ideal of a truly composite art form is a worthwhile one. Why must a legitimate composite abide by such inflexible standards of equality between the constituent media? Often in nineteenth-century ballet the music was not so distinguished as the dancing, since the point of this form was to direct attention to the movement. Does this imply that ballet, or at least ballet done in this format, is not a truly composite art? But if ballet is not a truly composite art and neither is opera, then one suspects that Arnheim is defining the category of composite art out of existence. Moreover, if the example of nineteenth-century ballet is taken seriously, one horn of Arnheim's dilemma can be neutralized. It may be perfectly acceptable to have composite art forms where one medium is subservient to another. Specifically, there may be many sound films that, although their scripts do not make edifying reading, have perfectly serviceable dialogue supporting the visuals. Films like *Citizen Kane, Psycho*, and *Rules of the Game* surely are examples of this sort. Thus, questioning Arnheim's criterion for a truly composite medium dispels half of the dilemma.[30]

The other half can be dispelled by questioning whether it is impossible to combine language and visuals so that each is given full honor. Surely the opening scene of Olivier's *Henry V* fully honors both action and poetry. Other examples also come to mind, Polonsky's *Force of Evil* for one—a film whose highly poetic script was rhythmically integrated with the action.

30. Interestingly, Arnheim differs from other specificity theorists like Panofsky who are willing to accept functional dialogue as the proper means of keeping cinema pure while at the same time using sound.

Furthermore, several objections raised against the specificity thesis in general can be applied to its use in the context of
the sound film. Undoubtedly, great moments in dialogue
film—for example, Groucho's speech to the ministers in *Duck
Soup*—are not begrudged because they were seen on celluloid
rather than on stage. If the specificity thesis entails cutting this
scene, then so much the worse for the specificity thesis. Of
course, it may be held that the specificity theorist is not committed to disparaging this scene. Rather, such a theorist
might praise the scene, but as theater rather than film. But
this seems wrong. For part of what is excellent about the
scene is that it is delivered by that man, Groucho Marx, with
that voice, at that period of time (the Depression). These
things fit together in a powerful expressive ensemble. Indeed,
part of what is valuable about the scene is that it is a *recording*
of a performance, exactly the aspect of cinema Arnheim is
most disposed to denounce. Moreover, the black and white
photography, the cut of the actors' clothing, their diction,
their bearing all conspire to evoke a powerful feeling of "thir-
ties-ness" that could not be replicated today on stage or
film—not only because many of the actors are dead but also
because films don't look and sound that way any more, and,
in all likelihood, theater never did. That that specific performance is on film—film of a certain technological vintage—
is part and parcel of the scene's power, no matter that it is
dominated by speech.

Summary and Conclusions

Rudolf Arnheim's theory of film exemplifies a main tendency
in the theory and practice of the silent film era that may be
called *creationist*. Faced with the dismissal of film, the progeny
of photography, for being a mere mechanical reproduction of
reality, Arnheim, like other silent-film theorists and filmmakers, strove to show that film could creatively reconstitute
reality, rather than only slavishly copying it. In demonstrat-
ing the specific ways in which this could be done, he not only
defeated the philosophical prejudices that confronted the nas-

cent art of film, but provided many invaluable analyses of particular cinematic structures.

In the process of defending film from its detractors, however, Arnheim mobilized a number of philosophically suspect presuppositions: that art is necessarily expressive; that art must diverge from the mere copying of reality; and that each art form has a specific area of invention defined primarily by the limitations of the specific medium (here, notably film) in question. Undoubtedly, these presuppositions were more extravagant than the case for film art required, though their adoption was certainly not wayward within the theoretical context in which Arnheim operated. Much of this chapter has been spent contesting these presuppositions. The point of this exercise is not to chasten Arnheim, who performed an enormous service for film theory and for film itself, but to challenge the underlying presuppositions that, though perhaps understandable in the theoretical and philosophical milieu of the twenties and thirties, continue today only as unexamined prejudices.

One of Arnheim's major assumptions—that art forms such as film are to be analyzed in terms of the specificity of their medium—is a theme that will continue, though in very different ways, in the ensuing chapters. In each of its manifestations, this thesis will be rejected. Given the critical bent of my exposition, it is especially crucial to note that although medium-specificity analyses are consistently challenged here theoretically, it must be acknowledged that they have, as a matter of fact, performed a salutary service in enhancing our understanding of film. For even if such theories are motivated by wrong (essentialist) reasons, their tendency is to direct attention to a close examination of characteristic cinematic structures. Arnheim's elucidation of camera angulation in this chapter is but one example; Bazin's discussion of depth-of-field cinematography in the next is another.

Chapter Two

Cinematic Representation and Realism: André Bazin and the Aesthetics of Sound Film

---

Bazin's Position in/on Film Theory

Bazin's importance

No figure is as important in the history of film theory as André Bazin. His influences on contemporary theory, though diverse, are unmistakable. Some contemporary theorists like Stanley Cavell follow a Bazinian line outright—claiming, with Bazin, that cinema is essentially a realist art.[1] Other theorists, such as V. F. Perkins, while diverging from Bazin on many crucial points, nevertheless attempt to incorporate central aspects of Bazin's theory into their own work; in Perkins's case, this can be seen in his elaboration of the concept of credibility.[2] Thus, while rejecting Bazin's theory as a whole, such authors seek to preserve some of its parts. Even contemporary film theorists who might be called ciné-Brechtians and who would consider themselves violent opponents of Bazin oddly enough buy into central parts of Bazin's theory.[3] Indeed, they often more or less accept Bazin's characterization of the spectator's response to the screen image as the accurate account. Bazin pictures the viewer of mimetic cinematography as accepting that he or she is witnessing a slice of reality—the film viewer is said to regard the image as the representation of some event or state of affairs from the past. Although ciné-Brechtians denounce this phenomenon as ideologically pernicious—a species of politically motivated, deceptive illusionism—they nevertheless hold as correct something very like the Bazinian story of how normal spectators regard mimetic images. They agree with Bazin on the putative facts of the case, but disagree on how these should be morally evaluated. What Bazin sees as the glory of cinema— its *purported* capacity to move viewers to accept that they are

---

1. Stanley Cavell, *The World Viewed* (New York: Viking, 1971).
2. V. F. Perkins, *Film as Film* (Baltimore: Penguin, 1972). This point is discussed at length in the next chapter.
3. Ciné-Brechtianism is discussed in my "Address to the Heathen," *October*, no. 23 (Winter 1982), 103–9.

in the presence of the referent of the image—ciné-Brechtians bewail as film's disgrace. Yet, they must accept the Bazinian spectator as the normal spectator before they can mount their attack upon the classical, mimetic, narrative cinema.[4]

Bazin's influence was also strongly felt by the generation, often called auteurists, that immediately preceded the present crop of film theorists. The authors I have in mind include Godard, Truffaut, Chabrol, Rivette, and others who, before they became filmmakers, were polemicists on the pages of the magazine called *Cahiers du cinéma* (which was cofounded by Bazin). In America, Andrew Sarris was and is the most distinguished *auteur* theorist. This theory—which attributes value to films insofar as they manifest or clearly evince the personal vision or stamp of their director (*auteur*/author)—was not propounded explicitly by Bazin (though in his criticism Bazin does lean toward the great-genius approach to art). What the auteurists learned from Bazin, however, was a sensitivity to *mise-en-scène*. And when one examines the pantheons erected by auteurist critics, one immediately sees the influence of Bazin, insofar as the directors most honored by these critics are often those, like John Ford, who excel as *metteurs-en-scène*, tending to favor long takes over pyrotechnical editing.

Not only is Bazin important for his influence. He is also the major representative of the change in direction that cinema took after the sound film survived its first decade and a half. That direction is often summarized by the word "realism." The film theory associated with the silent film was preoccupied with showing that film could be more than the mere recording of reality. Through editing, lighting, camera angulation, and the like, the filmmaker could reconstitute reality, offer interpretations of reality, and make statements about, rather than only copy, reality. Silent-film theorists—for ex-

4. Bazin's writings are also gaining contemporary importance in the newly developed debates concerning photography where he is taken—along with Sontag and Barthes—as one of the major proponents of the view that the camera image is a replica of some sort of reality. This position is addressed in my "Concerning Photographic and Cinematic Representation," forthcoming in *Dialectics and Humanism*.

ample, Arnheim, Eisenstein, Vertov—favored highly stylized films. Often these theorists seemed to believe that the more a film diverges or departs from the way the world normally appears, the better. Bazin led the counterattack against this tendency of silent-film theory that I have called creationist. While the creationists located the truly cinematic wherever the medium diverged from a perfect recording of reality, Bazin argued that the truly cinematic film stays as close to recording as possible, eschewing the interpretation, recreation, or reconstitution of reality.

This debate between sound-film theorists and silent-film theorists was in large measure precipitated by the introduction of sound in film. Sound enhanced the recording capacity of the medium—the dimension that the silent-film theorists held in lowest esteem. As the sound film evolved from the late twenties to the early forties, a gap developed between the undeniable international accomplishments of the sound film and the established film theory. The theory no longer seemed adequate to the task of accounting for cinema's newest achievements. A new type of theory was called for. Bazin offered such a theory, one sensitive to the masterpieces of sound film, and in the process he reversed the evaluative priorities of established film theory. Where Arnheim deprecated the recording aspect of film, Bazin chose this dimension of the medium as the major source of value in film. Where established film theory urged that the filmmaker be highly interventionist or creationist—that is, manipulating and rearranging images of reality almost like a poet manipulates words—Bazin advocated the adoption of formal strategies of composition, lighting, camera movement, framing, and narration such that meaning would not be imposed on reality but would rather seem to emerge from the interaction of the recorded event with a participant (rather than a passive) spectator. Where silent-film theorists often read as if they are embarrassed by the photographic, mechanical, recording components of the medium, Bazin, in the forefront of the realist movement in film theory, looks to exactly those elements of film to discover "the cinematic." From the perspective of the history of film theory, Bazin is a watershed figure. His theory marks the most decisive moment in the transition from the silent-film paradigm to the sound-film paradigm. Moreover, since this is the most important shift in the history of film theory, Bazin's central role in it guarantees him a privileged place in the study of film theory.

Bazin was not an academic theoretician. He was a journalist and a polemicist. Although he wrote for newspapers, he also contributed lengthy articles to intellectual reviews and general interest journals. His literary output was vast and varied, including theoretical pieces, film history, and film criticism. Many of his critical pieces and his observations about individual films and filmmakers have stood the test of time. They are the first and last word on the subject. But Bazin is also important as a historian of film style. In many ways his accomplishment is comparable to that of the art historian H. Wolfflin.[5] Bazin essayed a stylistic history of the medium that he was concerned with—his is the first major effort to encompass the stylistic development of both silent *and* sound film. In the course of tracing the logic and structure of the evolution of film history, Bazin mobilized a battery of dubious philosophical and metaphysical presuppositions. It is possible, however, to reread Bazin while ignoring these excessive theoretical commitments so that his observations about the evolution of film style can be de-mythologized leaving us with several insights about the progress of film history that have lasting value.

Once Bazin is de-mythologized, he can be reread as claiming that the advent of sound caused artists to reevaluate the possibilities of their medium. One avenue of response to sound can be seen in the early sound films of Rene Clair—for example, *À Nous la liberté*. This is a kind of formalist response. Another response was to embrace the acquisition of sound as an addition to cinema's capacity to record events. This attitude, in turn, changed the approach of artists to their

5. H. Wolfflin, *Principles of Art History*, translated by M. Hottinger (London: 1932).

medium *as a whole*. They sought techniques and strategies that would emphasize the recording aspects of film and thereby concord with the *telos* inherent in film's newest recording element, synchronized sound. That is, sound, regarded as a realist element, fired the imaginations of artists in a way that sent them searching for other techniques to accentuate the recording dimension of the medium as a whole. As Soviet writings on film indicate, this "realistic" attitude was not the only attitude held toward sound in the thirties. But, in historical perspective, it was certainly *the* important attitude.

As we have seen, silent film of the twenties, in theory and often in practice, betrayed a horror of the idea that cinema is simply the mechanical recording of events. In this, cinema responded to the prejudices of the world of fine art which, with the arrival of so-called nonobjective painting, began to discount the value of representation as an artistic property. In defense of their medium as an art form, film theorists like Arnheim and the Soviets denied that film was a simple, reflex, automatic reproduction of reality. And at the level of film-making, expressionism (for example, of the German variety) and montage were highly assertive styles that emphasized that cinema was not merely a mechanical reproduction or recording of profilmic events. Both silent-film artists and theorists—committed to the notion that film is an art—were predisposed to foreground the constitutive and creative (as opposed to the reproductive) aspects of the medium.

Some theorists, notably Arnheim, refused to endorse the shift in film aesthetics. Sound for them was a return to canned theater, a regression to the pre-Griffith era before film had weaned itself from the stage. Others, however, embraced the new device and attempted to incorporate it into the aesthetic system of the silent film. Eisenstein, Pudovkin, and Alexandrov, in their famous 1928 statement on sound,[6] and Roman Jakobson, in a rarely discussed 1933 article entitled "Is the

6. In S. M. Eisenstein, *Film Form*, edited and translated by Jay Leyda (New York: Harcourt, Brace and World, 1949), 257–60.

Cinema in Decline?"[7] proposed that sound be understood as a montage element: aural units should be juxtaposed against the visuals just as shots should be juxtaposed against shots. Jakobson, ironically, answers someone like Arnheim in the same manner that Arnheim might have answered the anti-cinematic charges of a Clive Bell or a Benedetto Croce. Jakobson tells the opponent of sound that his opposition to the sound film is not based on a thoughtful look at the possibilities of the new medium. Jakobson argues that the sound element in a scene can be asynchronous and contrapuntal, thereby diverging from mere reproduction. This possibility enriches cinema because added to all the conceivable visual juxtapositions of the silent film are inestimably large reservoirs of sound counterpoints.

Coinciding with the theoretical endorsement of asynchronous sound, a number of films were produced that exploited this "montage mentality": Lang's *M* and *Testament of Dr. Mabuse*, Dreyer's *Vampyr*, Vertov's *Enthusiasm* and *Three Songs of Lenin*, parts of Pudovkin's *The Deserter*, Buñuel's *L'Age d'or* and *Land without Bread*, and Clair's early sound films, especially *À Nous la liberté*. These films might be called "silent sound films." This is not meant disparagingly. Each of these films represents a major achievement. Yet that achievement in each case derives from a penchant for asynchronous sound based on a paradigm of montage juxtapositions as a means to manipulate, to interpret, and to reconstitute profilmic events.

The montage or "silent-film" response to sound was conservative in one sense. It was an attempt to extrapolate the basic concepts of a silent-film aesthetic to a new development, recommending montage as a basic model for dealing with sound. By the forties another kind of recommendation was evolved, by a group of artists isolated by Bazin. This alternative was diametrically opposed to the general silent-film propensity toward stylization and manipulation, toward what has been called creationism.

7. In *Russian Formalist Film Theory*, edited by Herbert Eagle (Ann Arbor: Michigan Slavic Publications, 1981), 161–66.

In Bazin, the recording/reproductive aspect of film—that nemesis of silent-film artists and theorists alike—became the center of a theory that made recommendations about the types of composition and camera movement that would best enable the filmmaker to re-present reality in opposition to the silent-film urge to reconstitute it. The formation of Bazin's theory was closely related to the transition to sound, especially in terms of the gradual emergence of a certain realist tradition of sound films that defines itself against the aesthetics of the silent film—notably the tendencies toward montage and expressionism—and that for that reason may be said to comprise "sound sound films," in contrast to "silent sound films." In other words, in the thirties a filmmaker like Renoir responded to the introduction of sound as an augmentation of film's recording capacities, and he evolved a realist style that roughly correlated with the notion of film as recording.[8] Bazin described and sought foundations for Renoir's practice, and in doing so charted the predominating ethos of the sound film until the sixties.

That is, with the introduction of sound, the aesthetic pendulum gradually began to swing away from montage and expressionism and toward the affirmation of something said to be closer to a "recording" style. This is not to claim that much sense can be gleaned from phrases like "the mere recording of reality," but only to acknowledge that "recording" is one parameter of film. What is compelling about Bazin's writings is the way that he is able to pick out and explain the place of formal techniques, like long takes and deep-focus photography, in the process of the move from a conception of film art as assertive stylization to a reconception of the medium as more a matter of recording—rooted, Bazin would claim, in the photographic nature of film. For example, Bazin explicates the work of Renoir in terms of specific strategies, such as irregular panning and deep-focus composition, that can be understood as *associated* with the recording/reproduc-

8. In my "Lang, Pabst and Sound" (in *Ciné-tracts*, no. 5), I discuss the film *Kammeradshaft*, which I take to be a forerunner of this tendency for handling sound that predates even Renoir's experimentation in this direction.

tive capacities of film in the context of the international cinema of the thirties. We need not commit ourselves—in our de-mythologized account of Bazin—to his idea that recording is the essential characteristic of film. It is a possibility—just as the more stridently interventionist or creationist techniques of montage and expressionism are possibilities. But what has explanatory power in Bazin is the way that he points to the development of certain techniques, that, in the context of the thirties and forties, can and do come to emphasize the recording aspects of the film medium as a historical response to the aesthetic proclivities of silent film, where that response is predicated on the belief that sound should be exploited and integrated into film style as an additional increment of recording. This is not to say that sound is not still sound-recording in examples of assertive stylization, such as Clair's, but only to say that Clair's use of sound in audio-visual tropes emphasizes the constitutive creationist dimension of film over the recording dimension.

When analyzing Renoir's irregular panning, Bazin was at pains to show that by using slight lateral pans and zig-zag pans, Renoir subverted the traditional manner of composing a scene. Previous standard operating procedure had often involved setting up all the action in a scene or shot so that it could be photographed without camera movement. The actors were blocked in such a way that they never stepped out of the camera's perspective, that is, out of range of the viewfinder. Renoir, however, orchestrated scenes, notably in *Rules of the Game*, in such a way that the camera was often reframing laterally to keep the actors on camera.

As well, rather than constructing sets and blocking actors so that the camera could move through the profilmic environment in highly direct, geometrically striking, and elegant lines and arcs, Renoir favored awkward, geometrically irregular, and unevenly paced camera movements. Bazin seized on both these techniques and argued that, insofar as they broke with traditional schemas, they functioned as indexes of spontaneity. The techniques downplayed certain evidences of pre-production artifice common in average films of the period.[9] In this light, these techniques can be interpreted as emphasizing that possibility of film that is thought of as the "spontaneous recording of events." For instance, a cameraman committed to laterally reframing action is a cameraman committed to *following* the actors and action. This is not to claim that Renoir's shots are in fact spontaneous recordings of events. Rather, the claim is that in contrast to the corpus of ordinary films of the period, Renoir's films subverted certain standard techniques in a way that could be interpreted as dismantling a kind of artifice that marked prior styles of filmmaking as both theatrical and painterly.[10]

Bazin's analysis of deep-focus composition can be reread in a similar fashion. Depth-of-field photography historically defines itself against editing as a structurally divergent but in some ways functionally equivalent means of organizing scenes. In this respect, deep-focus composition offers itself as an alternative to traditional forms of representation. Deep-focus compositions have structure. Nevertheless, that structure, when compared to traditional editing, emphasized the recording dimension of film by articulating events in a spatially and temporally *continuous* manner. And it is this concern with the possibility of film as a recording that makes depth of field, along with the analogous phenomenon of "lateral depth of field" (the taste for lateral reframings and irregular pannings), a meaningful option for film realists in the period that Bazin describes. Thus, Bazin can be read as offering a reconstruction of the logic of an (aesthetic) situation—in the Popperian sense of that phrase—an account of the rational choices and alternative "moves" open to the ambitious filmmaker in the circumstances of the advent and evolution of the sound film. Moreover, Bazin was able to connect the emergence of this realist sound style with a heretofore overlooked tradition of silent film—including the works of Stroheim, Murnau, Keaton, Flaherty, and Chaplin—as well as with developments

9. Andre Bazin, *Jean Renoir*, edited by Francois Truffaut, translated by Halsey and W. Simon (New York: Simon and Shuster, 1973), 89.
10. Ibid.

that were contemporary with the maturation of his own theory—the work of Welles, Wyler, and the Italian neorealists. In terms of offering an overview of the history of film style, Bazin's attention to film realism represents a discovery of the first order.

In the preceding paragraphs I have rewritten Bazin's position in a way that I think captures what is useful in his work. One result of my rewriting is to make Bazin sound less the theorist and more the historian of film style. And this, of course, corresponds to my view of Bazin—his talent was not for theorizing, but for perceiving and articulating broad stylistic movements. Most of this chapter will be devoted to undermining Bazin's theoretical speculations. I have taken this opportunity at the outset, however, both to explain my admiration for Bazin and to avoid leaving the reader with the mistaken conclusion that I think Bazin's work is worthless. Also, before proceeding, another disclaimer is necessary. As I have already indicated, Bazin wrote a great many articles. The majority of these were not theoretical. Moreover, the relation between the straight-forwardly theoretical articles and his critical reviews is sometimes especially complex and obscure. Often the reviews have little to do with his explicitly stated theory. And at times, Bazin says things that are quite at variance with what one would expect from a proponent of Bazin's theory. In fact, sometimes Bazin's critical "results" contradict his theory. Furthermore, often his critical conclusions have nothing to do with the theory. One way to deal with this problem would be to attempt an in-depth exegesis of Bazin's corpus of writing aimed at rendering all criticism and theory consistent, perhaps by invoking deep principles that Bazin never develops in his text and by offering subtle reinterpretations of Bazin's central tenets in ways that dispel apparent contradictions. This is not how I will approach Bazin's theory. Rather, I will take the theoretical articles at face value, ignoring the contradictory criticism. I do not take my task to be that of reconciling all the different things Bazin wrote at different times. It is Bazin's theory as it is explicitly stated rather than the theory that might be implicit in or presupposed by his criticism that is most important historically for film theory. Thus, I will set forth the outline of Bazin's theory as it is usually conceived in film circles rather than attempting to discover a more compelling version that might be developed by working through all his writing with the purpose of making it consistent.

It is often remarked by defenders of Bazin that he was willing to violate a theoretical precept in order to acknowledge cinematic achievements. If it came down to a choice between hardlining his theory or honoring a cinematic accomplishment, Bazin would opt for the film, not the theory. Some therefore claim that Bazin was not an absolutist but rather regarded his work as a conjecture.[11] And from this observation it might be argued that detailed criticism of Bazin—of the sort that I intend—is really beside the point. The missing premise of this argument is probably something like—"since Bazin knew his theory wasn't perfect, why bother to bring to light its imperfections?" I have three answers to this sort of objection. (1) A theory presented as a conjecture is no less deserving of criticism than a theory presented as incontrovertibly true—indeed, why submit a conjecture if not to see whether it should be abandoned or improved as a result of criticism? (2) Advocates of this line of thought seem to confuse criticism of Bazin the person with criticism of Bazin's theory. (3) Even if Bazin and everyone else know that this highly influential theory is false, spelling out its precise imperfections still seems worthwhile, since this will give future film theorists a deeper appreciation of the logical pitfalls along certain avenues of speculation.

An overview of Bazin's position

Perhaps the best way to begin a sympathetic account of Bazin's theory is to narrate the sequence of events leading to its

11. Bazin himself refers to his view of the evolution of film history as a "working hypothesis." See André Bazin, *What Is Cinema?* vol. 1, translated by H. Gray (Berkeley: University of California Press, 1967), 24. Henceforth I will abbreviate references to this book as *WIC* 1.

formation. Bazin began writing on film in the early forties, as a student,[12] and he continued working until his death in 1959 at the age of forty. One of the major films of the period when Bazin began to be concerned with cinema was Renoir's *Rules of the Game*. (Much of Bazin's theoretical work represents a sustained meditation of Renoir's films, especially *Rules of the Game*.) What Bazin perceived there was a style of filmmaking distinct from the dominant international styles of filmmaking.

Some of the features Bazin came to see as central to Renoir's achievement were: (1) the use of medium-long shots—shots in which the whole bodies of actors were visible on screen, often with space between the top of their heads and the upper frame line; (2) the use of deep focus—every point in the image was in hard focus, as opposed to the soft-focus techniques of Hollywood thirties' composition (the background of Renoir's shots were legible, visible, and recognizable rather than blurred); (3) the use of multiplanar compositions—since Renoir's images were in deep focus, he could situate dramatic details and contrasts on several pictorial planes, while more typical soft-focus films of the period situated action only in the foreground (at times Renoir would deploy as many as four planes of discrete dramatic action in *Rules of the Game*); (4) the use of the long take—rather than break down a scene into a series of shots, Renoir tackled it in one shot of long duration (a long take), working out the dramatic action on multiple planes of a deep-focus shot—the action was not analytically fragmented into a series of shots but developed in a long-take, medium-long shot, what is sometimes called a sequence shot, since the entire sequence is done in a single shot; (5) the use of camera movement rather than editing to follow the action; (6) a nontheatrical, nonpainterly use of the frame—because Renoir's camera was often shifting to keep track of the actors, the frame lacked the kind of fixity or permanence found in ordinary films, where the frame was

12. Many of Bazin's early critical writings are anthologized in André Bazin, *French Cinema of the Occupation and Resistance*, translated by Stanley Hochman (New York: Frederick Ungar Publishing Co., 1981).

modeled on the proscenium arch of a stage or the frame of a painting.[13] In reference to this last point, it should be added that the proscenium arch and the picture frame are said to mark the boundary between what they contain and what is geographically adjacent to them; likewise, the film framing that was modeled on them. Renoir's cinematic frame, however, has a more fluid relation to what is off-screen. Constant reframing makes the relation between what is on-screen and immediately off-screen seem more continuous than the centripetal framing of ordinary films. Renoir's frame, Bazin stressed, is not modeled on anything; it is merely homothetic to, that is, coextensive with, the viewfinder of the camera.[14]

Bazin did not claim that every shot of every Renoir film had all of these characteristics. But many of the most important images did, especially in such mature works of the late thirties as *Grand Illusion* and *Rules of the Game*. One way to capture Renoir's style is through the often obscure concept of continuity. The Renoir scene is *continuous* in the sense that the space and the action have not been broken up and elliptically resynthesized through editing (*WIC* 1, 48–52). The action is continuous—we see the whole action, without gaps, so to speak. What might be called the integrity of the space is respected. At the same time, the space of the action has a quality of *continuousness* that is quite different. It arises from Renoir's framing technique, which creates a continuity between on-screen and off-screen space that is constantly reaffirmed by the slight pannings and lateral reframings of the shot.[15] By exploiting these various dimensions of continuousness the Renoir image approaches a realistic representation of space. It projects an image that is certainly more like our ordinary ex-

13. Renoir himself acknowledged his awareness of the long take, medium-long shot, hard focus, multiplanar style when he said in a famous article: "The further I advance in my profession, the more I abandon confrontations between two characters neatly set up before the camera, as in a photographic studio. I prefer to place my characters more freely, at different distances from the camera and make them move. For that I need great depth of field" (quoted in Bazin, *Jean Renoir*, 90.)

14. Bazin, *Jean Renoir*, 87.

15. Bazin, *Jean Renoir*, 84–91.

perience of space than the constructed, artificially bounded, elliptical space found in most other films of the period, which synthesized scenes by means of editing and soft focus.[16] These "sequence shots" *might* be said to traffic in real space and real time rather than the constructed space and time of edited scenes (although "real space" and "real time" here ought not be taken too literally, but as terms of art signaling a stylistic contrast and thereby functioning like the term "depth" as it is applied to paintings).

Bazin further argued that deep-focus, long-take sequence shots place spectators in a relationship to the image that is *more* like their relationship to an actual—rather than a representational—perceptual manifold than what is available in edited film. Viewers scan the scene from foreground to background, making connections for themselves rather than having every relationship in the drama spelled out for them by the editing. Thus, in *Rules of the Game* viewers "discover" ironic echoes as the same marital farce is played out by different sets of characters in the hallway *and* in the room behind the hallway. (In the average film of the thirties the same point would be hammered home by cutting from the hallway to the room.) Using the long-take, deep-focus shot, Renoir could present simultaneously occurring dramatic events simultaneously rather than sequentially, as is done via editing. Renoir's commitment to work in a continuous dramatic space, Bazin thought, allows a certain freedom to the spectator that is more like our ordinary experience of actual events than is the highly directed manner in which we assimilate an event that is edited and shaped by classical montage. Rather than convey information through unambiguous close shots, for example, the director working with medium-long shots allows spectators to discover the dramatic point of a scene for themselves. Moreover, since Renoir's camera follows the actors, Bazin felt this lent the image the feeling that the event filmed seems somewhat "independent" of the camera (that is, rather than

16. Bazin discusses the interrelation of editing and soft focus in *WIC* 1, 33–34.

palpably staged for the camera).[17] And this, of course, corresponds to our ordinary experience of perceptual manifolds. Thus, because of these qualities of independence, perceptual freedom, and "continuity" of the space in Renoir's sequence shots, Bazin called Renoir's style "realist."

In the aftermath of World War II, American films began to flood into Paris again. Bazin noted that some major stylistic shifts were evident in American filmmaking during the war. These shifts were most evident in the work of directors Orson Welles and William Wyler and cinematographer Greg Toland. The American cinema in general seemed to be inching toward an aesthetic based more and more on the sequence shot, and, in the work of Welles, Wyler, and Toland, these shots were often articulated by using deep-focus, multiplanar medium-long shots and moving the camera. Certain American films—including *Citizen Kane*, *The Magnificent Ambersons*, *The Little Foxes*, *The Best Years of Our Lives*, *The Bishop's Wife*, and others—seemed to be evolving along the lines crystallized in Renoir's thirties films, particularly *Grand Illusion* and *Rules of the Game*. Due to American technological innovations, pioneered in part by Toland, the depth of field in these American films was crisper and more defined than it was in Renoir's films. And the camera movement, again partly due to the technological superiority of the Americans, was smoother then Renoir's. The aesthetic commitment to use sequence shots of continuous space, however, marked an affinity between these American *auteurs* and the French realist. This new aesthetic preference in American cinema engendered a number of famous scenes: Susan's attempted suicide in *Citizen Kane*;[18] the kitchen scene in *The Magnificent Ambersons*;[19] the marriage of Dana Andrews and Teresa Wright (in the foreground) while Frederic March and Myrna Loy echo their vows (in the background) in *The Best Years of Our Lives*; and the telling of the story of David and the angel in *The Bish-*

17. Bazin, *Jean Renoir*, 89.
18. Analyzed by Bazin in *Orson Welles*, translated by J. Rosenbaum (New York: Harper and Row, 1978), 77–78.
19. Ibid., 80.

op's Wife.[20] Bazin recognized in these American films a correlation with Renoir's experimental style in his late thirties'
films (*WIC* 1, 34). Bazin believed that he was witnessing the
emergence of a full-scale stylistic movement, one that he
would not only christen but also champion.

Along with the influx of American films, Paris after World
War II saw the appearance of the first fruits of the post-Fascist
Italian cinema. Most striking among these films were the
works of a newly coalesced movement called neorealism.
Rossellini, DeSica, Zavatini, Visconti, Fellini, Lattuada, and
De Santis all were participants in this tendency of Italian film.
Open City, Paisan, Bicycle Thief, and *Umberto D* are perhaps
their best known films. In many ways the realism of these
Italian films rested on factors different from the "spatial" realism of the American films.[21] The realism of the American
films was primarily a matter of cinematic style rather than
content—costume films and fantasies were counted as realist
insofar as they employed long takes. Neorealist films, on the
other hand, generally contained what could be thought of as
"classic" realist content—depictions of the contemporary
problems of the working class. Bazin also saw these Italian
films as realistic in virtue of: (1) their mixing of nonprofes-
sional and professional actors (*WIC* 2, 22–25); (2) their use of
location shooting; (3) their often episodic and open-ended
story construction;[22] and (4) their even lighting, which was
reminiscent of documentary filming in contrast to the dominant form of the studio fiction film (*WIC* 2, 33).[23] These fea-

---

20. The last two examples are my own, not Bazin's.
21. Bazin, of course, was well aware of the difference between the American realists and the Italian neorealists. See, for example, *WIC* 1, 37. Also
see André Bazin, *What is Cinema?* vol. 2, translated by H. Gray (Berkeley:
University of California Press, 1971), 29–30 and 33. Henceforth I will abbreviate references to the latter book as *WIC* 2.
22. See Bazin, *WIC* 2, 30–32, 34, 38–40, and 84. Related to the episodic
structure is what Bazin sees as key to neorealism—a downplaying of plot,
where plotting is seen as taking an a priori view toward reality. See *WIC* 2,
64–65.
23. Bazin also notes other similarities between neorealist camera style and
documentary style. He says, "The Italian camera retains something of the

tures, of course, have little in common with the style of realism that Bazin saw emerging in the Hollywood films of
Welles and Wyler. Yet, there was one point of congruence.
Like Renoir and the Americans, the Italians seemed to endorse a preference for elaborating scenes in continuous takes
rather than through editing. And in the clearly lighted back-
grounds of these Italian films shot on location, one could see
the daily flow of Italian life amidst the ruins of the war.
Whereas Renoir and the Americans used the background of
their long takes to develop dramatic detail, the Italians
amassed anthropological and archaeological detail there. The
Italians favored medium-long shots that gave the spectator
the freedom to peruse this wealth of detail and to see the contemporary problems of the Italian people played out in everyday locales, recorded in real—that is to say nonsynthetic, unedited—space and time. Bazin was quite aware that the films
of Welles and Wyler and the neorealists were not exactly the
same. Yet he also thought that in a broad but important sense
they were linked as representatives of a general tendency of
filmmaking. "They [the Italians and Welles] are aiming at the
same results. The means used by Rossellini and DeSica are
less spectacular but they are no less determined to do away
with montage and to transfer to the screen the continuum of
reality" (*WIC* 1, 37).

Though what Bazin had to say, as a positive generalization,
about the affinity between Renoir, Welles, Wyler, and the
neorealists at times seems strained, vague, or obscure, Bazin's
negative reasons for grouping these filmmakers together are
clear. The group coheres because it can be construed as standing against a style of filmmaking based on editing—whether
Soviet montage or the "invisible editing" of the classic thir-

human quality of the Bell and Howell newsreel camera, a projection of hand
and eye, almost a living part of the operator, instantly in tune with his
awareness." Bazin also sees the use of locale in neorealist films as documentary in the sense that it does not resort to the expressionist's mobilization
of the pathetic fallacy (*WIC* 2, 88). The comparison of neorealism and the
documentary can also be found on page 20.

ties' Hollywood film[24]—and because of a tendency to favor long-take, medium-long shots over editing.[25]

Bazin's arguments against montage of both the Hollywood and Soviet varieties (henceforth simply "montage") and in favor of spatial realism were based on a range of considerations. One was the aura of authenticity spatial realism imparted to certain scenes.

> Perhaps I shall make myself clearer by giving an example. In an otherwise mediocre English film, *Where No Vultures Fly*, there is one unforgettable sequence. The film reconstructs the story of a young couple in South Africa during the war who founded and organized a game reserve. To this end, husband and wife, together with their child, lived in the heart of the bush. The sequence I have in mind starts out in the most conventional way. Unknown to the parents, the child has wandered away from the camp and has found a lion cub that has been temporarily abandoned by its mother. Unaware of the danger, it picks up the cub and takes it along. Meanwhile the lioness, alerted either by the noise or by the scent of the child, turns back towards its den and starts along the path taken by the unsuspecting child. She follows close behind him. The little group comes within

---

24. For an explanation of "invisible editing," see the long quotation from Bazin beginning on page 117.

25. This claim, if it is to be empirically accurate, requires much more finesse than Bazin ever devotes to it. It is not the case that his preferred films lack montage altogether—for example, the hunt scene in *Rules of the Game*. One might say that these films eschew editing and adopt long takes in important or crucial scenes. But this is not an apt empirical generalization either—there is cutting, as well as deep-focus composition, in the wedding scene of *The Best Years of Our Lives*. To make the claim fit the facts, it would be best to say that Bazin's favored films use both long takes and editing to develop crucial scenes, but that the deep-focus and/or long-take images have a special, distinctive effect—are of greater importance or are more moving than the edited imagery—because of the sorts of qualities Bazin noted—for example, the accommodation of spectator discoveries. Moreover, it could be added that these cinematic structures would have been less probable in an earlier period of film.

sight of the camp at which point the distracted parents
see the child and the lion which is undoubtedly about to
spring at any moment on the imprudent kidnapper. Here
let us interrupt the story for a moment. Up to this point
everything has been shown in parallel montage and the
somewhat naive attempt at suspense has seemed quite
conventional. Then suddenly, to our horror, the director
abandons his montage of separate shots that has kept the
protagonists apart and gives us instead parents, child and
lioness all in the same full shot. This single frame in
which trickery is out of the question gives immediate
and retroactive authenticity to the very banal montage
that has preceded it. From then on, and always in the
same full shot, we see the father order his son to stand
still—lion has halted a few yards away—then to put the
cub down on the ground and to start forward again without hurrying. Whereupon the lion comes quietly forward, picks up the cub and moves off into the bush while
the overjoyed parents rush towards the child.

It is obvious that, considered from the point of view
of a recital, this sequence would have had the same simple meaning if it had been shot entirely in montage or by
process work. But in neither event would the scene have
unfolded before the camera in its physical and spatial
reality. Hence, in spite of the concrete nature of each
shot, it would have had the impact only of a story and
not a real event. There would have been no difference
between the scene as shot and the chapter in a novel
which recounted the same imaginary episode. Hence the
dramatic and moral values of the episode would be on a
very mediocre level. On the other hand, the final framing which involved putting the characters in a real situation carries us at once to the heights of cinematographic
emotion. Naturally the feat was made possible by the
fact that the lioness was half tamed and had been living
before the filming in close contact with the family. This
is not the point. The question is not whether the child
really ran the risk it seemed to run but that the episode

was shot with due respect for its spatial unity. Realism, here, resides in the homogeneity of space. Thus we see that there are cases in which montage, far from being the essence of cinema, is indeed its negation. The same scene then can be poor literature or great cinema according to whether montage or a full shot is used. (*WIC* 1, 49–50)

If slapstick comedy succeeded before the days of Griffith and montage, it is because most of the gags derived from a comedy of space, from a relation of man to things and to the surrounding world. In *The Circus* Chaplin is *truly* in the lion's cage and both are enclosed within the frame-work of the screen. (*WIC* 1, 52, italics added)

From these examples, it is clear that Bazin believes that these scenes acquire a quality of authenticity by making use of ho-mogeneous, unedited space as opposed to the synthetic, con-structed space of editing. "It is simply a question of respect for the spatial unity of an event at the moment when to split it up would change it from something real to something imaginary" (*WIC* 1, 50). Moreover, Bazin does not see this as merely a reason why some scenes should be spatially unified, but rather believes that such scenes reveal the essence of cin-ema—"Essential cinema, seen for once in its pure state, on the contrary, is to be found in straightforward photographic re-spect for the unity of space" (*WIC* 1, 46).

Bazin also supports what I am calling spatial realism over editing for what could be thought of as moral reasons. Mon-tage, according to Bazin, tells the spectator what to think about the action on the screen. But with a medium-shot, long-take composition, as I noted earlier, the spectator is free to discover the meaning of the action independently. Bazin's thesis is that montage compels passive spectatorship while spatial realism induces active spectatorship. The spectator scans the image and derives the meaning of the action on his own. The spectator of films of spatial realism is a participant in the meaning structure of the film—he is free in opposition to the enforced passivity of totalitarian montage. Bazin says the deep-focus, medium-shot, long-take style implies, "consequently, both a more active mental attitude on the part of the spectator and a more positive contribution on his part to the action in progress. While analytical montage only calls for him to follow his guide, to let his attention follow along smoothly with that of the director who will choose what he should see, here he is called upon to exercise at least a minimum of personal choice. It is from his attention and his will that the meaning of the image in part derives" (*WIC* 1, 36).

Bazin calls this criticism of montage a psychological consideration, but, although psychological observation is involved in stating the case, Bazin's emphasis on freedom of choice for the spectator makes the conclusion of the argument more a matter of moral evaluation than of applied psychology pure and simple.

Bazin had another charge to level at montage, one that he calls metaphysical but is again, better thought of as moral.

> In analyzing reality, montage presupposes of its very nature the unity of meaning of the dramatic event. Some other form of analysis is undoubtedly possible, but then it would be another film. In short, montage by its very nature rules out ambiguity of expression. Kuleshov's experiment proves this *per absurdam* in giving on each occasion a precise meaning to the expression on a face. . . .
>
> On the other hand, depth of focus reintroduces ambiguity into the structure of the image, if not of necessity—Wyler's films are never ambiguous—at least as a possibility. Hence it is no exaggeration to say that *Citizen Kane* is unthinkable shot in any other way but in depth. The uncertainty in which we find ourselves as to the spiritual key or the interpretation we should put on the film is built into the very design of the image. (*WIC* 1, 36)

In Roberto Rossellini's *Paisan* and *Allemania Anno Zero* and Vittorio DeSica's *Ladri de Biciclette*, Italian neorealism contrasts with previous forms of film realism in its stripping away of all expressionism and in the total absence of the effects of montage. As in the films of Welles and in spite of conflicts of style, neorealism tends to give

back to the cinema a sense of the ambiguity of reality.
(*WIC* 1, 37)

Bazin appears to be arguing that (1) since reality is ultimately
ambiguous—at least in terms of the judgments we make
about people—and (2) since this sort of ambiguity is possible
(but not necessary) in the long-take, medium-long shot style,
but not even possible in montage, then (3) the long-take style
is superior to montage insofar as it can reflect reality more
truly. This seems to be a species of moral argumentation,
since the type of ambiguity in question revolves around a belief in the "ultimate mystery of the human heart." Connected
with this is the injunction that such mystery demands that we
must refrain from judging and interpreting others. Editing,
in turn, is seen as a form of immoral interpretation.

At the same time that Bazin identified spatial realism he
also looked backwards to the history of film to find forerunners of this tendency. These included not only Renoir, but
also Stroheim, Murnau, and Flaherty (*WIC* 1, 26). "In their
films," he wrote, "montage plays no part, unless it be the
negative one of inevitable elimination where reality superabounds" (*WIC* 1, 26–27)[26] To see the type of thing that Bazin
found important about these filmmakers, consider what he
has to say about Stroheim.

> Stroheim's films could not have the same meaning *before*
> or *after* Griffith. This language [that is, Griffith's popu-
> larization of the conventions of editing] had to exist be-
> fore its destruction could be called an improvement. But
> what is certain is that Stroheim's work appeared to be a
> negation of all the cinematic values of his time. He will
> return the cinema to its main function; he will have to
> relearn how to *show*. He assassinated rhetoric and lan-
> guage so that evidence might triumph; on the ashes of
> the ellipse and symbol, he will create a cinema of hyper-
> bole and reality. Against the sociological myth of the

26. I take the obscure phrase "where reality superabounds" to refer to the
framing that amounts to something being "edited out" when the cinematographic images are strung together.

star—an abstract hero, the ectoplasm of collective dreams—he will affirm the most peculiar embodiment of the actor, the monstrosity of the individual. If I had to characterize Stroheim's contribution in one phrase, I would call it "a revolution of the concrete."[27]

If Stroheim's narrative could not, for obvious technical reasons, escape the discontinuity of shots, at least it was not based upon this discontinuity. But, on the contrary, what he was obviously looking for was the presence of simultaneous events and their interdependence on one another—not a logical subordination as with montage, but a physical, sensual, or material event. Stroheim is the creator of a virtually continuous cinematic narrative, tending toward permanent integration with all of space.[28]

These quotations show—as did his analysis of sound film realists—that what Bazin found striking about silent-film realists was an explicit contrast with the montage style. These "opponents of montage" were dubbed realists because they could be seen as developers of a film style that was an alternative to montage and because that style could be seen as an affirmation of the continuity of "real" space through the use of long-take composition.

The isolation of a lineage of spatial realists gave Bazin the wherewithal to reconceive the entire history of film style. He divided filmmakers into two broad camps: those who put their faith in the image—montagists and German expressionists (who resort to distorted imagery);[29] and those filmmakers

27. André Bazin, *The Cinema of Cruelty* (New York: Seaver Books, 1982), 7–8.
28. Ibid., 9–10.
29. Bazin's twin enemies are the expressionists (notably the German variety) and the montagists. The expressionists commit the same general type of error that the montagists do. Bazin spends less time chastizing expressionists, however, than he does montagists. Perhaps the reason for this is historical; by the time Bazin was writing, expressionism was a defunct and generally disparaged tendency in filmmaking.

who put their faith in reality—those committed to the realism of "continuous" space. He writes:

> . . . I will distinguish, in the cinema between 1920 and 1940, between two broad and opposing trends: those directors who put their faith in the image and those who put their faith in reality. By "image" I here mean, very broadly speaking, everything that the representation adds to the object there represented. This is a complex inheritance but it can be reduced essentially to two categories: those related to the plastics of the image and those that relate to the resources of montage, which, after all, is simply the ordering of images in time.
>
> Under the heading "plastics" must be included the style of the set, of the make-up, and, up to a point, even of the performance, to which we naturally add the lighting and, finally, the framing of the shot which gives us its composition. As regards montage, derived initially as we know from masterpieces of Griffith, we have the statement of Malraux in his *Psychologie du Cinema* that it was montage that gave birth to film as an art, setting it apart from the mere animated photography, in short, creating a language.
>
> The use of montage can be "invisible" and this is generally the case of the prewar classics of the American screen. Scenes were broken down just for one purpose, namely to analyze an episode according to the material or dramatic logic of the scene. It is this logic which conceals the fact of the analysis, the mind of the spectator quite naturally accepting the viewpoints of the director which are justified by the geography of the action or the shifting emphasis of dramatic interest.
>
> But the neutral quality of this "invisible" editing fails to make use of the full potential of montage. On the other hand, these potentialities are clearly evident from the three processes generally known as parallel montage, accelerated montage, montage by attraction. . . .
>
> Whatever these may be, one can say that they share

that trait in common which constitutes the very definition of montage, namely the creation of a sense or meaning not proper to the images themselves but derived exclusively from their juxtaposition. (*WIC* 1, 24–25)

Through the contents of the image and the resources of
the montage the cinema has at its disposal a whole arsenal of means whereby to impose its interpretation of an
event on a spectator. By the end of the silent film we can
consider this arsenal to have been full. On the one side
the Soviet cinema carried to its ultimate consequences
the theory and practice of montage, while the German
school did every kind of violence to the plastics of the
image by way of sets and lighting. Other cinemas count,
too, besides the Russian and the German, but whether in
France or Sweden or the United States, it does not appear
that the language of cinema was at a loss for ways of saying what it wanted to say.

If the art of cinema consists in everything that plastics
and montage can add to a given reality, the silent film
was an art on its own. Sound could only play at best a
subordinate and supplementary role: a counterpoint to
the visual image. But this possible enhancement—at best
only a minor one—is likely not to weigh much in comparison with the additional bargain-rate reality introduced at the same time by sound.

Thus far we have put forward the view that expressionism of montage and image constitute the essence of
cinema. And it is precisely on this generally accepted notion that directors from the silent days, such as Erich von
Stroheim, F. W. Murnau, and Robert Flaherty, have by
implication cast a doubt. (*WIC* 1, 26)

From these passages it is evident that Bazin is working up
his observations about the development of a forties' style spatial realism and his isolation of forerunners of this style into a
grand evolutionary scheme of film history, one that is pro-
gressive in nature. That is, Bazin's history sees the forties
style of spatial realism as a goal that was inherent in the me-

dium from the start. Stroheim, Murnau, Flaherty, et al. were glimmerings of film's destiny in the days of German expressionism and Soviet montage. At times, Bazin seems ambivalent about how to judge these early "art" cinemas. Sometimes he appears willing to honor them—at least some of the montagists, though not the expressionists—as necessary and respectable (though infantile and now exhausted) stages in film's development. In fact, occasionally it sounds as if he is willing to regard the Soviets as representatives of some early sort of realism, despite their employment of montage. More often than not, however, when Bazin speaks of realism he has his variant of spatial realism in mind. And, since he sees evidence of it as early as the teens (in, Stroheim for example), it naturally follows that this style, in Bazin's view, is the most correct one throughout film history—even if at times Bazin has kind words for some of the montagists of the twenties, notably Eisenstein. In any case it is at least clear that by the forties, for Bazin, adherence to the constraints of spatial realism is a necessary condition for cinematic achievement. Indeed, in Bazin's articles on his contemporary, Alfred Hitchcock (the montagist exemplary of the sound film), the firm but gentle resistance to Hitchcock—against the importunings of younger auteurist critics—is underwritten by Bazin's belief that cinema's destiny, determined by its essence, is against the increasing sophistication of montage.[30]

Bazin was not satisfied to chart the emergence of a distinctive style of filmmaking and to adumbrate its special qualities. Rather, he wished to establish that style as the most important and the only legitimate cinematic style. He recast film history in a particular evolutionary mold to suggest that spatial realism was the ultimate style of film—the destiny of the medium. In order to ground this extreme form of advocacy, he attempted to show that his beloved style best exemplified the essence of cinema. Bazin argued that spatial realism followed logically from an understanding of the unique representa-

30. Bazin's struggle with the problem of Hitchcock can be reviewed in his *Cinema of Cruelty*, 101–80.

tional nature of cinema. He also argued for spatial realism on the basis of claims about the objectivity of the photographic process, the moral inferiority of montage to spatial realism, and the psychological genesis of the urge for cinema.

A Critical Look at Bazin's Theory

Bazin's concept of cinematic representation and the argument for spatial realism

There is no single concept of representation. Aside from the multiplicity of uses it serves in ordinary language, "representation" also is used as a technical term in communities of discourse as distinct as art, law, politics, and psychology. Even within a single community, such as art, one finds a diversity of uses. It can be used, in the broadest sense, to express the evocation of an impression—"This music represents to me the Russian spirit."[31] Less broadly, it can refer to a mode of depiction, such as that used by a novelist or a dramatist.[32] Even more specifically, the term may refer strictly to pictorial representation.

In what follows, I will be concerned almost exclusively with pictorial representation, specifically pictorial representation in cinema. What has been said about representation in general, however, also plagues discussions of pictorial representation. It is not clear that pictorial representation (henceforth simply "representation") has only one meaning, that is, a single set of invariant, necessary, and sufficient conditions. Clearly, representation has a range of different applications, from cave paintings to the canvases of Courbet. Furthermore, the matter is complicated by the fact that there are not only several uses of "representation," but there are also many theories of what constitutes representation.

In this section, I will examine Bazin's theory of cinematic representation and his attempt to defend the cinematographic

31. John Hospers, *Meaning and Truth in the Arts* (Chapel Hill: University of North Carolina Press, 1946), 49.
32. Ibid., 40.

style of spatial realism. When speaking of Bazin's theory, it is important to emphasize that he is concerned primarily with what is uniquely cinematic representation. Thus, one must not be surprised by the fact that the explication of representation he proposes is radically distinct from that of theorists concerned with representation in the fine arts. Nevertheless, there are two reasons why it is helpful at this point to make a short digression into the theories of representation in fine art. The first reason has to do with highlighting what is logically distinctive and original in Bazin's theory. The second reason is more substantive than heuristic. Although Bazin's theory is logically distinct from fine art theories, Bazin seems sometimes to confuse what his theory entails with what certain fine art theories properly entail. Thus, since a conceptual equivocation lies at the heart of Bazin's theory, it is essential to get clear on exactly what is being confused with what.

Two traditional explications of the nature of representation are the illusion theory and the resemblance theory. Most often these two positions are joined together because one form of the illusion theory explains illusion in terms of resemblance. However, one can maintain an illusion theory without reference to resemblance. One might argue that for a painting x and its subject y, x represents y if and only if x causes normal viewers to believe that y is before them. "Before" should be read in the sense that Macbeth saw a dagger "before" him. Thus, according to this theory, a picture of Attila is a representation of Attila if and only if it (the picture) causes viewers to believe that Attila is before them. Here, resemblance is not used to explicate illusion. Rather, deception is the underlying concept.

Of course, the mode of deception involved in viewing representational paintings must be analyzed in a highly circumspect manner. First of all, it must be made clear that the viewers' state is not one of delusion or hallucination, because normal viewers of paintings always know they are looking at paintings. If a painting depicts a battle, normal viewers are not deceived into believing they are in the presence of warfare. They see no movement, hear no cannon, smell no smoke. In this respect, the use of the picture frame is a convention that, by means of articulating the edge of the painting, emphasizes the discontinuity of the subject and the adjacent physical environment. Given these considerations, it should be immediately apparent that whatever mode of deception is offered, the illusion theorist must allow for the fact that in normal picture viewing "believing that y is present" must be conjoined with "knowing that y is not present."[33]

Combining these two conditions is not an easy task, because "knowing that y is not present" requires clarifying the sense of belief that is employed in "believing that y is present." Indeed, the suspicion arises rather quickly that the sense of belief in this formula is without substance or, at least, without any relation to the kinds of dispositions and conditions we ordinarily find requisite for the ascription of belief.

Even in exclusively visual terms, paintings and photos are not very powerful illusions. Viewers cannot see around objects in paintings and photos by shifting their viewpoint. Furthermore, the surface of paintings and photos support irregularities like scratches, grain, uneven applications of paint, thick impastos, and glare from varnish that viewers must "see through" in order to comprehend the scene.[34] The idea that viewers must know how to "see through" surface distortions sits uneasily with the idea that they have somehow been deceived.[35]

At this point, the fine arts theorist has the opportunity to drop deception as the defining characteristic of representation and replace it with resemblance. Representation is now analyzed with a formula like: for a painting x, and its subject y, x represents y if and only if x appreciably resembles y.[36] That is, a painting of Attila represents Attila if and only if it (the painting) resembles Attila. This kind of theory appears under

33. Max Black, "How Do Pictures Represent?" in *Art, Perception and Reality* (Baltimore: Johns Hopkins University Press, 1972), 114.
34. Ibid., 116.
35. Ibid.
36. Nelson Goodman, *Languages of Art* (Indianapolis: Bobbs-Merrill, 1968), 3.

many labels, including mimesis, imitation, and verisimilitude.

It is important to note that resemblance theories are not rendered problematic by the fact that many paintings have fictional entities as subjects. Confronted with a picture of Zeus, the resemblance theorist could estimate the picture's representational value in terms of the degree to which the picture appreciably resembles a powerful old man, since Zeus was conceived of as a figure with human form.

A further complication could arise if our picture of Zeus also appreciably resembled John Jones, the artist's model for the picture. Such a complication, however, does not wreck the resemblance theory. It simply points to the fact that under the rubric of representation there are a range of denoting relations and that these denoting relations are not always mutually exclusive. A painting of an ancient Roman scene by David may depict that scene and at the same time afford excellent likenesses or portraits of the models who posed for the painting. Thus, depiction and portraiture can be seen as two distinct but not necessarily exclusive sub-types of representation. Any resemblance theory worth its salt will differentiate and define the sub-types of representation.[37]

To see where nettlesome problems arise in resemblance theories it is not necessary to trace through elaborate sets of distinctions between the different denoting forms or sub-types of representation. Rather, one need only attend to the surface grammar of the theory's core formula. "For a painting x and its subject y, x represents y if and only if x appreciably resembles y." This formula states that a case of resemblance supplies both necessary and sufficient conditions for cases of representation. Stated in this simple manner, the proposition can only be false.

The first way of seeing this is to compare the logical structure of the relations of resemblance and representation. Resemblance is a symmetric relation.[38] That is, if x resembles y,

37. Cf. Monroe Beardsley, *Aesthetics: Problems in the Philosophy of Criticism* (New York: Harcourt, Brace and World, 1958), 269–78.
38. Goodman, *Languages of Art*, 4.

then y resembles x. In this respect, resemblance is formally isomorphic with the mathematical relation of equality: if x equals y, then y equals x. Any relation that takes the form "if xRy, then yRx" (where "R" stands for "is related to") is symmetrical. If this grid is applied to the idea of representation, however, we immediately discover that representation is not a symmetrical relation.

If Jones resembles Smith, then Smith resembles Jones. Yet, representation, unlike resemblance, is not a symmetric relation. Therefore, resemblance and representation cannot be equivalent relations. In virtue of this, resemblance cannot be a sufficient condition of representation. That is, we cannot use resemblance as grounds for recognizing representation. To understand this, one need only remember that resemblance *is* symmetrical. Consequently, taking a pictorial example, if resemblance were a sufficient condition of representation, then if a painting of Attila resembles Attila, then it is also true that Attila, the man, resembles the painting of Attila; thus, if resemblance were a sufficient criterion for representation, we would be forced to infer that since Attila resembles his picture then Attila represents his picture. But this is absurd. Thus, there are a multitude of cases of resemblance that are not cases of representation.

To determine whether resemblance is a necessary condition of representation, reference to non-art uses of representation may be helpful. To be a necessary condition of resemblance means that, though not all cases of resemblance are cases of representation, all cases of representation are cases of resemblance. That is, resemblance is a necessary component of the definition of representation.

To hold this and this alone would be to hold a weak form of the resemblance theory. Nevertheless, even this weak form seems highly suspect in that, apart from the case of pictorial representation, there does not seem to be any putative relation between representation and resemblance. The pope represents Christ but no more resembles Christ than James St. Clair resembled Nixon when St. Clair represented Nixon before the Supreme Court. Likewise, a pin on a military map may represent an army but hardly resembles one. Certainly the concepts of representation in religion, law, and art are different. Yet, they do seem to share a common thread in that the relationship denoted by "representation" is that of something (x) "standing for" something else (y). If anything is a candidate for a necessary condition of representation, the relationship of "standing for" seems to be the likeliest candidate. And if this is the case, x can stand for y without resembling y. An engraving of a fasces on a coin can stand for the power–through–unity of the state but not resemble the state or its power. That is, representations understood as proxies in no way imply resemblance as a necessary condition. Thus, even the weak form of the resemblance theory seems suspect.[39]

Though resemblance theorists are most often concerned with painting, they would also apply their explication of representation to photography, cinema, and television. Bazin's concept of representation, however, involves only photography and cinema. This limitation in domain affords Bazin the opportunity to maintain a copy (copy of the world) theory of representation that does not evoke the kinds of objections enumerated above against the resemblance theory.

The basic problem with the resemblance theory is that the relationship it maintains between the artwork and its model is resemblance. In Bazin, the relationship between the cinematic artwork and its model is not a resemblance relation, but an identity relation. Bazin writes:

> The photographic image is the object itself. . . . It shares by virtue of the process of its becoming, the being of the model of which it is a reproduction; it *is* the model. (*WIC* 1, 14)

> The objective nature of photography confers on it a quality of credibility absent from all other picture making. In spite of any objections our critical spirit may offer we are

39. I do not take these brief remarks to settle the matter; but for the purpose of illuminating Bazin's concept of re-presentation I think that the issue of resemblance has been pursued far enough.

forced to accept as real the existence of the object reproduced, actually re-presented, set before us in space and
time. (Ibid.)

Before the arrival of photography and later of cinema,
the plastic arts (esp. portraiture) were the only interme-
diaries between actual physical presence and absence.
Their justification was their resemblance which stirs the
imagination and helps the memory. But photography is
something else again. In no sense is it the image of an
object or person, it is its tracing. Its automatic genesis
distinguishes it radically from the other techniques of reproduction. The photograph proceeds by means of the
lens to the taking of a luminous impression in light—to
a mold. As such it carries with it more than mere resemblance, namely a kind of identity—the card we call by
that name being conceivable only in an age of photography. (*WIC* 1, 96–97)

It is important to note that there are two key elements in
Bazin's explication of representation in cinema and photography. These are that (1) the film image is identical with its
model because (2) the film image is directly produced from
its model "to a mold." The expression "to a mold" is somewhat vague. I take it that it must refer to the raw film stock.
The metaphor of the film stock as mold, it seems to me, spec-
ifies the way Bazin construes the identity relation between the
model and the developed film image. That is, the mold "fits"
both the image and the model. The latter two are related as
two subway tokens are related. One way of unpacking this,
albeit a "strong" way that Bazin does not explicitly state, is
that Bazin's identity claim holds that patterns of light from
the image are identical with the pertinent patterns of light
from the model, which also served as causal factors in the
production of the image.[40] To formalize this version of Ba-

40. I will examine a weaker interpretation of Bazin's identity claim later.
Also, the reason for speaking here of "pertinent" patterns of light is to forestall objections based on most films probably having been made in black
and white.

zin's theory of representation, we can write, "For any photographic image x and its model y, x represents y if and only if (1) x is identical to y (in terms of pertinent patterns of light) and (2) y is a causal factor in the production of x."

This account of cinematic representation has certain advantages over the resemblance theory. First, it is easier to establish identity than it is to establish unequivocally compelling resemblance. And second, by making reference to the causal process of photography, the theory uses the symmetrical nature of identity while not entailing that "if model y is identical with picture x then model y represents x" because it is not the case that picture x is a causal factor in the production of model y. That is, a picture of the Empire State Building was not a factor in the making of the Empire State Building.

The inclusion of the causal process of photography in the concept of representation gives Bazin's characterization a temporal dimension. Bazin writes, "we are forced to accept as real the existence of the object reproduced, actually re-presented" (*WIC* 1, 13). That is, the film image is identical with its model except in terms of temporality. The film image re-presents or *presents again* a manifold of light patterns to perception. This does not mean, however, that the film image must be nonfictional. A film image can represent the inside of a rocket ship because the studio set that existed in the past can be re-presented. For Bazin, a film has existential import. It is a re-presentation of something that existed in the past. Here the problem of establishing how something two-dimensional can resemble something three-dimensional is putatively bypassed with the assertion of perceptual identity. The film image *is* the model (that is, is perceptually identical to the model), even though the model may have been a studio set.[41]

Another consequence of including the automatic or causal process of photography as a defining characteristic of cine-

---

41. It is often pointed out that realist theories of film such as Bazin's and Cavell's have no way of accounting for many types of cartoons. This objection is, I believe, correct. But rather than belabor the point, I will assume in the arguments above that Bazin means to exempt cartoons from his account.

matic representation is to impute to all cinematic images the property of being representational. In other words, Bazin is claiming that cinema, in virtue of its process of production, is *essentially* representational or re-presentational. This, one assumes, is supposed to follow from Bazin's characterization of cinematic representation.

Bazin uses this premise, that cinema is essentially representational, to argue that cinema is a realistic art. He says, "The realism of cinema follows from its photographic nature" (*WIC* 1, 108). This inference on Bazin's part is more complex than it appears. Broadly, he is attempting to deduce a stylistic attribute, realism, from the mechanical process of photography. In this respect, it is not clear whether Bazin's proposition—that cinema is realistic—is a simple declaratory sentence, that every cinematic image is automatically realistic because it is automatically representational, or an injunction that every cinematic image ought to be realistic because realism maximizes the essential characteristic of the medium.

Of these two alternative formulations, the injunctive version appears more plausible in the context of Bazin's writing. Bazin analyzes the idea of cinematic realism in terms of a commitment to the spatial realist (or what is sometimes called the "phenomenological") style of photography. The spatial realist style, however, is clearly a matter of artistic choice rather than an automatic effect of the causal process of photography.

What emerges from Bazin's characterization of cinematic representation is nothing less than an attempted deduction of the style of spatial realism from an analysis of the nature of cinema. The salient points in this putative deduction are:

1. The film medium, given the nature of its mechanical processes, is essentially representational.
2. Representationalism implies realism.
3. A commitment to realism implies a commitment to the cinematographic style of spatial realism.[42]

42. This schematization of the argument is clearly not valid as it stands; all I mean to represent by it are its major moments.

The first point ostensibly is derived from the definition of cinematic representation. Since the mechanical process of cinema supplies necessary and sufficient conditions for cinematic representation, all cinema images must, in some sense, be representational. The second point—that representation implies realism—is much more complex. It supports three different interpretations, each of which will be analyzed later. For the present, however, I will read this step in terms of the injunctive sense already discussed. In this regard, the second part of the argument evolves as a result of a kind of reasoning analogous to the argument "All things being equal, you shouldn't use a thoroughbred race horse to pull a plow." That is, cinema is essentially representational, and representationalism is best suited for realism. A style such as German expressionism goes against the grain, or more specifically, against the natural purpose of cinema.

The last point—that a commitment to realism implies a commitment to the photographic style of spatial realism—is analogous to the second point in that its justification is also premised on the idea that a specific style, spatial realism, maximizes the essential realistic capacity of cinema.

It is important to note that Bazin's defense of aspects of spatial realism, such as deep-focus photography, differs from that offered by someone like Greg Toland. Toland supported deep focus on the basis of "physical" realism. That is, he believed that deep-focus images (images with sharp focus at all points on the visual field) replicate the way the human eye actually sees.[43] But the human eye, contrary to Toland, has qualitatively different focal areas. The vision of the retina as it leaves the center of the visual field is less distinct than that located in the fovea. Thus, Toland's commitment to sharp focus at every point in the image, based as it was on a false understanding of how the eye sees, was quite misconceived.

Bazin does not explicate spatial realism in terms of physical realism, but in terms of phenomenological realism. Deep fo-

43. Greg Toland, "How I Broke the Rules in *Citizen Kane*," in *Focus on "Citizen Kane,"* edited by R. Gottesman (Englewood Cliffs: Prentice-Hall, 1971), 74.

cus, for example, is not an imitation of the physical structure of retinal images. Rather, it putatively affords a relationship between screen and viewer that is more like ordinary, perceptual experiences than soft-focus or montage techniques.[44]

The specific relationship Bazin has in mind is cognitive; it is the propensity of a subject to scan and in the course of scanning to make discoveries.[45] This is the characteristic human response to the natural environment. Analogously, deep focus, unlike soft focus, makes possible scanning from background to foreground. It affords an experience of the image where scanning and an active mental attitude are operable. This is not to say that looking at a Renoir set in *Grand Illusion* is equivalent to viewing some natural, nonartistically designed environment, but only to say that the active mode of experience set in motion by a Renoir image is more like our typical perceptual attitude than, say, a Borzage close-up. And, for Bazin, montage is problematic just because it interferes with—indeed, it pre-empts—the phenomenological experience of scanning and discovery.

The experience of scanning and discovery is the bedrock of Bazin's defense of depth-of-field composition. This experience, however, is not the same as what Bazin calls "ambiguity." Bazin prizes ambiguity above all aesthetic qualities. Yet he does not rest his case for deep-focus photography on a belief that this style guarantees ambiguity: "Composition in depth, on the other hand, brings ambiguity into the structure of the image; this is not automatic (Wyler's films are hardly ambiguous at all), but it is certainly a possibility."[46] This is a significant point in refuting much unwarranted criticism of Bazin.

Many critics attack Bazin by arguing that it is quite possible to compose in depth in such a way that the shot is unambiguous. Imagine a shot in which a telephone looms large and close in the foreground while a man fifteen feet away stares at

44. André Bazin, "The Evolution of Film Language," in *The New Wave*, edited by Peter Graham (Garden City: Doubleday, 1968), 45.
45. Ibid.
46. Ibid., 46.

it anxiously. Why, a critic of Bazin might ask, is this any more ambiguous than cutting between close-ups of the phone and the man? But it is very difficult to read this question as a criticism of Bazin. There is no reason to suppose that deep-focus composition will necessarily be more ambiguous than editing. Bazin, however, does not make this claim, but only that the basic virtue of deep-focus composition vis-à-vis realism is that it is a structure that preserves and facilitates the phenomenological mode of scanning and discovery.

From the discussion that has preceded, it should be clear that Bazin attempts to ground much of his theory on his concept of representation. For that reason it is important now to review that concept in a critical rather than an expository fashion to see if it can support the role Bazin ascribes to it.

The first point to emphasize is that Bazin's concept of cinematic representation is merely homonymous with our ordinary sense of representation, including representation in cinema. One way to see this is to consider cases of process shots, especially where these shots are made in an optical printer. Certainly, we ordinarily think of these shots as representational. When Gary Cooper gallops along on his horse to the accompaniment of a back-projection, that is representational. Moreover, the image would remain representational if the image were achieved by means of an optical printer rather than by back-projection. Indeed, all the optically constructed images in *Star Wars* are representational in terms of our ordinary concept of representation. Yet if we read representation as re-presentation, a problem immediately arises, viz., what is the existential import of printed shots? That is, what exactly is being re-presented by the image made by optical printing? What is the *one* place in the world that is being re-presented? Even if there is an answer here, it certainly is a radically different sort of answer than the one we normally supply to the question of what is represented by such "trick photography," process shots. My own guess is that certain types of process shots will not count as representations under Bazin's dispensation because of the requirement of existential import that is presupposed by re-presentation. In this respect,

Bazin's theory is narrower than our ordinary concept of representation, because there are cases like process shots that we ordinarily regard as representations but that are not representations (re-presentations) in Bazin's sense.

Bazin's concept of representation is also, in ways, broader than our ordinary concept. Bazin maintains that a shot and its model are identical because the image is a causal effect of the light reflected by the model. It is in this sense that cinema is re-presentational. Yet, by this standard, we must endorse many kinds of shots that we do not ordinarily count as representations as representational. A flash pan or a close-up of a square inch of bare, undifferentiated white wall are re-presentations but they are hardly the kinds of things we generally call representations. Recognizability is key to our ordinary concept of representation; customarily, I would argue, pictorial representations are the sort of symbols that we recognize just by looking—sans any process of decoding, inference, or reading. Re-presentation, however, proposes itself as a physical analysis without psychological dimensions. Therefore, all manner of shots—like our close-up of the wall—satisfy the requirements of re-presentation without being what we generally think of as representational images, because they will not be recognizable. Here we find that Bazin's concept of representation is in some cases broader than our ordinary concept in that certain shots that we would count as non-objective and contrary to the style called representationalism, Bazin must count as representational in terms of his very special sense of that word.

One may believe Bazin's stipulation that cinematic representation is defined by identity of light patterns between image and model will enable Bazin to pick out only recognizable images with his theory. This, however, is not true. Angle and distance from the subject may preserve the identity of light patterns, but they in no way guarantee recognizability. This is especially true of very close shots, very long shots, and unfamiliar camera angles.

The whole notion of the identity of patterns of light between model and image is murky. Bazin seems to propose identity of light patterns as a condition for re-presentation. Yet, such identity is not a sufficient condition for re-presentation because it is not enough to show that an image and a model deliver identical light patterns to a station point in order to establish that the image re-presents a given model. The reason for this is that many models will have identical patterns of light.[47] The Ames experiments have shown that we can, for example, build all sorts of distorted rooms that, among other things, will deliver to a pre-arranged monocular viewing point or camera position the same retinal image and the same patterns of light as a normal room.[48] In this respect, in terms of identity of light patterns alone, one cinema image could be identical with many models. Which one would it re-present?

Bazin might answer that it re-presents the model that was involved in its causation. But this proposal is easily controverted. Let us gather three shots of three different Ames-type rooms, each of which delivers an identical batch of light patterns to a camera. We have three different shots, each re-presenting a different place. Now let us superimpose these three shots in printing. The shots, though of different places, are all identical. And by superimposition, each place becomes a causal factor in producing a fourth image, which in turn is identical with the other three shots. In such a case, it is impossible to say that image x (our fourth image) re-presents model y (*one* of the models for the first three shots), even though x and y are identical in terms of light patterns and y is a causal element in x's production. Therefore, identity and causal efficacy are not jointly sufficient conditions for Bazinian re-presentation.

It is also the case that identity of light patterns is not a necessary property of all re-presentation. Let us photograph a man, using a 16-mm camera. Let us take three shots in which we will keep the man the same size in the finished frame while also varying the focal length of the lens and the subject-to-

47. Goodman, *Languages of Art*, 12.
48. W. H. Ittleson, *The Ames Demonstrations in Perception* (Princeton: Princeton University Press, 1952).

camera distance. We may take one 9-mm shot, one 17-mm shot, and one 100-mm shot—one shot with a wide-angle lens, one with a normal lens, and one with a telephoto lens.[49] The result will be three shots, each of which, all things being equal, Bazin would accept as re-presentations of the self-same subject. As a matter of empirical fact, however, the patterns of light of these shots will differ grossly enough that the disparities can be detected even by an untrained eye. They all re-present the same subject, yet each delivers a different pattern of light, not because of physical changes in the subject but because of changes in the focal length of the lens. This counterexample is quite damning. Bazin is committed to each of these shots being a re-presentation of its subject. Thus, each is identical "to a mold" with its subject. However, identity is a transitive relation—if x is identical to y, and y is identical to z, then x is identical to z. Hence, each of the shots, if identical to the model, must also be identical to each other. But the shots will not be identical in terms of the light patterns they deliver. This means that Bazin's explication of representation as re-presentation is incoherent and results in a formal contradiction.

The problems that are cropping up here are quite serious for Bazin insofar as Bazin must supply some evidence to show that cinema images and their models are equivalent in some way. Otherwise what sense does it make to speak of re-presenting? We have already noted that Bazin's concept of representation is a special or technical concept with an extension radically different from traditional interpretations. The difficulty in establishing some identity relation like identity of light patterns between the cinema image and its model has the force of suggesting that the special sense re-presentation is purported to have is, in fact, inoperable.

Barring identical patterns of light, the only plausible reading of Bazinian re-presentation seems to be that the process of projection re-presents the exact impression or imprint of

49. For a concrete example of this, see Plate 44 in Edward Pincus, *Guide to Filmmaking* (New York: Signet, 1969). This countercase was derived by considering the photographs in Plate 44.

light that was reflected by objects and people in the past. This is probably true enough, but it makes out-of-focus shots, shots with vaseline on the lens, in fact, every kind of shot, no matter how distorted, representational. That is, to define re-presentation in terms of an imprint of light from the past defines every shot of cinema whether it is of the variety we normally call representational or not. The consequence of this explication of re-presentation is that any image that results from placing objects or people in front of an operating camera is a representation. In fact, in this sense, representation becomes trivialized; it is any shot in any style. An out-of-focus Brakhage close-up whose model even Brakhage can no longer remember or identify is still a projected imprint, and, therefore, still a Bazinian representation. Obviously, this is not a strong starting point from which to launch an attack on German expressionism.

A summary of the preceding analysis includes several points. First, Bazin's concept of cinematic representation is merely homonymous rather than synonymous with our ordinary concept of representation. This is important in terms of Bazin's deduction of spatial realism insofar as the possibility that the deduction proceeds through equivocating different senses of "representation" becomes likely. and, since Bazin's explication makes no use of the concept of recognizability, it is not a very strong conception of representation. Because Bazin wants to derive the essential nature of cinema, he restricts his analysis to the physical process of cinema. Recognizability is not a simple physical property of an image. It is something that is either achieved or not achieved. As anyone whose photos have ever turned out as faint grey blurs knows, a recognizable image is not something a camera automatically produces. The camera must be modified and adjusted. When we understand that recognizable images, what we ordinarily call representational images, are achievements, then we see that representation is not the essence of cinema but one of its many possibilities. Distortion and abstraction are possibilities, as well. The point here is that representation is a decision about how to use cinema. Bazin's interpretation radically differs in that he maintains that representation defines the nature of cinema rather than simply one purpose or use of cinema.[50]

In order to support his claim of the essentially representational nature of cinema, Bazin proposes an analysis of representation in terms of re-presentation. Its limitations are manifold. First, it does not have the same extension or domain as our ordinary concept insofar as it, for example, entails that certain process shots are not representational. In this respect, the theory has dubious explanatory power as an analysis of even cinematic representation. Furthermore, the most likely readings of the theory put it on the horns of a dilemma. Alternately, the theory is incoherent and leads to a contradiction, or it is trivial. The reading in terms of identical patterns of light leads to a formal contradiction, whereas the reading in terms of an imprint of light is trivial. There are more or less identifiable fingerprints at the scene of a crime, but they are all fingerprints. [Every cinema image is made by the imprint of light (save special cases of handprinted images, scratch films, or films like *Mothlight*[51]), but not all are recognizable. We usually call the recognizable ones representational. If Bazin calls them all representational, then "representation" loses all descriptive content.]

If these observations are true, Bazin's deduction begins to collapse. The first premise states that the film medium is essentially representational. This premise is only as good as Bazin's concept of representation—which is to say, it is either self-contradictory or trivial. If Bazin opts for the "re-presentation of impressions of light" version, this first premise, though trivially true, will stop his argument before it starts because it will not support the second premise, that representation implies realism. That is, the trivial reading implies every possible cinematic style, by necessity.

Some may feel that Bazin is being unduly parodied, on the

50. This argument is similar to but not the same as the one Black uses in *Art, Perception and Reality*, 100–104.
51. *Mothlight* is a film produced by encasing parts of insects between clear celluloid strips.

grounds that Bazin is certainly entitled to add all sorts of stip-ulations about lenses and focus to his conditions for cinematic representation. Such a maneuver will save his concept from trivialization. But this cannot be done without begging the question. The analysis of something called the essence or na-ture of cinema must be demonstrably apart from the individ-ual purposes and styles it can be used to implement. To use Bazin's own terms, the nature of cinema must be what is "au-tomatic" to cinema. But the point that must be made against Bazin is that those automatic processes warrant possibilities beyond what we normally think of as representation.

Now it is true that representation was, historically, the first purpose of cinema. But this is a contingent fact that has to do with the culture that invented cinema. Logically, there is no reason why abstraction might not have preceded representa-tion. Cultural needs determined the use of cinema. Analo-gously, the atomic bomb was developed to use against Japan. But obviously the mechanics of the A-bomb are neutral as to its use, whether cutting canals or bombing civilian popula-tions. If Bazin wants to analyze representation on the basis of the mechanics of film, then he cannot restrict the mechanical process by stipulating lenses, subject-to-camera distance, fo-cusing procedures, and lighting techniques. He must be pre-pared to include every mechanical possibility in his analysis. If he does not do this, then he is begging the question by de-fining the mechanical process as the style he intends to de-duce. In that case, there is no reason for the deduction at all since the style that is to be justified has been built into the conception of the process from the start.

The next move in Bazin's deduction—that realism follows from the representational nature of film—has three possible interpretations. Two of them can be seen to be false by an immediate application of the account thus far. The first read-ing is that realism follows from representation automati-cally—that the nature of the medium makes every shot real-istic. This is not the case; consider out-of-focus shots. Furthermore, if re-presentation defines cinema then ob-viously it is the case that a German expressionist film like *The*

Cabinet of Dr. Calagiri re-presents its distorted sets. Here Bazin's theory teeters on the border of self-contradiction again.

The second reading is as an injunction—since film is essentially representational, one should maximize this attribute by adopting a realist style, which is the style that best accords with representation. This is a prudential argument; its prototype is something like the aforementioned "All things being equal, don't use a thoroughbred race horse for plowing." The problem with mobilizing this argument form in this context, however, is that we really don't know if cinema is a thoroughbred. That is, Bazin has failed to demonstrate cinema's essential representationalism.

The last reading may have some plausibility. That is, apart from Bazin's very special concept of representation, we do ordinarily agree that there is some relation between representation and realism, at least "realism" in a certain sense of the word. This is probably true in virtue of the influence of the resemblance theory of representation.

The resemblance theory maintains that "x represents y if and only if x appreciably resembles y." A key word here is "appreciably." A statue may be smaller than its subject but at the same time maintain the same proportion of parts as its subject. On the resemblance theory, to avoid having the size disparity count against representation, the word "appreciably" is added. "Appreciably" can be thought of as modifying resemblance in terms of certain pertinent categories of resemblance; that is, the resemblance a painting, for example, bears to its model is not absolute but restricted to certain pertinent categories of resemblance. In terms of our statue, the resemblance theorist would claim that "a statue x appreciably resembles a man y in respect of proportion." Proportion is a pertinent category of resemblance for sculpture, but size is not. A list of all pertinent categories or respects of resemblance for a given art form (painting, sculpture, and so forth) will be built into the concept of representation in each form, according to this type of analysis. "This statue is a representation" (on this approach) will entail "This statue resembles its model in respect of proportion." In turn, such categories of resemblance can readily be seen as constituents of a stylistic canon, a canon of production that is often identified with realism in one sense of that term.

If the preceding paragraph is correct, then for some resemblance theories it will be true that representation implies realism. Bazin's concept of representation, however, is quite distinct from that proposed by resemblance theorists. Consequently, even if realism of a certain sort did follow from representation on some readings, this entailment is not open to Bazin. The difference between the concepts of representation in the resemblance theory and in Bazin's theory are too different for Bazin to simply adopt an entailment of the resemblance theory without modifying his concept of representation. In all probability Bazin did not understand that the divergence between the logical structures of his theory and the resemblance theory meant that the entailment from representation to realism was closed to him. A German expressionist set is re-presented even if it does not appreciably resemble any environment in pertinent respects. Thus, it seems that the second move in Bazin's argument is based on a fallacy of equivocation. That is, Bazin confuses re-presentation with representation to derive the relationship with realism that may be appropriate to some interpretations of representation but not appropriate to re-presentation.

Turning to the last stage of Bazin's argument—the claim that a commitment to realism implies a commitment to the style of spatial realism—we immediately note that the proposition has lost its sting insofar as it has been shown that filmmakers *are not* committed to realism because of the nature of the medium. Moreover, as I intend to show, there is no necessary connection between realism and the techniques, such as deep focus, that constitute the Bazinian style of spatial realism.

"Realism," of course, has many meanings. Calling a film realistic may simply be a way of saying it is very brutal. And as a means of referring to content, realism may more narrowly designate attention paid to generally ignored stratas of society, for example, the lives of the proletariat. Realism may also be used to apply strictly to formal technique. Here realism can merely mean a degree of what is called "verisimilitude." Realism can also refer more specifically to the style of Courbet, Manet, Jules Breton, and others. These different senses of the word make it difficult to apply without qualification. Neither Dali nor Bosch usually count as realists, though by certain readings of the resemblance theory one might be tempted to call them realists in terms of technique. Whether content or technique has more weight in determining what is realistic is difficult to evaluate.

In Bazin's account, spatial realism pertains primarily to technique, and as an ensemble of techniques it does not determine content nor is it restricted to realist content (consider, for example, Murnau's *Faust*). If spatial realism has some necessary relation to something called realism-as-such, then it must be to the idea of a realist technique. The question then arises whether there is somethng called *the* realist technique, which has an invariant set of defining properties.

Consider the case of Georg Grosz. He is a man who stood at the fore of a realist movement—called The new Objectivity—in Germany in the twenties. His style is representational and figurative, and his social themes are of the critical variety historically associated with left-wing realist sensibility. Yet Grosz uses distortion—look at the exaggerated mouths of his capitalists. Moreover, this distortion is symbolic in intent—it is a means of identifying capitalism with conspicuous consumption. The issue here is whether the techniques of distortion and symbolism work against Grosz's being counted as realist. If decided against Grosz, the case creates a dilemma, for then we would have to strike off the roster such seminal realists as Zola (for symbolism) and Manet (for distortion).

Grosz is a realist, but the grounds for this claim are not a set of transhistorical conditions constituting realist technique. Rather, Grosz is a realist when compared with the expressionists of his day. Many of these expressionists shared Grosz's socialist sympathies, while Grosz in turn used techniques of distortion and symbolization. Yet, there is a difference between Grosz and the German expressionists. That dif-

ference cannot be marked simply by pointing to this or that
technique. Rather, it has to do with the function of technique
in Grosz's work. Grosz's works present themselves as documents of the social life of Weimar Germany. That is, the most
plausible way of looking at his sketches is in terms of the observation of social life and the criticism of Weimar society.
Unlike the expressionists, Grosz does not use symbolism and
distortion as emblems of intense personal crisis. In this respect, compared to the expressionists, Grosz counts as a realist.

There are many more similar examples. Thomas Mann
may use quasi-stream of consciousness techniques; con-
versely, Robbe-Grillet may be a worthy descendent of Zola's
preoccupation with description. Yet Mann is a realist and
Robbe-Grillet is not. One cannot talk of realist technique
apart from both the total design of a work and the art historical context of the work.

Consider the preceding observation in relation to the Bazinian spatial realist style deep-focus shots of the typing pool
in Orson Welles's *The Trial*. Clearly the possibility of scanning and discovery is formally preserved in these shots. Yet,
it seems that what is emphasized by these shots is scale—identical typewriter desks as far as the eye can see—rather than the
possibility of scanning and discovery. The function of these
shots is exaggeration, for the purpose of revealing the Taylor-
ization and industrialization of clerical work. Deep-focus
composition makes this oneiric image particularly compelling. One could scan the image from desk to desk but not
only would that be monotonous, it would merely reempha-
size the immediately apparent uniformity of the composition.
In this respect, the aim of the technique is not realism but an
abstract form of symbolism that emerges through the use of
deep focus and set design. Moreover, this analysis of the shots
of the typing pool is certainly much more consistent with a
general analysis of the total film than an analysis in terms of
realism. Indeed, in the context of the narrative, editing,
sound, and use of lenses in *The Trial*, an analysis of these

shots in terms of realism strikes me as the most implausible one imaginable.

Though the preceding examples do not prove the point conclusively, I do think that they make highly suspect the idea that there is an invariant realist technique. Rather, there are techniques that can be adopted for realist purposes. Applied to elements of the spatial realist style such as deep-focus photography, this implies that there is no necessary relation between such techniques and realism. What constitutes realism, both in terms of technique and content, changes over the course of history. Realism is a useful comparative concept for both artists and art historians insofar as it supplies a means for both to distinguish one group of artworks from another. This, however, makes the extension of the concept very context and period dependent. In this regard, I hasten to add that I believe, along with Bazin, that deep-focus photography was used as a key realist technique from the thirties through the fifties. But I believe this on historical grounds and not because I agree with the theoretical presumption that deep-focus photography is a transhistorical, defining characteristic of something called film realism.

Though Bazin at times acknowledges that there are styles of cinematic realism other than spatial realism, he more often than not writes as though spatial realism is the only legitimate realist film form.[52] He appears to do this on the basis of his belief that this style is the most realistic because it corresponds most closely to the way reality really is. Here, Bazin seems to presuppose a view that realism is a two-term relation of correspondence between film and reality. That is, the theory of film realism is to be understood on an analogy to the correspondence theory of truth. And just as truth in such theories is truth for all time, so realism will be transhistorical.

52. This is a point of some interpretive tension in the text. At times, Bazin speaks respectfully of Soviet realism of the twenties, but for the most part he impugns that style as a sort of aberration. Throughout this section I am presupposing that Bazin rejects the montage style of realism and that his deferential bows to *Potemkin* and Eisenstein are nothing more than diplomatic gestures.

It is far from clear, however, that realism in any of the arts should be thought of as a simple relationship of correspondence between a representation and reality. Realism is, after all, a term used to point to stylistic differences between contrasting artworks. When we call a film or a movement realist, we are directing attention to certain characteristics the given films have that other films lack. *Rules of the Game* uses deep-focus cinematography to induce audiences to search the image for dramatic details that are lodged in the background of long-take shots. This mode of composition differs from the techniques prevalent in Russian films of the twenties and Hollywood films of the twenties and thirties. We signal this difference by using the word "realism." Why? Because the spectator's relation to the Renoir image—scanning it for detail—is a possibility that is not only inhibited by Soviet montage and soft focus but is also taken to be *more like* (not exactly like) our normal perceptual experiences than what we encounter in the alternative styles that existed when the deep-focus style crystallized. Deep-focus photography does not correspond to or match reality. Rather, it is more like some specified aspects of reality when compared to alternative styles. To call a film or a movement realistic means that the films in question deviate from a designated group of contrasting films in such a way that the deviation can be interpreted as analogous to some aspect of reality that was repressed or perhaps merely absent in the films or movements presented for comparison. Realism is not a two-term relation between a film and reality. Realism is at least a three-term relation among *a film or group of films* and *a contrasting group of films*, some of whose differences are interpreted in terms of the first group of films supplying a greater range of analogies to *reality* or, less grandiosely, to ordinary or everyday experience. If this is correct, then there is no single form of realism in film. Soviet films of the twenties were realist in virtue of their use of the mass hero and location shooting and their concentration on aspects of contemporary proletarian life—all of which were excluded from the Hollywood-studio, glamorous star vehicles of the day. When the deep-focus style of spatial realism crystallized, it emphasized a dimension of reality—of ordinary perceptual experience—that was not relevant to Soviet realism. But the success of spatial realism as a movement does not force us to disparage the realism of Soviet films. Instead, we merely acknowledge that a new type of realism has been introduced. Realism is a style concept whose use revolves around historically grounded comparisons and contrasts. Consequently, it is dangerous to speak of realism unprefixed. Rather, we should speak of types of realism—for example, *Soviet* realism or *neo*realism. Insofar as Bazin writes at times as though there were only one legitimate form of film realism—a form whose legitimacy rests on a straightforward correspondence to reality—he has drifted from the realm of stylistic analysis into that of metaphysics.

Bazin, Cavell, and the re-presentation of objects

As we saw in the preceding section, Bazin believes that a photo, and, by extension, a cinematographic image, has existential import. A photographic image is always an image of something—specifically, it is an image of the objects, places, events, and persons that gave rise to it. A photographic image re-presents its model. The image is rooted in reality. Thus, Bazinians hold that with regard to photographic images—in contrast to paintings and drawings—it always makes sense to ask what lies beyond the photographic image: what is *behind* the objects in the image and what is *adjacent* to the image.[53] Undoubtedly the belief that the photographic image is a slice out of the continuum of reality is one reason Bazinians champion the idea of lateral depth of field in opposition to the painterly and theatrical conception of the frame as a box. But it is important to recall that this stylistic choice is purportedly defensible by reference to an ontological fact about photographic images—that they re-present places, events, persons, and objects.

Bazin himself does not really supply an argument for this

53. Cavell, *The World Viewed*, 13.

point. The leading contemporary Bazinian, Stanley Cavell, however, does. Cavell initiates his argument by asking what it is that films reproduce. He sees two alternatives: either films reproduce the very objects that give rise to the image, or they reproduce the sight or appearance of the objects.

> We said that a record reproduces a sound, but we cannot say that a photograph reproduces a sight (or a look, or an appearance). A sight is an object (usually a large object like the Grand Canyon). . . . objects don't make sights or have sights . . . they are too close to their sights to give them up for reproducing.[54]

And apart from these ordinary language considerations, Cavell also argues that "sights" are rather queer metaphysical entities that might better be banished from one's ontology in the name of parsimony—indeed, imagine how very many sights each object, viewed from an infinity of angles, will have. But if it is not the sight or the appearance of the object that a photographic image represents, then it must be the object itself that is re-presented.

The obvious problem with this argument is the assumption of the premise that photographic images re-present either objects themselves or sights of objects. The problem here is not that Cavell has failed to give enough alternatives (though, of course, there might be more). Rather, the premise begs the question by assuming that the photographic image must re-present something from the past and that the task of analysis is simply a matter of determining what that something is—is it an object or a sight? But why must we believe that something or anything is in fact re-presented via photographic representation? The idea of re-presentation is doubtless a powerful metaphor for the phenomenon of representation. But we must ask whether it is literally true that anything—whether an object or a sight—is re-presented or reproduced by photography or cinematography. In fact, in the previous

54. Ibid., 24.

section of this chapter the very intelligibility of "re-presenta-tion" was called into question.

A representation, rather, *presents* a stand-in or a proxy of a model; it does not re-present either the model or the sight of the model. Cavell may be right when he says that the sight or appearance of the object is "too close" to the object to be pried off for re-presentation. But he is wrong to surmise from this that the only alternative is that the object is re-produced. For we may say instead that what photography does is to *produce* a stand-in for its model (at least in cases of what in the next section will be called physical portrayal; with what will be called depiction and nominal portrayal, what is stood for is more complex). Therefore, the image does not literally re-present anything whatsoever.

Bazinians are fond of connecting the supposed existential import of photographic images to an essential distinction be-tween paintings and films. It is argued that with paintings it does not make sense to ask what is adjacent to an image, but with film it always makes sense to ask what is off-screen. There are many confusions involved here, and none of them are settled by the ontological prejudices of Bazinians.

First of all, I see no reason to believe that it never makes sense to ask what is adjacent to the view portrayed by a paint-ing—that is, what we would see if the painting did not end where it does but continued on. Imagine a painting of the battle of Waterloo. I see Napoleon's grenadiers repulsed by Wellington's thin red line. I am taken by the historical accu-racy of the work. I turn to the painter and ask "Where are the Prussians?" It seems perfectly reasonable for the painter to point to a place on the wall two feet from the left of the paint-ing and say "They would be about here, given the scale of the painting." Indeed, since this painting is one that is committed to historical accuracy, this answer makes more sense than possible alternatives such as "In the world of this painting, there are no Prussians at the battle of Waterloo." I am not denying that a painter could portray a fictional battle of Wa-terloo where there were no Prussians. But this would be the special case, one the painter would have to flag in some way if viewers were supposed to delete the Prussians from this Waterloo.

On the other hand, it is not true that it always makes sense to ask what is adjacent to a photographic or cinematographic image. Here, the problem of fiction, to be taken up in the next section, looms in a way that makes this issue almost unintelligible. For Bazinians believe that cinema literally re-presents the models that give rise to the image. Thus, if it always makes sense to ask what is adjacent to cinema images, we may arrive at some very screwy answers. "What's next to the land of Oz?" "The MGM commissary." And apart from these obvious problems, there are films, just as there are paintings, whose internal structures are designed to imply that a viewer should not ask what is adjacent to what is on-camera because the film presents its imagery as that of a fantastic realm or of a realm completely constructed by conventions, rather than in terms of the mimesis of the normal space of physics. *Blood of a Poet*, *Andalusian Dog*, and *Heaven and Earth Magic* are examples of the former. Rohmer's *Perceval* is an example of the latter. Rohmer's images do not signal that they are to be regarded as realistic. They are completely conventionalized, making direct allusions to theatrical staging. We are best advised not to assume that there are spaces adjacent to those on camera; indeed, we are best advised to regard the frame line as like a proscenium, insofar as this accords with the overt theatricality of the rest of the film. Moreover, this theatricality is rigorously enforced to give the film its aura of artificiality, decorum, containedness, and delicacy. To say of *Perceval* that it always makes sense to ask what is immediately off-screen, is a profound mistake. It makes no more sense than to ask what is next to Swan Lake—that is, just beyond the leg curtains—in the ballet of the same name.

A note on cinematic representation

One of the most peculiar features of Bazin's concept of representation is the characterization it implies of what is represented by fiction film. Bazin believes that film images have existential import—the film image re-presents some x from the past. Film images, in supposed contrast to all painting, represent things in a unique way—that is, they re-present things—which compels us to accept their referents as real. Bazin would seem to have to defend this claim by saying something like "*Casablanca* re-presents Humphrey Bogart." But this is a curious thing to say since what is most relevant to viewing the fiction film *Casablanca* is that it represents Rick. It certainly does not re-present Rick nor does it "fictionally re-present" Bogart. If it does re-present Bogart, that seems beside the point if we are interested in appreciating the film as fictional representation—in which case it is about Rick and not about Bogart.

A photo of Tip O'Neill might, in some sense, be said to re-present Tip O'Neill—photos in our culture are generally used to document. Bazin extrapolates this conventional use of the photo—documentation—into an account of cinematic re-presentation. But the presupposition that photography—let alone feature films—can only be used to document or to literally re-present is quite mistaken. Richard Avedon's recent advertisements for Christian Dior are miniature fictions, replete with three characters: Wizard, Mouth, and Oliver. The character of Wizard is modeled by the avant-garde dramaturge André Gregory. When I look at one of these ads, I may be forced to accept the fact that the character The Wizard had to have some model who existed at some time and some place, but this admission does not entail that I characterize the ad as a representation of André Gregory. Indeed, the fact that André Gregory plays the role of Wizard is irrelevant to the fictional representation at work in the photo. Bazin's conception of photography, on the other hand, seems to say that what is important about any photographic image—whether in a fictional context or otherwise—is what it re-presents, that is, documents. Yet what is literally re-presented or documented in a photographic fiction may be irrelevant to what the fiction represents. That is, when confronted with fiction, Bazin's theory implies strange results by ontologically misplacing, so to speak, the focus of our attention.

This anomaly in regard to photography escalates when we turn to the issue of feature films. At least with photography, documentation rather than fictionalization was and possibly still is considered its primary role in our culture. It is easy to see how one could confuse the pervasiveness of the snapshot with the essence of photography. But it is harder to see how the theorist can overlook the possibility of fiction when it comes to the feature film, because fiction is surely the most visible purpose of cinema in our culture. What is most bizarre about Bazin's theory is that it is strangely ill-suited to account for what is represented in fictional films. Films seem to become records of actors and places; their fictional referents dissolve. *M* is about Peter Lorre rather than about a psychopathic child killer; *The Creature from the Black Lagoon* is not about a rivulet off the Amazon but about Wakulla Springs, Florida. Films you thought were representations of castles, graveyards, and forests are really about studio sets.

The problem with the issue of fiction is a function of Bazin's implicit assumption that there is only one form of cinematic representation. But as in other media, artistic and otherwise, there is more than one mode of representation in cinema. In fact, we can adopt some of Monroe Beardsley's terminology (without necessarily endorsing his resemblance theory of representation) to show that there are at least three types of representation in cinema that we must distinguish before we can appreciate the representational range of the medium.[55]

The first level of cinematic representation is *physical portrayal*. That is, every shot in a live-action photographic film physically portrays its model—a definite object, person, place, or event that can be designated by a singular term. It is in this sense that *Psycho* represents Anthony Perkins rather

55. Beardsley, *Aesthetics: Problems in the Philosophy of Criticism*, especially Chapter 6, section 16. Also see Goran Hemeren, *Representation and Meaning in the Visual Arts* (Lund: Scandinavian University Books, 1969), especially Chapter 2. A similar application to film appears in my "From Real to Reel; Entangled in Non-Fiction Film," in *Philosophic Exchange*, an annual edited at SUNY, Brockport, the 1983 issue, pages 5–45.

than Norman Bates—it was Anthony Perkins who served as the source of the image. Every live-action shot will physically portray its model. This is obviously the point Bazin has in mind when he speaks of films re-presenting the past. Because of the way such images are produced, every shot (save certain special effects) in a live-action film physically portrays whatever people, places, and things caused the image. Shots are called "recordings," in the most basic sense of the term, if the only representational function they perform is physical portrayal. A physical portrayal is a representation of the particular person, object, or event that caused the image. Traditional realist film theory is preoccupied with physical portrayal to the extent that this mode of representation is taken to be either the only use of shots or the most essential, most important, or most fundamental one. As a result, the use of shots in fictional representation becomes utterly mystified and confused, since the realist must give an account of what is represented in a fiction film in terms of physical portrayal.

But physical portrayal is not the only mode of representation in film. A film not only physically portrays its source— a particular person, place, thing, event, or action—but it also *depicts* a class or collection of objects designated by a general term. A shot from *Psycho* physically portrays Anthony Perkins while also depicting a man; likewise, a shot of the Golden Gate Bridge in *Attack of the Killer Tomatoes* physically portrays *the* Golden Gate but also depicts *a* bridge. Every shot of a live-action film physically portrays its model—some specific individual—while also depicting a member of a class, describable by a general term—man, bridge, fire, cow, battle, and so on. A film may be important in terms of what it physically portrays—for example, a record of President Reagan's oath of office—or a shot may be important in terms of what it depicts. Imagine, for example, a montage introduction to an evening news program. Let us say that this montage includes an image of a fire—one that occurred on the northwest corner of Twenty-third Street and Lexington Avenue in New York City on December 11, 1972. But what is important in this prologue to the news program—important in terms of what is being communicated—would not be the portrayal of that particular fire, but the depiction of *a* fire, which is the *kind* of thing this program is concerned with. A film image can depict a class as well as physically portray an individual. And in some contexts of communication, it may be the case that only what the image depicts is relevant for communication. The shot's causal relation to its model will be, for the most part, irrelevant.

What is theoretically important about depiction is that it splits the shot from its source, and it is this split that makes the third mode of cinematic representation, *nominal portrayal*, possible. A shot that physically portrays Anthony Perkins in *Psycho* depicts a madman while, given its place in the context of the story, nominally portraying Norman Bates. A shot is a nominal portrayal of an object, person, place, or event when it represents a *particular* object, person, place, or event different from the one that gave rise to the image. Nominal portrayal in film is a function of such factors as voice-over commentary, titles, an on-going story, or editing. These devices establish that the things shown in the image "stand for" particular things other than the ones that caused the image. For example, in the fictional world of the story of *Psycho*, the images of Anthony Perkins stand for Norman Bates rather than for the actor whose presence in front of Hitchcock's camera contributed to bringing these images into existence. Nominal portrayal is the most important mode of representation in terms of the way our culture uses film—that is, feature films—since nominal portrayal is the basis of all fiction film.

Realist theorists like Bazin tend to concentrate on the phenomenon of physical portrayal, which is why their theories imply such strange accounts of the operation of fictional representation in film. On the other hand, their opponents, the montage theorists, are champions of the possibilities of nominal portrayal, particularly in virtue of the way editing can give a shot a meaning and a reference different from what the shot physically portrays. Montage theorists did not invent nominal portrayal in film, but they did polemicize its importance, especially in regard to editing. Perhaps montagists like

Lev Kuleshov at times became overly enthusiastic in their claims for montage, sounding occasionally as if they believed that editing could make any shot—its photographic content notwithstanding—stand for anything. But this is too extreme. No amount of cutting will make a shot of Gracie Allen look like a nominal portrayal of a pencil. Undoubtedly, what a pictorial representation depicts constrains the range of what it can be used to nominally portray. However, despite their excessive sloganeering, the Soviets were more correct about the way film is used in our culture than was Bazin with his curious allegiance to physical portrayal as the essential form of cinematic representation. As a result, the Soviets have little problem handling fictional representation, but it is Bazin's greatest embarrassment.

The automatism argument

Bazin's defence of realism is obviously suggested by his tendency to see the camera as an agency for documentation. Realism and documentation, at least on the surface, both seem to be connected to standards of veracity. And Bazin believes the camera has some special purchase on the truth that should predispose us to a realist style in cinema (where "realist" is given primarily an epistemic gloss). I have already challenged this string of associations; however, it is useful to consider Bazin's reasons for attributing a special purchase on objectivity to the camera, because those reasons articulate a not uncommon prejudice about photography.

For Bazin, it is extremely significant that the photographic process is a mechanical process. Bazin believes that since cinematic images are made automatically via photography, they are objective in a way that is impossible in painting. This objectivity, moreover, commits the filmmaker to realism as the proper aesthetic direction for the film medium.

Bazin writes:

> Originality in photography as distinct from originality in painting lies in the essentially objective character of

photography. (Bazin here makes a point of the fact that the lens, the basis of photography, is in French called the "objectif," a nuance that is lost in English.—Tr.) For the first time, between the originating object and its reproduction there intervenes only the instrumentality of a nonliving agent. For the first time an image of the world is formed automatically, without the creative intervention of man. The personality of the photographer enters into the proceedings only in his selection of the object to be photographed and by way of the purpose he has in mind. Although the final result may reflect something of his personality, this does not play the same role as is played by that of the painter. All the arts are based on the presence of man, only photography derives an advantage from his absence. Photography affects us like a phenomenon in nature, like a flower or a snowflake whose vegetable or earthly origins are an inseparable part of their beauty. (*WIC* 1, 14)

From these considerations, Bazin surmises that "the cinema is objectivity in time" (Ibid.) And it is this connection with objectivity that determines the proper use of the medium.

> The aesthetic qualities of photography are to be sought in its power to lay bare the realities. It is not for me to separate off, in the complex fabric of the objective world, here a reflection on a damp sidewalk, there a gesture of a child. Only the impassive lens, stripping its object of all those ways of seeing it, those piled-up preconceptions, that spiritual dust and grime with which my eyes have covered it, is able to present it in all its virginal purity to my attention. (*WIC* 1, 15)

Bazin's argument appears to be that since cinema is a mechanical/automatic process, it is objective—both in the sense that it is an object, the product of a natural process, and in the sense that it is not subjective, not a personal vision. This objectivity makes a certain kind of realism possible—namely, it makes possible the showing of things without preconceptions. Given that this is a unique power of cinema—and given Bazin's evident predisposition to medium-specificity arguments—it follows for Bazin that cinema should be used to implement a realist project.

The first thing to note about this argument is that it does not give logical support to a style of realism as specific as spatial realism. At most, the conclusion favors a form of realism conceived as the showing of things without preconceptions. This corresponds to the way Bazin characterizes some aspects of Italian neorealism, but it does not entail endorsement of stylistic choices such as long takes and medium-long shots. Nor does this notion of unpreconceived presentation correspond to some enshrined variety of realism as such; Zola, for example, thought that the realist was committed to the scientific viewpoint rather than to an eschewal of all viewpoints.[56] Thus, even if cinematic images were such that they show the world without preconceptions, no particular style of realism can be grounded on this fact and this fact alone.

Of course, the argument also errs in attempting to infer that given photography's purportedly unique capacity to show the world without preconceptions, the role of photography is only to "lay bare realities." This portion of the argument presupposes the sort of medium-specificity myth discredited in the first chapter.

An even deeper error seems to beset the argument from the start. The argument's basic premise is that some sort of objectivity is built into the photographic medium because it is a mechanical or automatic process. Bazin claims that the automatic nature of photographic reproduction is objective in the sense that the photographic image is a natural product—like a snowflake—and that once the photographic process is set in motion, subjectivity is excluded from the machine, so to speak. These dimensions of objectivity are said to be special to the photographic medium. But are they special to photog-

56. Emile Zola, "The Experimental Novel," in *Modern Literary Realism*, edited by George Becker (Princeton: Princeton University Press, 1969), 162–96.

raphy and film in any way that marks a real difference between the photographic arts and other representative arts?

When I write a novelistic description of a room and my
fingers touch the keyboard of my IBM typewriter, the process of printing the words is automatic. Is the mechanical process between me and the final text any less automatic with the
typewriter than with the camera? Indeed, there is a way in
which it is appropriate to describe a typewritten (or even a
handwritten) page as a natural product, if what one means by
that is that the page is a result of a causal process. Likewise,
painting also has a physical, natural, causal dimension. As
Douglas Lackey points out, "once the painter touches his
brush to the canvas, there are certain things that will happen
automatically. The paint, for example, must flow at a certain
rate given the condition of the brush."[57] That is, the medium
has a physical dimension whose mechanical manipulation involves a natural, causal process. Every medium that involves
representation involves causation in the process of physically
manifesting the representation in question. Every representation in every media is, in some sense, a product of a causal
process. Cinema and photography are not alone in this respect. Every medium in some degree has a physical-process
dimension and, therefore, has some aspects of "the automatic" about it. Thus, at best, the sort of objectivity that Bazin attributes to cinema can differ only in degree rather than
in kind from a similar type of objectivity to be found in all
representational media.

But one wonders whether Bazin can sustain even this mild
claim. One problem with this claim is the peculiar notion of
"objectivity" it supports. What we really want to know is
whether cinema's mechanical process either guarantees objectivity or excludes subjectivity, where those terms are used in
their normal epistemic sense and not in the sense that the photographic image can be called a natural product or object. But
it is not true that cinema's mechanical process either guaran-

57. Douglas Lackey, "Reflections on Cavell's Ontology of Film," in *Journal
of Aesthetics and Art Criticism* 32 (1973), 271–73.

tees objectivity or excludes subjectivity. The process cannot guarantee objective results because the process in and of itself does not guarantee any sort of success, objective or otherwise. An attempted photo of a room may be overexposed beyond all recognition—as an automatic result of the process of photography. That is, photography as a set of physical reactions does not guarantee objective results insofar as it does not guarantee any recognizable results. Getting recognizable results requires a photographer adjusting the camera mechanism, the lighting, and so forth. Once this is admitted, however, then it is clear that the photographer can set the "automatic" process in action in such a way that the results are highly subjective and personal. Imagine a photographer with a vegetable phobia—following Weston's monumentalizing examples, he could easily transform a green pepper and some carrots into a giant threatening insect, armored and horned. This is not to say that there cannot be objective photographs—for example, those of Cartier-Bresson. The point is rather that the question of the objectivity or subjectivity of a photograph or a film cannot be settled by reference to the automatic mechanical process of the medium. Thus, realism does not follow from the supposed "automatic objectivity" of the medium because there is no such automatic objectivity. Even if Bazin had succeeded in establishing that the cinematic image is, in some distinctive sense, objective in terms of being the product of a natural process, this would have no implications for realism. It would show, correctly enough, that cinematic images were *real* in some respect, not that they are or should be *realistic*.

This last point deserves some further amplification. It touches upon an issue that recurs often in Bazin's writing—a tendency for equivocation that centers on the concept of the "real." From the fact that the cinematographic image is real— that is, a physical fact resulting from lawlike chemical and mechanical operations—a connection with realism is suggested. Likewise, when Bazin notes that the long take traffics in *real* time, a correlation is made with realism. Whenever Bazin can tag some concept with the adjective "real," he seems to believe that he has presented further evidence for the realistic style he advocates. But, the logical distance between such items as the real image—the image as a real thing in and of itself—and a realistic image—for example, a shot in the Renoir style—is being papered over by a cluster of equivocations on terms such as "real," "reality," "realism," and the like, which are rampant in Bazin's writings.

Bazin's Arguments against Montage

Bazin does not only promote the cinematic style of spatial realism by means of attempted derivations from the nature of cinema. Bazin also advocates spatial realism by advancing negative arguments against spatial realism's nearest challenger—the montage style, whose proponents also defend it as having some special relation to the nature of the medium.

Throughout his writings, Bazin pictures montage as an elementary form of cinematic trickery. Of Jean Tourane's *Une Fée pas comme les autres*, Bazin writes,

> For it is very important to note that Tourane's animals are not tamed, only gentled. Nor do they ever actually do the things they seem to be doing. When they do, it is by a trick, either with a hand off-screen guiding them, or an artificial paw like a marionette on a string. All Tourane's ingenuity and talent lie in his ability to get animals to stay put in the positions in which he has placed them for the duration of the take. The environment, the dissimulation, the commentary are already sufficient to give to the bearing of the animal an almost human quality which, in turn, the illusion of montage underlines and magnifies to such an extent that at times it makes the impression almost complete. In this way, without the protagonists having done anything beyond the remaining perfectly still in front of the camera, a whole story is built up with a large number of characters in complicated relationships. . . . The apparent action and meaning we attribute to it do not exist, to all intents and purposes,

prior to the assembling of the film, not even in the form of fragmented scenes out of which the set-ups are generally composed. (*WIC* 1, 44)

Here, Bazin appears to be arguing that there is something wrong with a film where, for example, a dog's retrieving of the hero's gun is represented by three shots—one of the dog sitting; one of the dog walking; and one of the dog with the gun in his mouth. Bazin prefers that the action be performed in a long take—a Lassie type struts from the foreground to the background, picks up a gun with its mouth and walks forward to the camera with the gun clamped between her jaws. But what is the difference between these two schemes of representation? At times, Bazin appears to be suggesting that in the edited version the dog did not really retrieve the gun, but that in the long-take version, the dog really did retrieve the gun. But is this a distinction in kind or merely in degree? For in neither case does the dog *really* retrieve the *hero's gun*—each appears to retrieve an object that nominally portrays the hero's gun in the world of fiction. Both of these representations are fictional, so neither dog really retrieves the hero's gun. Both are instances of nominal portrayal, the difference between them being that in one case the nominal portrayal is executed by means of the editing as well as the ongoing story, whereas in the case of the long-take, the ongoing story alone establishes the significance of the dog's action. But since both sequences are cases of nominal portrayal, the difference between them is a matter of degree, not kind. The long-take scene does not have a closer connection with what is really going on. It—like the edited scene—is fictional. Here again, we see how fiction wreaks havoc with Bazin's theory.

Another way to distinguish the two scenes would be to say that the edited scene was "faked" and the long-take scene was "not faked." But the question then becomes whether we can give any consistent sense to "not faked" other than "not edited." I say this because in scenes such as these it may very well be the case that though the action is performed in a single take, trickery of some sort may still be employed to enable the canine to retrieve the gun. Imagine a case where the hero's gun has been carved out of a steak bone. The dog leaps to it not out of training, but instinct, and then turns to the camera, gun in jaw, slavering in doggy ecstasy. In the context of the story, it will appear that the dog has retrieved the hero's gun. At the same time, the shot is executed in a long take. But one cannot say that since the shot lacks editing, it is devoid of fakery or trickery. Again, the attempted distinction between this shot and an edited one is one of degree, not kind.

Bazin seems somewhat aware of this problem, but his attempts to grapple with it are virtually incoherent. He compares Lamorisse's *Le Ballon Rouge* with *Une Fée pas comme les autres*. The Lamorisse film sets out the zoomorphic hijinks of its eponymous balloon in long takes. Yet it took a great deal of patient experimentation to produce the stunts "performed" by Lamorisse's magical red balloon. Indeed, as might be expected, there was not *one* red balloon, as the film implies— Lamorisse spent more than 500,000 francs on red balloons. Given this degree of "fakery" in Lamorisse's long-take approach, how is the long-take method to be discriminated from the montage approach in terms of trickery? Bazin writes:

> What does it matter, you will say, provided the result is the same—if, for example, we are made to accept on screen the existence of a balloon that can follow its master like a little dog? It matters to this extent, that with montage the magic balloon would be nonexistent, whereas in the film by Lamorisse we are dealing with an existing balloon. (*WIC* 1, 13)

But what could this possibly mean? In both versions there would be a red balloon—or a collection of identical red balloons—that gives rise to the action photographed in the images. In both cases, the red balloon (or the collection) would exist. How can it be that the red balloon of the montage version is nonexistent? Because it is not truly magical—because it does not truly follow the protagonist? But neither does the

red balloon—or more accurately, the collection of red balloons—in the long-take version. Again, Bazin seems at a loss
to spell out intelligibly the difference between the montage
and the long-take versions.

Earlier I cited several of Bazin's examples showing that the
long-take approach can impart a greater sense of authenticity
to the action than a scene constructed on an editing table. In
The Circus, because of the camera set-up, we see that Charles
Chaplin is literally in a cage with a lion. Had the scene been
shot in such a way that we saw Charlie with a look of terror
on his face, followed by a cut to the lion—with no shot con-
taining both Charlie and the lion—then Bazin would claim
that the scene would not be as suspenseful as the long-take
version. This is a psychological claim, and it sounds intui-
tively plausible. The issue of the risk in the lion scene hinges
on spatial proximity and, therefore, our sense of risk is
heightened when the space is laid out as perspicuously as possible. This might not be achievable through editing. Note
that the contest between these variant approaches cannot be
one of fakery, since even with a long-take approach, the film
asserts that Charlie is standing next to a ferocious lion when
he is really standing next to a studio-tamed lion. Apart from
the issue of utter fidelity, however, there is another quality
that this long-take shot has—call it authenticity—because the
long take makes the represented risk more compelling.

Now even if Bazin is correct (and I think he is) that in certain instances the long-take approach has qualities of authenticity and suspensefulness that could not be achieved by a
montage version of the same scene, it is still not obvious that
this implies any general conclusions about the relative
strengths and weaknesses of the two styles. Nor does it establish the propriety of the long-take style. For it is not clear that
in every case it is appropriate to strive for the authenticity effect above all others; and certainly not every scene is such that
it can or should be played for Bazinian suspense. A scene
might be developed for qualities that are more readily available through editing, for example, the intensity of the gun-
fighters communicated by the montage of giant close-ups of

eyes in *The Good, the Bad, and the Ugly*. If authenticity—of the sort imparted by spatial realism—were the only or the most important quality achievable in cinema, then montage obviously would be problematic. But authenticity is only one quality among the great many available to cinema, and its appropriateness depends not on the ontology of film but on the way it serves the scenes where it is used.

Undoubtedly, Bazin's most famous arguments against montage are moral in nature. Bazin argues, on the one hand, that montage denies the spectator freedom of choice—freedom to discover the meaning of a scene for oneself—while concomitantly imposing a preordained viewpoint on the action, events, and states of affairs in films, especially films that involve human characters. Bazin believes that the montage style excludes the possibility of ambiguity—the openness of an action to more than one interpretation—and compels the spectator to adopt a single point of view—the director's—on the action represented by the film.

It is not easy to make complete sense of Bazin's remarks in this area of speculation. He speaks of the montagist as imposing a preordained viewpoint on actions, in contrast to the spatial realist, who lets the event speak for itself. This makes it sound as though the event in question has some existence independent of its form of representation. But remember that here we are speaking, for the most part, of fictional events. To what extent does it make sense to speak as though a fictional event is independent of its representation in such a way that the director can be said to be imposing his view on it? Certainly the idea of imposition here is a strange one—no fictional event could conflict with or resist an author's imposition. And also, does it make sense to say that a spatial realist is not imposing a preordained viewpoint on a represented event? That seems to presume that there is an event independent of the representation that is being allowed to unfold. But in fact, the "event," with either spatial realism or montage, is constituted by the process of filming. Thus it seems strange to think of that process as either imposing or not imposing a viewpoint. But even if some sense can be made of this, an-

other problem will arise in working out whatever Bazin believes accounts for the correlation of ambiguity with spectator freedom and the lack of authorial compulsion. For is it not
the case that ambiguous or multiple viewpoints in works of
fiction are authorial effects? If montage is morally problematic, then why are ambiguous viewpoints or perspectivism
not problematic? Perspectivism—seeing characters nonjudg-
mentally from several vantages—is still an authorial viewpoint; and a technique that enhances it—such as the long
take—disposes a spectator to take the author's moral/philo-
sophical viewpoint. Intentionally arranging a fiction so that
no single moral judgment must be made—especially where
this is the thematic point of the story—is still exerting control
over the spectator. Indeed, it is hard to imagine anything
worth calling a style that would fail to direct the spectator in
some way.

Bazin often sounds as though he is claiming that montage
correlates with authorial control and spectator constriction,
whereas the long-take correlates with lack of authorial control and spectator freedom. As an empirical law, these corre-
lations are false, though they may somehow metaphorically
capture our feelings about the balance of control in a scene.
However, our feelings about the balance of control in a scene
cannot be the basis for condemning a style such as montage
for moral improprieties.

Of course, the Bazinian may respond that the point is not
to claim a constant variation between authorial control and
apparent spectator freedom but only to make the weaker
claim that the long take makes some sort of spectator freedom
possible (not necessary) and that the same sort of spectator
freedom is not possible with montage. This, however, is not
true. It may be the case that most of the montage in the history of cinema has been unequivocal and unambiguous in its
meaning. But this is not, as Bazinians suggest, because montage as a technique is automatically univocal in its meaning—
no more than the fact that most long-take shots have been
unambiguous excludes the possibility of ambiguity for spatial
realists. Montage elements can be juxtaposed in such a way

that the shots in question can have more than one meaning and can be ambiguous—for example, in the film *Last Year at Marienbad*. Shots in montage can also be arrayed in a manner that is (1) not immediately apparent to the spectator and (2) that calls on the active participation of the spectator to infer their meaning, for example, the sequence of the gods in *October*. Indeed, it is interesting to note that the Soviets prized active spectatorship and audience participation in constructing the meaning of the film as much as Bazinians do. But they saw montage as a means of achieving this. And there is no reason to believe that the montage technique cannot be adapted to induce participation any less successfully than the long take of the spatial realist. Of course a given case of montage, like a given case of long-take, can be simple-minded. But there is no reason why audience participation cannot be a function of montage. Montage may be brutally demonstrative, blatant, and manipulative, as it is in the *Why We Fight* series. But it can also be suggestive, allusive, multilayered, and ambiguous, as it is in *Murder Psalm*. If audience participation and ambiguity are indices of the moral worth of technique as such, there is no reason in principle to demote montage in favor of the long take.

Before concluding this section, a brief historical remark may be useful. The rhetoric of freedom suffuses Bazin's discussion of montage; spatial realism is constantly advocated over montage because if affords the spectator the opportunity of choice. Bazin's obsession with choice and freedom is, of course, very intelligible within the cultural context of Bazin's writings. For, as Annette Michelson has pointed out, Bazin's career corresponds to what might be called "the period of Sartre's ascendency."[58] Bazin's fetishization of freedom and choice, then, can be seen as a correlate to the central values of existentialism.

58. Annette Michelson, review of *What Is Cinema?* vol. 1, in *Artforum* (Summer 1968), 68. This article is particularly helpful for situating Bazin within the intellectual life of mid-century Paris. Michelson relates Bazin's work to existentialism and to the related movement of phenomenology, while elucidating as well the influence of Catholicism on Bazin's writing.

This connection is not indirect or conjectural. In "Theater and Cinema—Part One," Bazin writes: "The importance of depth of focus and the fixed camera in Welles and Wyler springs from a reluctance to fragment things arbitrarily and a desire instead to show an image that is uniformly understandable and that compels the spectator to make his own choice" (*WIC* 1, 92). Immediately preceding this comment, Bazin had alluded to Sartre's attack on François Mauriac as an expression that accorded with Bazin's own dismissal of classical film editing—a practice whose presuppositions Bazin contemptuously maintains are the "same as those *peddled* by the traditional novel" (Ibid., italics added).

Sartre had charged: "M. Mauriac has put himself first. He has chosen divine omniscience and omnipotence. But novels are written by men and for men. In the eyes of God, who cuts through appearance and goes beyond them, there is no novel, no art, for art thrives on appearances. God is not an artist. Neither is M. Mauriac."[59]

For Sartre, part of the problem is that Mauriac's authorial omniscience deprives his characters of freedom, despite Mauriac's attribution of freedom to them; but Sartre also feels that this "Godlike" style of authorship deprives the reader of freedom, since no mysteries are left for decipherment—Mauriac has provided a complete and determinate interpretation. Similarly, though wrongly if my arguments above hold, Bazin feels that film editing is likely to preclude spectator interpretation.

That Bazin's allegiance to freedom is connected to existentialism does not, of course, enhance its philosophical respectability. For in all probability, the existentialist's concept of freedom is unacceptable, insofar as it is so extreme. Moreover, it is by no means clear that the phenomenon labeled "freedom" in the relation between writer and reader (and filmmaker and viewer) is really morally significant in the

59. J. P. Sartre, "François Mauriac and Freedom," in Sartre's *Literary Essays*, edited and translated by Annette Michelson (New York: Philosophical Library, 1957), 23. Sartre's piece was published in 1939 and might have been read by Bazin quite early in his intellectual development.

ways Sartre and Bazin would have it. The correlation between
Bazin and Sartre, however, may suggest an interesting line of
speculation about Bazin's reception in America. For the enthusiastic response to Bazin in the late sixties was prepared,
so to speak, by nearly a decade of fascination with existentialism in the US, a fascination that itself had interesting relations
to the brewing cultural revolution.

The Psychological Origins and Purpose
of Cinematic Realism

Readers familiar with Bazin's writings will probably be surprised that I have saved comment on Bazin's remarks about
the psychological function of cinema until the very end of this
chapter. One reason for this surprise may be that Bazin's psychological speculations constitute the opening chapters of his
collected writings—at least as they are anthologized in English.[60] And, given this prominent placement, they would
seem to represent the cornerstone of the system Bazin is
about to put forward. I, however, find these speculations to
be the weakest point of his writing. And if it is true that there
is a way in which these speculations do connect with Bazin's
central preoccupations, then it is also true that there is a way
that Bazin's central points can be stated without reference to
his comments on the function and origin of cinema. Thus, I
have refrained from discussing these speculations when it was
not absolutely necessary to do so. Yet, this aspect of Bazin's
theorizing cannot be dodged completely. So, I now briefly
turn to it.

Bazin argues that the psychological power of cinema originates in cinema's perfection of the great dream or wish underlying all the plastic arts—the fantasy of defying time.

> If the plastic arts were put under psychoanalysis, the
> practices of embalming the dead might turn out to be a

---

60. These psychological speculations are contained primarily in "The Ontology of the Photographic Image" and "The Myth of Total Cinema" in
WIC 1.

fundamental factor in their creation. The process might reveal that at the origin of painting and sculpture there lies a mummy complex. The religion of ancient Egypt, aimed against death, saw survival as depending on the continued existence of the corporeal body. Thus, by providing a defense against the passage of time it satisfied a basic psychological need in man, for death is but the victory of time. To preserve, artificially, his bodily appearance is to snatch it from the flow of time, to stow it away neatly, so to speak, in the hold of life. It was natural, therefore, to keep up appearances in the face of death by preserving flesh and bone. (*WIC* 1, 9)

Bazin goes on to suggest that all the arts of verisimilitude arise as magical measures taken to forestall the march of time, and all the plastic arts are preservatives of sorts, of which cinema is the most potent.

Besides, painting is, after all, an inferior way of making likenesses, an *ersatz* of the processes of reproduction. Only a photographic lens can give us the kind of image of the object that is capable of satisfying the deep need man has to substitute for it something more than a mere approximation, a kind of decal or transfer. The photographic image is the object itself, the object freed from the conditions of time and space that govern it. No matter how fuzzy, distorted, or discolored, no matter how lacking in documentary value the image may be, it shares, by virtue of the very process of its becoming, the being of the model of which it is the reproduction; it is the model.

Hence the charm of family albums. Those grey or sepia shadows, phantomlike and almost undecipherable, are no longer traditional family portraits but rather the disturbing presence of lives halted at a set moment in their duration, freed from their destiny; not, however, by the prestige of art but by the power of an impassive mechanical process: for photography does not create eternity, as art does, it embalms time, rescuing it simply from its proper corruption. (*WIC* 1, 14)

Because of its success—via photography—at embalming the moment, cinema is the ultimate satisfaction of the realist urge, the desire that from mummification through mannerism has led artists to attempt to reproduce nature. Bazin writes, "Photography and cinema on the other hand are discoveries that satisfy, once and for all and in its very essence, our obsession with realism" (*WIC* 1, 12).

Here Bazin attempts to endorse realism in film by showing that it satisfies a human need for immortality (of a sort) that reaches back to prehistory. Indeed, Bazin writes as though the realism of the film medium were tantamount to its destiny. And if something is the destiny of the medium or is the need that determined its precise evolution, then we have a *prima facie* reason to regard the medium as *particularly* fitted for that something—in this case, realism.

From the perspective of these broad anthropological-psychological speculations, we can discern the outlines of what might be called Bazin's "mummy theory of film." Bazin sees the purpose or function of film to be the immortalization of the past. Knowing this purpose—here a matter of film's destiny—enables Bazin to pick out and to focus on the determinant characteristic of film, which Bazin identifies as the recording of reality via its re-presentation. Bazin then goes on to examine various articulatory processes of the medium—such as depth of field photography and montage—which he evaluates positively and negatively in terms of how well they serve the realist requirements of the project of re-presentation.

There are many problems with Bazin's mummy theory of film's destiny. The first and most obvious is establishing that a drive to immortalize the past, or just to have the past immortalized (the audience's portion), is in operation with all types of film. Although it seems an apt motive to account for the existence of home movies, it does not seem to account for the ubiquitous interest in fiction films. But even if Bazin were able to show that the mummification drive were at work with every type of film, the argument would still be incomplete. The crux of this incompleteness is the relation between mummification and realism. Bazin tends to write as though film as an embalming process—the process of re-presentation—were identical with what is being called realism. Our obsession for realism becomes, in the previous quotations, synonymous with our obsession for the immortalization of the past through its re-presentation. This argument, however, proceeds only by sleight of hand, because a style of realism—especially one as specific as what Bazin advocates—cannot be equated with a vague yearning for the immortalization of the past. For the past can be photographically re-presented—if there is any sense to that term—without the image even approximating a style we would call realist.

Even if it is true that something like the deep psychological drive for immortalizing the past gave birth to the medium, why is it still the case that the medium must be responsive to only this psychological need? That is, suppose we agree with Bazin and say that it was the obsession with mummifying the past that gave rise to cinema. Why do we have to say that cinema still responds to this need either exclusively, primarily, or even at all? One drive might have given rise to the actual discovery of cinema, but after its discovery another drive or set of interests—ones the medium could readily satisfy—could have replaced the initial drive. Here I have in mind an analogy of the following sort. Fear of teachers may engender a child's initial perserverance in mathematics, but after a time that initiating cause may recede in influence and the maturing child may come to prize the field for the kind of self-generating curiosity that the discipline is famous for. Likewise, is it not possible that even if cinema first garnered allegiance because it satisfied an interest in the re-presentation of the past, once the medium was in place (albeit as a result of the mummification drive) it continued to be of interest because of potentials other than those that first attracted attention. So, if recording was what first struck audiences about cinema, it may be (indeed, I think it is) that other interests—

fiction, rhetoric, abstraction, and the like—replaced the original source of interest in cinema with newer, and perhaps even more sophisticated, dimensions of audience appeal. That cinema got off the ground, so to say, by satisfying the mummy drive does not imply that cinema stays aloft that way.

Bazin's deepest problem, like that of many classical film theorists, is that he seems to feel compelled to name a single purpose that cinema can serve. Bazin gives pride of purpose to the first end the medium persued—recording. Yet the important point to make, is that a medium like cinema can serve more than one purpose, and, most interestingly, these purposes need not always be compatible—even where they all may have some claim to being essential possibilities of the medium, whatever that might be taken to mean. Even if it is true that cinema has the capacity to re-present the past—perhaps, thereby, satisfying a psychic need—cinema *also* has the seemingly incompatible potential to fabricate—not to record the world but to create worlds—which satisfies an at least equally pressing psychic need. Nor would these appear to exhaust the alternatives.

Summary and Conclusions

André Bazin is perhaps the most influential figure in the history of film theory. He regarded cinematic representation as essentially distinct from the verisimilitude available in other representational media, notably painting. For Bazin, cinematography re-presents objects, persons, places, and events from the past due to its basis in the causal processes of photography. This process of re-presentation, metaphorically speaking, puts cinematic representation "closer to its referents," or "closer to reality" than the modes of representation found in other media. Due to this putative ontological fact, Bazin believes cinema to be committed artistically to realism. In this attempted linkage of ontology to style, Bazin not only repeats the medium-specificity argument challenged in Chapter One, but also articulates theoretically familiar prejudices within our culture, namely, that photography has some special relation to the factual, and that film should be a realistic art form.

Furthermore, Bazin argues that the type of realism most appropriate to the medium of cinema is what might be called spatial realism. This style emphasizes long takes, depth-of-field cinematography, medium-long shots, multiplanar composition, lateral panning, camera movement (often of the zig-zag variety), and a continuous relation between off-screen and on-screen space, all of which enhance the impression that the image is a spontaneous recording and encourage the spectator actively to scan the image. Spatial realism is contrasted to expressionism, on the one hand, and to styles rooted in editing (both Soviet montage and Hollywood-type invisible editing), on the other.

In the course of this chapter, I have argued that Bazin's metaphysics of cinematic re-presentation appear either incoherent or trivial, and I have proposed that, rather than taking cinematic representation to have a single, unique structure, rooted in the nature of the medium, we should agree that there are a number of different types of representation available in film, types determined by and best analyzed in terms of the uses they serve.

Bazin's assertion that the realism of cinema follows from the representational nature of the medium was analyzed as a likely fallacy of equivocation, and an alternative approach to film realism was proposed. Likewise, Bazin's belief that there is a special connection between deep-focus cinematography and realism is disputed.

Although most of this chapter has been spent contesting Bazin's philosophical claims, I have also attempted to stress the usefulness of his theory. Bazin's theory can be de-mythologized or, perhaps more aptly, de-metaphysicized, to show that Bazin had an astute appreciation of an important stylistic shift that was occuring, quite literally, before his very eyes.

Specifically, Bazin was attuned to a gradual movement, occasioned by the introduction of sound, away from the overt stylization of silent film and toward a style that might, in one sense of this word, be said to approximate recording. This transition can be grossly marked by opposing expressionism and montage to spatial realism, the most sophisticated variant of the recording tendency. Bazin isolated the key features of spatial realism and situated its rationale in the history of film style; these analyses are of lasting value. At the same time, however, Bazin attempted to defend the accomplishments of spatial realism with a theory redolent with spurious metaphysical trappings.

Like Arnheim's, and like Perkins's (as will be shown in the next chapter), Bazin's theory of film is in many ways a thinly veiled brief in favor of a certain style of film. This negative observation, however, also has a positive side. For the connection between classical film theorists like Bazin and specific stylistic movements promises that such theories are likely at least to provide insight into the ways of appreciating the kinds of cinema the theories are designed to elevate. What fails as theory may excel as criticism.

Chapter Three

Film Theory as Metacriticism:

V. F. Perkins

——

___

An Outline of Perkins's Project

V. F. Perkins's *Film as Film* was published in 1972.[1] It was the product of a period of a renewed interest in as well as an unprecedented attitude of seriousness toward film theory and film art. In the sixties, perhaps as a result of the broadcasting of old movies on TV in the fifties and the emergence of the French New Wave, a passion for film and film history developed in the English-speaking world. The celluloid muse was elevated from the rank of handmaiden to empress among the arts. The number of people claiming or seeking expertise in film history and aesthetics multiplied a thousandfold. The classics of film theory were republished or translated for the first time. Of particular interest during the sixties and early seventies was a critical method, called the *auteur* theory, that, among other things, attempted to establish that Hollywood contract directors like Howard Hawks and Alfred Hitchcock might be the artistic peers of the likes of Shakespeare. Perkins's book appeared in the midst of this movie boom. It was an attempt to dispell what Perkins believes are the myths of classical film theory, which were being recirculated in the sixties, and to erect a competing theory, one that would be far more sensitive to the achievements of certain films—notably, what might be thought of as the "standard" Hollywood production—than were the classical film theories. Also, although Perkins never mentions it explicitly, his book fundamentally questions and departs from the *auteur* theory by pressing a strongly anti-intentionalist bias—that the value of a film resides in *the individual film as it is seen*. To my mind, Perkins's book was the most thoughtful, ambitious, and original attempt to construct a film theory in the seventies. Unfortunately, mine is a minority opinion. For Perkins's book was forgotten by film scholars almost as soon as it was published. The main direction that film theory took in the seventies was

1. V. F. Perkins, *Film as Film* (Baltimore: Penguin, 1972). Henceforth I will abbreviate references to this book as *FAF*.

scientific, or pseudoscientific (the synthesis of semiology, psychoanalysis, and Marxism),[2] whereas Perkins's approach was aesthetic—that is, he was concerned with the "artistic quality" of films, a concept that many a contemporary film theorist would laugh out of court as primitive mysticism. Also, the "scientific" turn in film theory represented itself as the successor to both classical film theory and the *auteur* theory. Thus, Perkins's book was regarded as an unscientific attempt to do what the reigning semiologists did far more rigorously. The result was that *Film as Film* never got a proper hearing. The purpose of this chapter is to rectify that omission.

In the literature of film theory, no other book bears the trace of post–World War II Anglo-American analytic philosophy more unmistakably than *Film as Film*. This claim requires some clarification. *Film as Film* was published in 1972, so, as one might expect, it does not incorporate the philosophical debates that were roughly contemporary with its writing—for example, the so-called Goodman questions and the disputes surrounding the institutional theory of art. Nevertheless, the book does reflect a number of biases that dominated philosophical aesthetics immediately prior to them. These biases include (1) the use of an open-concept-type argument to reject the conception of film theory espoused by Perkins's predecessors—that is, at least an avowal of anti-essentialism; (2) a belief that film theory should be reconceived as a species of metacriticism; (3) formalism: a film's value is located in its organization and not in its moral or intellectual content; (4) anti-intentionalism: the meaning available on the screen is what is important, rather than possible authorial meanings; and (5) anti-geneticism: what the film is, not how it was made, is what film theorists and critics should attend to. Items (4) and (5), of course, both reflect a deeper bias, what might be called "aesthetic phenomenalism," the belief that the way the film appears, rather than factors con-

2. This type of contemporary film theory is discussed in my "Address to the Heathen," *October*, no. 23 (Winter 1982), 103–9.

cerning its production, is all that has to be taken into account when evaluating a film. Perkins does not cite any Anglo-American philosophers in his footnotes; therefore, it is not clear that he arrived at these premises by reading primary sources. These ideas, however, were "in the air" throughout the fifties and sixties, especially since several of them were tenets of the dominant approach to literature, the New Criticism.

Film as Film opens with an attack on preceding film theory. Perkins directs his criticism at two groups that correspond to what he believes is the major division among classical film theorists. The first group of theorists—which includes Arnheim, Balasz, Eisenstein, Pudovkin, Rotha, Lindgren, Manvell, and Kuleshov—I have called creationists. They are united in championing a point of view in which "the decorative and expressive use of pictorial space was given precedence over the dramatic use of real space. Established theory commands the camera to *create* and denies its right to observe" (*FAF*, 19). The creationists were responding to charges that film could not be an art because it was *merely* a mechanical reproduction of reality. The creationists met this charge by showing all the ways that film diverged from the perfect recording of reality. Furthermore, they asserted that the potential for film art resided in expressively exploiting the limitations of film as a recording instrument—that is, wherever cinema fell short of or diverged from a perfect duplication of reality, there the filmmaker would find the stylistic variables to generate art. Editing, which allowed the filmmaker to rearrange reality rather than to simply record it as it unfolds in time, was the most esteemed cinematic technique for creationists for obvious reasons. A second group of theorists, called realists, including Bazin and Kracauer, arose in response to the creationists. Like the creationists, the realists believed that film had both a creative capacity and a recording capacity. The realists, however, reversed the priorities of the creationists; they regard the recording capacity of film, which was rooted in the photographic/cinematographic base of the medium, as the essence of film. For the realists, the facility of film to mechanically reproduce views of the past was not disparaged but celebrated, while the assertive stylization of the creationists was rejected as going against the grain of the film medium's most essential constituent, photography.

Perkins condemns both the creationists and the realists for misconceiving the role of film theory. His basic theme is that the classical theorists each attempted to identify a sine qua non for film that, in turn, became a prescriptive standard for the kind of films that ought to be made. What were proffered as theories of the nature of the medium were really pieces of advocacy-criticism that lauded preferred styles of film. This type of theorizing imposed restrictions upon the evolution of film art—dictating what artists were supposed to do rather than accounting for what was original and valuable in what artists were in fact producing. Perkins believes that film has no single essence (it is a hybrid of multiple, often conflicting, potentials) and that attempts to define the nature of the medium are at odds with artistic creativity. He concludes that the classical conception of film theory rested on an error—the belief that film theory should define the essence of film art.

Perkins's argument against the classical approach to film theory is not exactly like Morris Weitz's open-concept argument in regard to art,[3] but it bears enough resemblance to be thought of as a popularized version of the open-concept idea. Perkins is not, like Weitz, speaking of art theory in general, but only of film theory. The complaints he brings against classical film theory, however, are similar to Weitz's against art theory: past theories have never been able to accomplish satisfactorily what they have set out to do—provide an essential definition of film—and have only been covert film criti-

3. Morris Weitz, "The Role of Theory in Aesthetics," *Journal of Aesthetics and Art Criticism* 15 (1956). Weitz also recapitulates his case in "Wittgenstein's Aesthetics," in *Language and Aesthetics*, edited by Benjamin Tilghman (Lawrence: University of Kansas Press, 1973), 27–35. Other papers in the same vein as Weitz's include: Paul Ziff, "The Task of Defining a Work of Art," *Philosophical Review* 62 (1953), 58–78; W. E. Kennick, "Does Traditional Aesthetics Rest on a Mistake?" *Mind* 67 (1958), 317–34; and Stuart Hampshire, "Logic and Appreciation," in *Aesthetics and Language*, ed. William Elton (Oxford: Blackwell, 1967), 161–70.

cism despite their theoretical trappings. Perkins attacks classical film theory by saying that film has no single essence (in an argument I will rehearse later) and that the implicit prescriptions of film theory stifle creativity. Perkins' picture of classical film theory stifling the artist, of course, is not the same as the logical point that Weitz upholds, namely, that the concept of art, insofar as it prizes creativity, is incompatible with the enterprise of defining art. Perkins's version, however, is a popularized, dramatically portrayed representation of the sentiment behind Weitz's theory—depicting the rigid theorist imposing a conceptual straitjacket on the artist. What Perkins leaves out of his argument—which is key to Weitz's— is a statement to the effect that our concept of art is such that it involves creativity and the latitude for unexpected invention of the sort that would frustrate an attempt to define the compass of film art. But I suspect that Perkins believes this goes without saying.

Unlike Weitz, who feels that his arguments show there can be no theory of art, Perkins does not say that film theory is impossible, but only that its focus must be redirected. Instead of searching for the quiddity of cinema, Perkins proposes an alternative role for film theory—to derive a set of principles that film critics can use to rationalize their critical judgments. Rather than stipulate rules that filmmakers must abide by, Perkins tries to establish certain axioms of cinematic value to which the critic may advert. In short, Perkins believes that film theory should be metacriticism—it should concern itself with elucidating the underlying principles that must guide film criticism. "This book," Perkins writes, "aims to present criteria for our judgments of movies. It is written in the belief that film criticism becomes rational, if not 'objective', when it displays and inspects the nature of its evidence" (*FAF*, Preface, 7). This aim is to be contrasted with the essentialist project of classical film theory.

> I do not believe that the film (or any other medium) has an essence which we can usefully invoke to justify our criteria. We do not deduce the standards relevant to

Rembrandt from the essence of paint; nor does the nature of words impose a method of judging ballads and novels. Standards of judgment cannot be appropriate to a medium as such but only to particular ways of exploiting its opportunities. That is why the concept of the cinematic, presented in terms of demands, has stunted the useful growth of film theory. Helpful criteria are more likely to be based on positive statements of value than on prohibitions. To regard criticism positively, as a search for the most satisfactory definitions of function and value, allows an escape from academic systems of rules and requirements. Criteria then relate to claims which the critic can sustain rather than to demands he must make. The clarification of standards should help to develop the disciplines of criticism without seeking to lay obligations on the filmmaker. (*FAF*, 59)

Perkins himself putatively supplies a film theory of the sort he endorses. It is a theory of evaluation that is explicitly restricted to the narrative fiction film. It is meant to provide the critic with criteria for telling whether a film is good or bad and, if the film is good, how much good there is in it.

The identification of film theory with metacriticism echoes, with special reference to film, an idea about the proper role of philosophical aesthetics that prevailed in the fifties and sixties. In distinguishing the philosophy from the criticism of an art form, Monroe Beardsley wrote:

> . . . one can ask questions about criticism itself, about the terms it uses, its methods of investigation and argument, its underlying assumptions. These questions obviously belong to philosophical aesthetics. When Socrates asks in the *Greater Hippias* what "beauty" (*to Kalon*) means, or when Aristotle asks in his *Poetics* when defenses may reasonably be given for a tragedy that has been disparaged as implausible, the philosophical concern is central and evident.[4]

4. Beardsley, *Aesthetics: From Classical Greece to the Present* (New York: Macmillan, 1966; Alabama: University of Alabama Press, 1975), 14.

What Beardsley thinks of as the terrain of the philosophy of an art form, Perkins appropriates as the subject matter of film theory. Of course, the purview of Perkins's theory is more limited than Beardsley would envisage as a philosophy of film, since Perkins narrows his project to isolating only the *evaluative* criteria that are applicable exclusively to narrative fiction films. Perkins, however, does present a characterization of film theory that at least *appears* to depart radically not only from that of classical film theorists, but also from the conception of film theory presented in chapters one and two. Thus, one of the tasks of this chapter will be to determine whether, in fact, Perkins has truly invented a new type of film theory.

The underlying evaluative principle that Perkins finally offers is rather like a compromise, struck between realists and creationists. Perkins himself does not put it precisely this way, but speaks instead of finding a balance between conflicting tendencies of the medium. But on identifying these conflicting tendencies, one immediately realizes that they are nothing but extrapolations from the preferred creationist tendency— that films shape or meaningfully reconstitute the world—and the preferred realist tendency—that films observe, record, and reproduce reality. Perkins does not attempt to choose between these two conceptions. Rather, he says that the medium is hybrid and has at least these two tendencies. Moreover, he notes that the two tendencies, when followed rigorously, result in styles that preclude each other. A filmmaker cannot be a radical creationist and a radical realist at the same time. Extreme purism as regards one tendency contradicts extreme purism as regards the other. So, since Perkins accepts both tendencies as legitimate features of film, it is his task to find a principle that reconciles the potential for conflict between the creative and reproductive capacities of the medium. This is how Perkins frames the problem:

> The movie is committed to finding a balance between equally insistent pulls, one towards credibility [realism] and the other towards shape and significance [creation-

ism]. And it is threatened by collapse on both sides. It may shatter illusion in straining after expression. It may subside into meaningless reproduction presenting a world which is credible but without significance. (*FAF*, 120)

The way that Perkins deals with this inherent tension in the medium is to acknowledge the claims of both realists and creationists, and to set out their conflicting demands in an ordinarily ranked formula in which a narrative fiction film must *first* satisfy the realist requirement of credibility, *after which* it may go on to be as creative in terms of shaping meaning and significance as it can, while abiding by the basic restraint of credibility. In order to be good, a film must be credible—that is, in order to be a candidate for positive evaluation, the film must be credible. Credibility gets the film into the ballpark, so to speak, as an object that may qualify for commendation. "But when we've said that a film is credible, we've not said much. We have established the soundness at only one end of its balance" (*FAF*, 123).

A narrative fiction film will be credible or not according to whether its images are consistently derived from the fictional world it depicts (*FAF*, 121). A film does not lack credibility because it fails to correspond to the world. That birds do not organize and attack human civilization does not count against the credibility of Hitchcock's *The Birds*. For within that fictional world, birds, en masse, do attack humans. Therefore, the images of birds besetting schoolhouses are not incredible, according to Perkins's formula, because they are consistent with the rest of the fictional world proposed by *The Birds*. On the other hand, due to certain imperfections of the matting process used in achieving the special effects, one often notices that the enraged avians in the film are swathed in a luminous blue hue. Nothing in the story accounts for this. We are not told, for example, that hot and bothered fowl stew blue as a matter of biological law in Hitchcock's fictional world. So, the flawed special effects in this film are not credible and are bad-making features of the film (*FAF*, 122). Moreover, what happened accidentally to Hitchcock because of the ineptness of his special effects crew resembles a certain kind of incredible effect that is often consciously sought after by many directors. In Huston's *Moulin Rouge*, "When the director characterized his hero's jealousy by flooding the set with, in the film's own terms, inexplicable green light, he broke down the essential structure of his picture's relationships and thus destroyed the world within which his hero *existed*" (*FAF*, 122–23). That is, for the sake of heightened significance, the credibility of the film was violated. For Perkins, the director can add significance to the film only as long as his manner of presenting his comment does not endanger the credibility of the film. To add significance without respect for credibility prevents a film, or at least the part of the film in question, from being called good.[5]

If a film, or a segment of a film, is credible, then it is a candidate for positive evaluation. But credibility alone does not make the film or film segment good. It is a necessary condition for goodness, but it is not a good-making feature. The degree of goodness a film has depends on how much shaping or meaning it has, while still remaining credible. To evaluate whether a film or a film segment is good, two ordinally related tests must be brought to bear. First, the film must be weighed against the credible/incredible standard. These measures are binary opposites; the film or film segment is either one or the other. If the film is credible, then it may have some good in it. How do we tell how much? To answer this question, the second standard—coherence (alternatively called "significance," "meaning," "shape," or "pattern")—must be applied. Coherence is a degree concept. The more

5. Throughout *Film as Film* Perkins gives examples only of sections of films that he finds unacceptable. He never explicitly characterizes an entire film as unacceptable. Thus, I am not sure whether one instance of a breach of credibility, such as the case in *Moulin Rouge*, disqualifies the film from the order of the good. I am assuming, however, that, although Perkins doesn't say so outright, a number of (I don't know how many) breaches of credibility, especially for the purpose of heightened significance, debars the film from being considered good.

coherence a film has, the better it is. Of course, each added increment of shaping or coherence that the film has must also be credible in terms of the fictional world of the film. Coherence at the cost of credibility is a bad-making feature. The narrative fiction filmmaker must balance the simultaneous demands of credibility and coherence. And "In this process, the maintenance of credibility acts as a necessary discipline" (*FAF*, 97). The procedure for evaluating a good film is a two-step operation: first, check its credibility. Then, if it is credible, see how much coherence it has. The degree of coherence will correspond to the degree of goodness.

To understand this formula, we need some sense of what Perkins means by coherence. *Film as Film* is full of examples of "coherences"; one chapter especially, the longest in the book,[6] is a catalogue of cases showing how each articulatory dimension of film—camera movement, framing, blocking, lighting, camera angle, color, sound, actor's gestures, setting, and so forth—has been used to produce coherence. Perkins's samples of coherence are very similar in nature. In each case, they involve the introduction of a formal variation (a camera movement or a variation in lighting or framing) or a detail (of the action or the setting) that can be deciphered symbolically as making a comment—of either a dramatic or thematic variety—on the narrative or the characters in the film, especially in terms of rendering the inner lives of characters through graphic objectifications. For instance,

> In Nicholas Ray's *Johnny Guitar* a funeral party becomes a lynch mob when the mourners set out to capture the dead man's suspected killers. The victim's sister, Emma, rides with the posse. As she forces up the speed of the pursuit the wind carries her black-veiled hat to be trampled in the dust beneath galloping hooves. The "action" of the hat amplifies our view of the character: grief for the loss of her brother is not the motive guiding Emma's action. . . . (*FAF*, 78)

6. "The World and Its Image," *FAF*, 17–116.

Of Preminger's *The Cardinal*, Perkins writes:

> Stephen Fermoyle has been granted a year's leave of absence from the priesthood and has taken a teaching post in Vienna. During the summer vacation he is shown the scenic and architectural beauties of Austria by Anne-Marie, a gay and flirtatious woman who is unaware of his profession. The sequence opens with the two of them cycling down a hillside in the country. The camera turns to follow their descent as they glide round a bend in the road, its movement embracing a wide sinking arc until it comes to rest on a huge open landscape spread out before them. The movement amplified by the composer's expansive waltz theme, conveys to us the exhilaration and release that Fermoyle discovers in his relationship with the girl, his sense of new and attractive possibilities opening up for him.
>
> Here Preminger is using for its emotional effect the transition from an enclosed to an open image and the physical impact of camera movement projected onto a large cinema screen. The image conveys a feeling of exhilaration and release which we transfer to the dramatic situation. (*FAF*, 88)

And of Brooks's *Lord Jim*:

> The hero, a dreamer haunted by his vision of inhuman grandeur, is standing on a fog-bound raft in the middle of a river. By his side is Gentleman Brown, the cynical chief of a gang of cut-throats. Brown is trying to persuade Jim to arrange his escape from an ambush; his remarks repeatedly hint at bonds, recognized or obscured, that make Jim "one of Us." While they talk, Jim, fair-haired and dressed in light colours faces out across the water, raising his right hand to lean against the raft's guiderail. Then Brown, a swarthy, black-bearded figure in a bowler hat and a dark suit, takes up the same position—except that he holds onto the rail with his left hand. The image is briefly shown, but it lasts long

enough for us to appreciate the psychological implications of its structure: Brown is Jim's dark reflection, his unrecognized mirror-image, so much his opposite as to be almost a replica. (*FAF*, 82)

And commenting on Minnelli's *The Courtship of Eddie's Father*—a film about a father and son readjusting after the death of the mother—Perkins says:

> During this brief episode Eddie is perched on top of a kitchen stool, taking down a cup and a saucer from the wall-cupboard. This action is in no way dictated by John Gay's script. It presents the director's view of the moment in the relationship between father and son. Firstly, it puts their shared bereavement in a very ordinary context: the day-to-day household routine of preparing the dinner table. At the same time it presents, in the most direct way, the empty strangeness of their situation: Eddie is doing something which, ordinarily, would have been left to mother. The action also takes us graphically inside Eddie's mind and feelings by stressing the instability of his emotional balance. Eddie's precarious physical position on the stool, his careful handling of two fragile objects, counterpoint his attempt at emotional poise. (*FAF*, 76)

What all these examples have in common is what might be thought of as a double use of a formal device or of a detail of the action or setting. The second or ulterior purpose of the device or detail is to comment on the story or the characters. If the element in question is a detail of the action or setting— for example a hat trampled by horses—Perkins believes that it must be naturalistically motivated within the story. This means that it must be part of the narrative exposition in the sense that it is a credible piece of information about the fictional world of the film. First and foremost, it must fit into the sequence of events that comprise the ground-floor level of reality in the story. Second, the detail may have extra-representational, or symbolic, portent. That is, the image may be not only representational—"Emma's hat is trampled"—but commentative as well—"Emma's bereavement has changed into something horribly other." This second use of the detail is not a representation of a visible fact *within* the fictional world but an authorial comment *about* the fictional world (an outward rendering of Emma's inner psychological state).

Where the element in question is a formal device—for example, a camera movement—Perkins believes that it must be operating functionally first and commentatively second. That is, the formal device must first be unobtrusively performing some expositional task. Unobtrusive exposition as a requirement for formal devices parallels the requirement of naturalistic motivation for commentarial details. The formal device must have some denotative function—it must present or inform the viewer of some facts, states-of-affairs, or events belonging to the fictional world of the film—as well as have a commentative function. Perkins, for example, criticizes the "stone lion" segment of Eisenstein's *Potemkin* because it is an unmitigated authorial aside that is not connected to the story, action, or location of the rest of the film (*FAF*, 103–4).[7] The lions are sheer metaphors; they have no effective existence in the fictional world of *Potemkin*. They are edited in not to represent any action that is happening in the world of the film; they are, rather, symbols of Eisenstein's outrage with the behavior of the czarist generals. If the filmmaker wishes to use editing to comment on the action, the images must exist plausibly within the fictional world of the film. Perkins cites a favorable example of symbolic editing from Brooks's *Elmer Gantry*: as the faith healer, Sharon, begins to pray there is a cutaway to a worker throwing a lit cigarette stub onto a pile of paint rags; as the fevered pitch of the revival meeting mounts, so does the fire. Brooks comments on the frenzy and destructiveness he sees in the faith-healing business via the fire, which is rooted in the world of the film (*FAF*, 100–103).

7. For an analysis of the stone lion segment see my "Toward a Theory of Film Editing," *Millennium Film Journal*, no. 3, (1978), 79–99, and my "Language and Cinema: Preliminary Notes toward a Theory of Verbal Images," *Millennium Film Journal*, nos. 7/8/9 (1980), 186–217.

If a label were needed for Perkins's position, one might call him an expressive realist.[8] That is, he is a realist who appreciates added symbolic meanings and asides in a film. He refers to these as cinematic elaborations, and I will refer to them as commentative saturation. These expressive flourishes, however, must be restrained by a commitment to realism, which amounts to the demand that every commentative formal device also serve a narrative function—that is, present information about the fictional world. It is the commitment to realism, I believe, that leads Perkins to call his book *Film as Film*. That is, the kind of commentative saturation Perkins favors could be a source of value in any narrative art. But his insistence on the criterion of credibility for film art seems to be, to some degree, a medium-specific standard. Perkins's evaluative criteria for film could not be used for other arts such as opera or painting or theater because of the credibility criterion, which is predicated on the *photographic component* of the film medium.

Like many classical film theorists, Perkins spends a great deal of time providing examples of how commentative saturation has been achieved (in specific films) in regard to each dimension of filmic articulation. Perkins contrasts his view to that of classical theorists, however, by claiming that he is reviewing cinematic articulation in terms of the "opportunities" (*FAF*, 98) afforded artists, as opposed to theorists who placed demands on artists. Perkins says that his theory does not oblige the artist to do anything in particular. His review of the articulatory processes only shows what the artist *can* do with the medium rather than what the artist *must* do.[9] Per-

8. Perhaps Balazs might be another example of this tradition of expressive realism. Basically I see this tradition as one that prizes symbolism at the same time that it demands that the world of the film be, broadly speaking, in accord with our (Kantian) conceptions of space and time.

9. In a curious passage on pages 97 and 98 of *Film as Film*, Perkins notes that many of the great film comedies do not evince the kind of cinematic elaboration that he advocates in his criteria. I am not convinced that this is empirically accurate. But if it is, it would appear to create some incongruities for Perkins's theory. For how will these putatively great films be good ones according to Perkins. Perkins says of these films that "The purely

kins, I take it, sees the major thrust of his exercise as showing critics where and how to look at films in order to see the value that, as a matter of fact, is in them.

Undoubtedly *Film as Film* can be very instructive to critics, especially about the aesthetic dimension of the type of film Perkins most often discusses—the post–World War II Hollywood film. These were mass audience films that, perhaps because of their financial need to be widely accessible, led their directors to prefer the sort of hidden or unobtrusive symbolism that Perkins is so adept at ferreting out. There is no question that many filmmakers, especially Hollywood directors from the forties through the sixties, embellish their narratives with the type of nondemonstrative cinematic elaborations Perkins adduces. And Perkins, more than any other film theorist, has shown critics how to appreciate the often understated expressiveness of this style of filmmaking. Indeed, *Film as Film* might be thought of as a guidebook for learning how to watch a certain kind of Hollywood film, on a par with a handbook for deciphering Byzantine icons. But it is far from clear that Perkins's criteria don't place any demands on filmmakers. True, Perkins represents the type of cinematic elaborations he discusses as opportunities rather than obligations. On the other hand, since he has not identified any other source of value for the narrative fiction film, one wonders whether the attention Perkins gives to instances of commentative saturation is indeed merely a highlighting of opportunities. For presumably, the filmmaker wishes to create good films. And how will the filmmaker make good films according to Perkins's two criteria unless he employs commentative

'filmic' criteria fade into irrelevance. That is why the great comedies with their insistence on action and their indifference to cinematic elaboration have proved so difficult to assess within the terms proposed by traditional film theory." But the nagging question is not how traditional film theory will evaluate such comedies but rather how Perkins will evaluate these works. That is, if there are great works of film comedy or other genres that lack cinematic elaboration, by what criterion will the rational critic call them good? Later I will discuss Perkins's inability to evaluate narration as such. Perhaps his problem with comedy is connected to his problem with narrative.

saturation? By speaking exclusively of commentative saturation as the source of value in a film, it seems to me that Perkins turns it into a requirement for any filmmaker who wants
to make good films. Perkins might say his theory does not
demand that filmmakers produce good films. But this is irrelevant. For in a sense, no film theory demands that filmmakers *must* make good films. Rather, the film theories that
are evaluative begin with the presupposition that filmmakers
want to produce good films and then the theories go on to say
how this can be done. It is true that Perkins says there are
some great fiction films (for example, comedies) for which
the criterion of cinematic elaboration is irrelevant.[10] But this
is an anomalous remark within the totality of Perkins's book,
since he nowhere suggests by what criteria such films are to
be evaluated. (Is the critic, then, irrational when he calls such
films "good"?) And, since Perkins has not specified how films
can be good without it, cinematic elaboration appears to be at
least a prima facie demand confronting any filmmaker interested in making good films.

But even if Perkins is correct in asserting that his coherence
criterion places no demands on the filmmaker, can the same
be said of his credibility criterion? Perkins criticizes a scene in
Losey's *The Criminal* in which the background lighting goes
black in order to draw attention to the monologist in the foreground (*FAF*, 83). Similarly, he attacks a scene in Antonioni's
Red Desert where a bedpost gradually turns red in order to
symbolize the heroine's increasing madness (*FAF*, 85). In
both cases, the symbolic effects in question involve changes
in the film's physical environment that have no mechanical
causes in the world of the fiction. Both effects are thought
to mar the films they are in. I cannot see how this can be
construed as not placing a demand on the narrative fiction
filmmaker. Moreover, it is the sort of demand that medium-
essentialist film theorists were said to saddle artists with, insofar as Perkins's credibility criterion is derived from the pho-

10. See note 24.

tographic/cinematographic (that is, an "essential") constituent of cinema.

The core of *Film as Film* is taken up with the elaboration
and exemplification of Perkins's two criteria for film evaluation. He also reviews, however, several other issues that,
though not essential to his theory, seem to flow from it. First,
he defends the spectator of the Hollywood variety of narrative
fiction films.[11] Such spectators are often dismissed as the willing victims of escapist fantasies. Perkins, on the other hand,
argues that the Hollywood spectator is sufficiently detached
from the film spectacle to develop an appreciation (predictably enough) of the commentative saturation that Perkins advocates. As a formalist—that is, one who sees the value of a
film in terms of its organization rather than its message—Perkins believes that the normal viewer of fiction films is in a
good position to develop the appropriate sensitivity to the
narrative fiction film because, unlike the art film viewer, the
Hollywood viewer does not insist on edifying or profound
content but is willing to accept films on their own terms
(*FAF*, 156).

Given Perkins's over-riding emphasis on coherence, he is at
pains to exclude the director's intentions as the source of value
in a film. He does this on the grounds that most narrative
fiction films are the result of a collaboration among many different people with many different specialties. Thus, the final
result is not the expression of a single mind, the director's
(*FAF*, 172).

> Provided that a film has its own unity, it seems unimpor-
> tant whether the unity was evolved through cooperation
> and compromise within the production team or con-
> ceived by one man and imposed on his collaborators.
>
> If the relationships established in a film are significant,
> it makes no difference to the spectator how they came or
> were brought about, or to what extent their significance
> was intended. A movie has a meaning for a spectator
> when he is able to interpret its pattern of actions and im-

11. In the chapter entitled "Participant Observers," *FAF*, 134–57.

ages. Provided that its relationships are coherently shaped, the film embodies—and can be shown to embody—a consistent meaning which may or may not have been sought, or sincerely felt, by the director. (*FAF*, 173)

The question of intended meaning, of sincerity, is left open by the film. Its effective meaning is all we can be sure of. And it is all we need to know. If as connoisseurs we wished to place the picture in the context of Tourneur's work and beliefs, it would be important to find out how far *Night of the Demon* embodies a sincere attitude to the occult. But so long as we are concerned, as critics, with the meaning and quality of this particular movie such information is irrelevant. (174–75)

By locating film criticism in the apprehension of patterns and coherences, Perkins believes that he has grounded the enterprise in something that is objectively observable.

If filmmaking is, as I've implied, a form of play—a problem-solving game of splendid intricacy and potential profundity—it takes on the nature of spectator sport rather than a private amusement like doodling as soon as it offers itself for public enjoyment and judgment. Its coherences exist to the extent that they are publicly perceptible. (*FAF*, 189)

Moreover, he argues that his version of film criticism avoids the pitfalls of other approaches to the subject. Perkins's emphasis on the organizational virtues of film short-circuits the type of film criticism that praises or condemns films on the basis of whether they are "thought provoking," a term of near derision for Perkins (*FAF*, 188); Perkins protests that this sort of content-oriented standard is insensitive to the actual (formal) values to be found in narrative fiction films. The other great error of film criticism that Perkins believes his theory averts, is the presumption of a prescriptive, theoretically charged standard of "the cinematic." Such a standard is found in authors like Arnheim, Lindgren, Bazin, and Kracauer. Against them, Perkins argues that "A theory of film is a theory of film *criticism* not of film*making*. We cannot lay down rules for the creators. If we insist on the concept of balance [between credibility and coherence] we do not thereby demand to dictate how or between what elements the balance is to be achieved" (*FAF*, 189).[12]

The Arguments for Perkins's Theory

The arguments that Perkins uses to support his theory fall into three broad categories. The first comprises arguments against classical film theories. The thrust of these arguments is purely negative. They are meant to show the shortcomings of classical film theory and the need for its replacement by some other kind of theory. These arguments, however, do not show that classical film theory should necessarily be replaced by the kind of theory that Perkins offers. The second category of argument is also negative. But the approach—a variant of an open-concept argument—implies that the type of theory that Perkins offers is the correct alternative to classical film theory. Lastly, Perkins attemps a positive argument to derive the twin evaluative criteria of credibility and coherence from the hybrid nature of cinema.

Perkins and the problems of classical film theory

Perkins opens *Film as Film* with a series of arguments that are designed to reveal the weaknesses of classical film theory but do not imply that a theory such as his own is what is needed to overcome these difficulties. Since Perkins's mode of exposition is historical, he first attacks those whom I have called creationists. One problem with these theories is that they fail to account for what is good in films that exploit the photographic/recording aspect of cinema. Here, Perkins's target is

12. This is an unfair contrast with classical theorists such as Arnheim, since they never attempted to dictate exactly how their various general recommendations were to be implemented. Arnheim believed that film should not mechanically record reality but he did not specify what elements of the medium the filmmaker had to use to achieve this task.

really a sub-category of creationists, the montage theorists, who hold that the central stylistic variable in film is editing. Perkins's point is that these theorists are so impressed by the effectiveness of editing that they ignore alternative means of cinematic exposition. This led them to ignore the accomplishments of directors like Renoir, Keaton, Welles, Murnau, and Stroheim who at times emphasized composition in the medium-long shot over editing (*FAF*, 22–24). Perkins believes that montagists cannot account for the achievements of these films. In making this objection, Perkins is repeating a line of argument used by realist theorists since the forties, and he is adducing as his evidence filmmakers who have been mentioned often in this respect by realists. The charge, however, does not appear equally damaging to every creationist or to every montagist. A montagist such as Eisenstein may in fact be able to account for these accomplishments, since he extends the idea of montage to include the juxtaposition of elements within a single shot.[13] Perkins undoubtedly has a better case against theorists like Kuleshov and Pudovkin, but it is not clear that his argument has isolated an irreparable, generic flaw, as opposed to having merely identified an oversight in the works of some montage-creationist theorists.

Another problem with the evaluative dimension of orthodox creationist theory, according to Perkins, is that it gives us no way to account for stylistically assertive creationist films that are nevertheless bad. The example Perkins offers is Riefenstahl's *Triumph of the Will*, a magnificently edited film that Perkins feels must nonetheless be condemned for being bombastic (*FAF*, 26). Furthermore, Perkins thinks that creationist theory, with its preference for assertive devices, has a natural inclination toward crude, gross, and rhetorical effects at the expense of subtlety and complexity. To a certain extent, with reference to the montage tradition, the historical record seems at first to bear out Perkins's charge. Many a crass propaganda film has trafficked in montage. A closer look at the

13. S. M. Eisenstein, "Montage and Conflict," in *Film Theory and Criticism*, edited by C. Mast and M. Cohen (New York: Oxford University Press, 1975), 79.

evidence, however, reveals many subtle and complex montage films: *Man With a Movie Camera, Song of Ceylon*, and *Our Trip to Africa*. A second aspect of Perkins's criticism is that creationist theories do not supply a criterion for identifying bombastic stylization. It is probably true that creationists don't outline such a standard. This is because, unlike Perkins, creationists were not designing evaluative theories. Most creationist theories were designed with one of two purposes in mind—either to establish that film could be art, Arnheim's theory for example, or to instruct filmmakers in the basic possibilities of the medium. In both cases the theorists stressed the importance of reconstituting reality via the film medium. But it seems only fair to read the call for manipulation as at most a necessary condition for aesthetic achievement in film. No creationist holds that using assertive stylization or montage-type editing will guarantee a good film. Yet, Perkins's example of *Triumph of the Will* seems to have such a view in mind. Perkins asks how creationists can account for the bombast in *Triumph of the Will*. Won't the creationist account for it the way any form of civilized criticism will—by pointing to the film's sentimentality, mindless repetition, and taste for endless parades? It is not clear that creationist theory has to have a *special* explanation of what went wrong in *Triumph of the Will*. For it is not committed to the proposition that all montage is good, but only to the proposition that montage is cinematic, which, of course, does not preclude some montage being bombastic or, for that matter, being trivial, gauche, vulgar, saccharine, obscene, or any of numerous other negative expletives.

Perkins also charges that creationists tend to make a fetish of the limitations of the medium—limitations vis-à-vis the perfect duplication of reality—at a given time. That is, they take the state of film technology at one point in history and regard it as an unchangeable given, assuming that the possibility of style and expressiveness emerges just where the medium is limited. Perkins writes that creationist theory is "distinguished by its reverence for the drawbacks, its insistence on the beneficent nature of mechanical limitations" (*FAF*,

54). Creationists are said to believe that "style and form are made possible by the observation of limitations" (Ibid.). The test case that Perkins appears to have in mind is the advent of the sound film. But the evidence is mixed. The Russian montagists, for example, were enthusiastic about the arrival of sound,[14] as they tended to be about technological innovation in general. Some creationists, like Arnheim, abhorred the innovation, and, as Perkins says, did believe that the verbal silence of the medium—a limitation of the medium's perfect duplication of reality—was a major source of expressiveness.

Perkins counters Arnheim's opinion by arguing that such creationists misconceive the relationship between style and technological innovation. Only limitations that artists freely choose—as opposed to impositions of the medium—can be relevant to style. Furthermore, he holds that technological innovations *increase* the stylistic options available to artists. Perkins contends that it is the overcoming of the limitations of the medium, rather than the surrendering to them, that makes style posible: "Devices can be molded into a style only when they have become inessential and, in the most favorable sense, gratuitous. In any medium, style is formed by a pattern of decisions; but decisions can operate only where alternatives exist" (*FAF*, 52). Perkins believes that technology provides alternatives. One example that he offers is color. Once color was easily available and widely used in all sorts of films, directors could choose to work with black and white cinematography to achieve special expressive effects—for example, *The Last Picture Show*, where the black and white connotes the sense of "pastness."

Perkins is undoubtedly offering an apt description of what happened to certain creationist theorists. They hypostatized the medium at a certain point in its development—believing that the limitations of silent film were what made it possible for film to be stylized (and, therefore, to be an art). But the

14. See especially the joint Soviet manifesto on sound entitled "A Statement on the Sound-Film by Eisenstein, Pudovkin and Alexandrov," in S. M. Eisenstein, *Film Form*, Edited and translated by Jay Leyda (New York: Harcourt, Brace and World, 1949), 257–60.

medium changed and, in fact, more stylistic options were opened by the technological innovations. Although this description is accurate for the case in point, it is unclear that it can be generalized into an argument that says it must always be wrong to remain committed to the limitations of a medium when technological innovations can remove them.

Built into Perkins's argument is the notion that for an element of an art form to be stylized, it must be the case that in some unrestricted sense the artist can choose it freely. But this seems unduly demanding. Consider the case of black and white photography. Even in the days when black and white was the dominant form of cinematography,[15] the black and white image was a stylistic element. For it could be used in alternate ways. One director might exploit the subtle modulations of the gray scale, suggesting gossamer softness, while another might oppose harsh blacks and whites to underpin some moral debacle. The fact that directors ordinarily were limited to black and white cinematography does not preclude style since a range of stylistic options is possible within these limitations.

This observation might be questioned, however, by saying that I have misconstrued Perkins's point. Perkins, it could be argued, is not denying that there can be stylistic invention within a given limitation of the medium. Rather, he is saying that the fact that an artist is working within a medium-imposed limitation means that the limitation itself cannot be considered a stylistic element, because the artist could not have chosen but to accept it. For example, if I make a film in 1920 and it is in black and white, Perkins holds that it is inappropriate to say that the black and whiteness of the film per se is a stylistic element of the film. That is, working in black and white only becomes stylistically relevant as soon as it is possible not to work in black and white.

This seems to be a doubtful hypothesis. For even during

15. I speak of the time when black and white was dominant rather than saying it was the only form of film because there were color films at the turn of the century, long before the innovation that made color films the dominant film form.

the period when most films were black and white, films were made that exploited the fact that they were in black and white for particular effects. The opposition of light and dark in Murnau's *Sunrise* is a case in point. It is used as part of a larger connotative system that contrasts the mother and the whore, the pure and the polluted. This use of style for expressive effect depends on the fact that the film is in black and white. Perhaps Murnau could not realistically have chosen to make *Sunrise* in color. Yet, it still seems appropriate to say that black and white cinematography per se is a stylistic element in *Sunrise*. Why? Well, many directors who were Murnau's contemporaries worked in black and white but were indifferent, so to speak, to using the black and white format to achieve any particular effect whatsoever. Consider any of innumerable, B-adventure programmers. For such films, black and white was a simple fact of life, a feature of the state of the art that was not employed in any distinctive way. But not so Murnau; he strove for effects that were especially legible and suitable for black and white cinematography. He used black and white photography as such as a stylistic variable. It seems arbitrary to deny this just because he could not have rejected the possibility of working in color.

Perkins's argument also presumes that the addition of stylistic options is always a boon for a medium or, at least, the beneficent line of direction that an art form should take. This seems questionable. Some media appear to stick with certain limitations even if a superior technology could do away with them. For example, we could, at this late date, certainly technologically counterfeit the beloved impression of flight in ways that would dwarf the antiquated leaps and lifts of ballet. Yet, in the main, ballet has foresworn technology in favor of its far more limited means. Creationists like Arnheim were betting that film—specifically silent film—was an art form like ballet. They were wrong. But I'm not sure that they were wrong in principle for the reasons Perkins produces. I say this not because I believe that the creationists were right in principle but because there does not seem to be any principle involved in the matter. In some cases, art forms will continue to abide by certain limitations despite prospects for techno-logical innovations. And those limitations may in fact mark off the range of available stylistic choice. In certain other cases, a technological innovation may eliminate a past limita-tion, which, in turn, allows the past limitation to accrue val-ues (especially expressive values) that it did not previously have. Of course, this, too, is a matter of high contingency. After all, though 3-D photography has been around for dec-ades, I know of no film that has attempted to use the fact that it is not in 3-D to particular stylistic advantage. In short, whether a medium sustains the technological limitations of a certain period of development in its history or whether a given technological innovation opens the possibility of new stylistic options for the use of previously imposed limitations is not an issue to be settled by a priori argument. Had Perkins been satisfied to attack creationists like Arnheim on these grounds—that is, by accusing them of attempting to legislate what is a matter of history, not of logic—he might have been more succcessful. But Perkins's argument is more ambitious. He opposes the creationist bias with his own theory of tech-nology, and he says innovations that transcend previous lim-itations represent the source of style. But neither alternative—Perkins's or the creationists'—has much, historically, to rec-ommend it as an exclusive theory of the relation of technol-ogy and style.

It is also Perkins's opinion that both creationist theory and realist theory commit genetic fallacies. Realist theory pur-portedly does this with its emphasis on the photographic con-stituent of the medium. For example, for a Bazinian, the greatest achievements of cinema are those in which the film-maker treats the film frame as merely homothetic with the viewfinder of the camera rather than as the analogue to the frame of a painting or the proscenium of a stage.[16] Perkins regards this prejudice as an instance of the theorist being overly concerned with how the film was made rather than

16. See Chapter Two of this volume for a full explication of this claim that Bazin makes in his book *Jean Renoir*.

how it appears. This violates the genetic fallacy, which states that it will "count as characteristics of an aesthetic object (the proper object of aesthetic criticism) no characteristics . . . that depend upon knowledge of their causal conditions whether physical or psychological."[17] Likewise, Perkins chides creationists for being too concerned with production factors such as montage. He writes: "A useful theory will have to redirect attention to the movie as *seen*, by shifting emphasis back from creation to perception. In order to arrive at a more accurate and inclusive definition of film as it exists for the spectator, it will need to concentrate not on the viewfinder or on the cutting bench but on the screen" (*FAF*, 26–27).

There are several problems with this line or argument. The first is the unargued assumption of the truth of anti-geneticism. Anti-geneticism seems to have the liability of either being false or unclear. Surely knowing that a musical piece now played on an organ was originally composed on and for a violin can and perhaps should be relevant to critical scrutiny of the piece. But if this is so, anti-geneticism is false. Of course, the anti-geneticist can respond by saying that this kind of knowledge is all right. But then the argument veers toward a lack of clarity. A principle is required to differentiate the kinds of knowledge of the physical production of the work that are legitimate from those that are not. And, as far as I can tell, no one has successfully produced such a principle. Furthermore, it is not apparent that Perkins's espousal of anti-geneticism is consistent with his beliefs about the relationship between technology and style. That is, since he believes that certain elements of film only become stylistic elements when technology makes their mobilization optional, it seems important for a critic like Perkins to know the state of the existing productive capacity of the medium at the time of each film's creation. But isn't that knowledge of the physical circumstances of the film's production?

17. Beardsley, *Aesthetics: Problems in the Philosophy of Criticism* (New York: Harcourt, Brace and World, 1958), 52.

Even if anti-geneticism were true, however, it is not the case that Perkins has won his argument. For though it is true that the photographic techniques that some realists advocate and the editing techniques that some creationists advocate are ways of making films, they cannot be divorced from the manner in which the spectator sees them. These techniques are readily perceptible on screen and their proponents championed them exactly because of their effectiveness in engaging the spectator at the level of perception. It is incorrect to construe the issue of deep focus versus editing as simply a debate about the best way of making a film—that is, a debate on a par with what fixative holds a splice together best. For deep focus and montage are techniques that are readily perceptible—they are observable structural elements in the art object—and, furthermore, are endorsed because of the way they organize perception. This is not said to concede the arguments of either realists or montagists but to contend that they cannot be defeated by the sort of facile, anti-geneticist dichotomy that Perkins draws between creation and perception.

Even if Perkins's arguments were successful, they would only demonstrate weaknesses within classical film theory. They might show the need to replace classical film theory with some other theory, but they do not compel us to accept the kind of theory Perkins supports as *the* successor to classical theory.

The open-concept argument

The majority of the previous arguments were directed at creationists. Perkins also has specific objections aimed at particular realists—for example, he complains that Bazin's theoretical statements often do not afford an adequate basis for his critical judgments (*FAF*, 38). Perkins, however, has far fewer independent arguments against the realists than against the creationists. Instead, he rests his case primarily on an argument that applies to creationists and realists alike.

Perkins believes that realist theorists such as Bazin performed an inestimable service by challenging the orthodoxy of creationist theory. Films like Renoir's *Rules of the Game* could now be appreciated despite their tendency to gravitate toward a cinematically noninterventionist style that often appeared merely to record the actors. Although Perkins agrees that the realists had some salutary influence, he also charges that their position degenerated into the same type of pernicious dogmatism encountered in the creationists (Ibid.).

> . . . realist theory becomes coherent only if we identify the cinema's "essence" with a single aspect of the film— photographic reproduction. In defining the film by reference to one of its features it [realist theory] resembles the orthodoxy [creationist theory], as it does in making a criterion out of a preference for particular aspects of film technique. Both theories discriminate in favor of certain kinds of attitude given cinematic form. The image dogma [creationist theory] would assess quality in terms of the artist's imposition of order on the chaotic and meaningless surface of reality. Object [realist theory] would derive its verdict from its discovery of significance and order *in* reality. Each of these positions presupposes a philosophy, a temperament, a vision—terrain which the theorist should leave open for the filmmaker to explore and present. (*FAF*, 39)

Commenting on a passage from Bazin, Perkins argues:

> This is accurate and illuminating about one aspect of Renoir's style. It is theoretically useful for its exposure of the orthodoxy's compositional dogma. But it is false and restrictive as a general, binding definition of the screen's *true nature*. As long as the screen has limits [is bounded on four sides] it is surely the artist's privilege to decide whether to exploit its sides as "mask" or "frame." His decision tells us much more about his attitudes and methods but nothing about the quality of his grasp of the medium.
>
> Bazin mistook his own critical vocation to the defence of realism for the "true vocation of the cinema." His the-

oretical statements threaten a purism of the *object* as narrow as that of the image. (*FAF*, 38–39)

Perkins's most emphatic brief against previous film theory is that it imposes rules, obligations, and limitations on filmmakers, thus hampering their creativity. Perkins sees this as the result of the attempt to define the essence of cinema. Furthermore, he regards these essentialist adventures as covert statements of the various critical preferences of the theorists in question. What theorists presented as objective theories were in fact special pleadings for particular styles of cinema—not definitions of cinema. The attempt to define cinema's essential feature is incompatible with the artistic exloration of the medium. This is Perkins's popularized form of the open-concept argument.

Perkins connects this variant of the open-concept argument with his argument that film theory should be metacriticism. He effectively eliminates the possibility that film theory can be a theory of filmmaking by means of his open-concept argument—thereby leaving a theory of film criticism as the only remaining alternative. In order for this strategy to be plausible, one must assume, as Perkins does, at least three things: that the only alternatives for film theory are the theory of filmmaking or the theory of film criticism; that a theory of filmmaking must perforce be an essentialist theory; and lastly, that any attempt at defining cinema is at odds with the imperative of artistic creativity.

Obviously, the division of the prospects for film theory between a theory of filmmaking and a theory of film criticism is not exhaustive. Perkins himself speaks about the spectator a great deal, though he never offers a theory of the spectator. Yet there seems to be no reason to believe that film theory might not be a theory of the film spectator, should the option of a theory of filmmaking fail. Likewise, Perkins often alludes to artistic decisions. But he doesn't show that there can't be an ex post facto theory of artistic decision making. And more options of this sort can be easily multiplied.

Of course, the above objection does not cut to the heart of

Perkins's argument. At most it shows that in order to make his demonstration ironclad, he will have to eliminate more options than simply a theory of filmmaking. Or, on the other hand, he might respond that he would be satisfied with acknowledging, for example, that film theory could involve both a theory of criticism and a theory of the spectator. That is, Perkins could say that his bottom line is only that film theory cannot be a theory of filmmaking.

The basic reason Perkins excludes the possibility of a theory of filmmaking is that he assumes such a venture must be essentialist (and, furthermore, that essentialism is incompatible with artistic novelty). But why must it be the case that a theory of film-making must be essentialist? For example, one can certainly imagine an approach to film theory that would be, so to speak, piecemeal. Instead of attempting to identify the essence of film and then analyzing each articulatory element of the medium in terms of its supposed essence, a film theorist might proceed by offering accounts of each articulatory dimension *ad seriatim*. That is, the theorist would offer a theory of editing, a theory of medium-long shot composition, a theory of the soundtrack, and so on. In each case, the limited theory would explain how the devices within each articulatory dimension function and describe the range of variation available, to date, within each articulatory process. The theorist need not attempt to unify all these discrete explanations into an overarching theory of film by reference to some putative cinematic essence. Nor do I see why the program I have just outlined would necessarily be covertly evaluative. Moreover, a program like this would certainly fall into the category of theories of filmmaking, but it would not be susceptible to the open-concept argument. Thus, we are not forced to accept metacriticism as the only alternative for film theory—though, unlike Perkins, we could admit that film theory encompasses both piecemeal theorizing about filmmaking *and* metacriticism.

What my preceding argument illustrates is that Perkins's attack on theories of filmmaking has a blind spot analogous to one found in Weitz's belief that the open-concept argument, if acceptable, would show that *all* art theory is impossible. Weitz holds that since he has shown that one cannot give a real definition of "art," he has also established that there can be no art theory. He believes this because he only conceives of art theory as the pursuit of real definitions of art. He overlooks the possibility that art theorists, approving his own open-concept argument, might reconceive their task, perhaps by making art theory more like scientific theory, or perhaps by directing art theory to more specific problems—for example, the nature of pictorial representation, the nature of musical expression, and so on. Ironically, the anti-essentialist Weitz says there can be no art theory because he himself has an essentialist definition of art theory—the pursuit of real definitions—and he refuses to see that art theory might be reconceived. Similarly, when Perkins believes he has defeated the claims of essentialist theories of filmmaking, he believes that he has shown that there can be no theories of filmmaking whatsoever. Insofar as Perkins has not shown that nonessentialist theorizing—perhaps of the piecemeal sort sketched earlier—is impossible, we are not forced to accept metacriticism as the only legitimate province of film theory.

So far I have granted Perkins his major presupposition: that defining an art form is inimical to artistic innovation. Here again Perkins's reasoning shares a limitation with Weitz's open-concept argument. Specifically, it overlooks the possibility that a theory that proposes a real definition of art or of film might be framed that either incorporates into its definition or, at least, acknowledges the creativity and search for innovation that is said to be part of the concept of art in general or film art in particular. In the realm of art theory, such real definitions have been offered under the rubric of the Institutional Theory of Art.[18] Whatever problems such theories confront, the imposition of rules on artists and the obstruction of creativity are not among them. Similar theories have

18. George Dickie, *Art and the Aesthetic: An Institutional Analysis* (Ithaca: Cornell University Press, 1974).

been offered for film art.[19] Thus, though Perkins may be right about the problems with the definitions of film offered by classical film theorists, he has not shown that every type of definition must be opposed to artistic creativity. Specifically he has not considered the possibility of definitions that have the logical space for artistic creativity built into them (if only implicitly). Therefore, he has not demonstrated that the aspiration of what he calls theories of filmmaking is so inherently incorrect that our only alternative is to abandon it in favor of metacriticism.

Perkins's positive argument for his criteria

Perkins's evaluative theory of film rests on the twin criteria of credibility and coherence. Credibility is explicated in terms of consistency, while coherence is concretized as the demand for what I previously called commentative saturation. A central question is how Perkins arrives at just these two criteria. His argument is long and elusive, and it involves detailed reference to the invention of cinema and its early history.

The argument begins with yet another attack on creationist and realist theories. Perkins contends that the fault with each is that it battens on one technical resource or constituent of cinema, thereby overlooking the fact that cinema is a hybrid invention composed of several different elements, without any of which the medium would not be cinema. Realist theories, for example, emphasize or, as Perkins would say, overemphasize the importance of photography. Yet cinema was not simply the result of photography. Rather, movies owe their existence to a peculiarly mixed marriage between the camera, the magic lantern, and the optical toys of the nineteenth century (*FAF*, 85). Perkins's point here is that photography is not a historically privileged component, since the medium is that of *motion* pictures and not simply that of pictures. And that motion has in its lineage such devices for pro-

19. Noël Carroll, "Film History and Film Theory: An Outline for an Institutional Theory of Film," in *Film Reader*, no. 4 (1979), 81–96.

ducing the illusion of movement as the Phenakistascope, the Heliocinegraphe, the Zoetrope, and the Praxinoscope. Perkins makes this point to underscore an underlying theoretical claim: the cinema is not reducible to one of its constituent elements. It is the product of more than one invention and it is made up of more than one element; each of these elements has an equal claim to being basic to cinema; each of these elements has different potentials (for example, illusion or recording); the exploration of any of the potentials of cinema is equally grounded in the hybrid origins of the medium.[20]

Perkins goes on to develop the notion of the hybrid nature of cinema through a discussion of the most important stylistic divisions of turn-of-the-century film—that between the brothers Lumière, on the one hand, and Georges Méliès, on the other. This is a contrast that is often invoked by film historians. The Lumières are considered the forerunners of the documentary tradition of film. Much of their production was centered on gathering and disseminating short newsreel clips of current events from far and near. Méliès, who began his career after the Lumières, is often credited as the father of the narrative fiction film. He came to specialize in often stagey, tableaux-like adaptations of stories such as *Cinderella*. Besides his pioneering work with the narrative fiction film, Méliès also exploited the medium's potential for magical effects, using stop-action photography to conjure up disappearances, transformations, gruesome dismemberments, and miraculous re-memberments. Thus, Méliès is not only regarded as the father of the fiction film but also of the fantasy film, the horror film, the science fiction film, and indeed of all films of lavish special effects in which the world is shaped according

20. Before continuing with Perkins's argument, it is useful to note that his attack in the paragraph above does not affect all creationists and realists equally. Arnheim, for example, never prized one technical element of cinema above all others. Instead, he claimed that any element of cinema must be used creatively rather than reproductively. Perkins can only have *some* creationists in mind—notably some montagists such as Kuleshov. Also, some realists like Cavell and Kracauer would be hard to pin down with this argument since they do not set restrictions on what techniques are legitimate.

to the filmmakers' wishes. Perkins uses the Lumière/Méliès contrast to underscore his point about the hybrid nature of the medium. From the onset of cinema, the Lumière/Méliès dichotomy implies that cinema can equally pursue the tasks of either documentation or fiction; recording or illusion (in the sense of prestidigitation); the reproduction of facts or the superimposition of magic; copying the world or creating a world. The oppositions associated with Lumière and Méliès likewise correlate with the potentials marked off by the different inventions that gave rise to cinema; the Lumières explored the viability of the camera to do what it was designed for—recording. Méliès mined the cinema's heritage of the tradition of the magic lantern. Thus, both realists and creationists can trace their ancestry to the early days of cinema, and even to the proto-cinematic devices that gave rise to the invention of film. Creationism corresponds to the Méliès/magic lantern potentials of the medium—the montagists, concerned as they are with the organization of the celluloid reel, are heirs to the inventors and showmen who popularized the various illusions of movement that evolved into the film-strip. Realists, on the other hand, derive from the Lumière tradition, which valorizes the photographic constituent of the medium. For Perkins, both creationists and realists can claim some connection to a basic feature of the film medium. But neither side can claim that its allegiance is more fundamental, since the cinema is *essentially* hybrid.

Not only is the medium essentially hybrid, but there is a potential for tension between its elements. Perkins describes this tension by means of a number of not always equivalent dichotomies. The creation-versus-copy opposition becomes (dubiously) the opposition between "the 'objective', factual elements being derived from the camera and the 'subjective', magical ones from the Phenakistascope and its relations" (*FAF*, 60). It is also the opposition between the power "to possess the real world by capturing its appearance" and "the presentation of an ideal image, ordered by the filmmaker's will and imagination" (Ibid.). And it is also described in terms of the contrast between reality and illusion, which in turn correlates respectively with the "solidity" and "malleability" of the fictional world. Dramatic illusion and heightened meaningfulness correspond to the creative potential of the medium; photography counterposes the creative potential while corresponding to the copying tendency. The fiction/documentary dichotomy, at times, is treated as homologous to the creation/copy distinction. Whether all these dichotomies are supposed to be identical or merely somehow related is not perfectly clear in Perkins. But it is clear that they all stand for a potential for conflict among cinema's capacities.

For Perkins, one set of cinematic capacities points the filmmaker in the direction of creating a world, while other capacities suggest that the role of film is to copy the world. These potentials cannot both be fully exploited at the same time. The filmmaker either must pursue one ideal (or the other) or must be bound to reconcile the two potentials. (Presumably, avoiding both creating and copying is not an option for the filmmaker, since one cannot but be engaged in one or the other or both when employing the medium, since these are entailed by basic constituents of the medium.)

Perkins believes that certain kinds of abstract cartoons (for example, Pintoff's *The Critic* and MacLaren's *Begone, Dull Care*) gravitate toward the pole of pure creation, while certain documentaries gravitate toward the pole of pure copy (perhaps *This Is Cinerama* is an example here). According to Perkins, however, the narrative photographic fiction film cannot opt to go in the direction of either pure creation or pure copy because it inherently involves both creating and copying—it involves the creation of a fictional world that it then records. Thus, the narrative fiction film must reconcile the conflicting tendencies of the medium. Perkins writes: "The photographic narrative film occupies a compromise where a fictional 'reality' is *created* in order to be *recorded*. Here the relationship between reality and illusion, object and image, becomes extremely complex; any attempt to isolate either in a 'pure' state becomes correspondingly inept" (*FAF*, 61).

The structure of Perkins's argument is plain to see: Cinema

is a hybrid medium with potentially conflicting tendencies; in order to avert said conflict, the filmmaker must either favor one tendency over the other, or reconcile the potentially conflicting tendencies; the narrative filmmaker—because of the nature of photographic narration (which records creations)— cannot favor one tendency over the other; therefore, the filmmaker must reconcile film's potentially conflicting tendencies. The credibility/coherence criteria supply guidelines for testing whether such a reconciliation has been achieved. Hence, the next stage of Perkins's argument is to show how the demand for reconciliation translates into the credibility/ coherence criteria.

Perkins appears to connect the conflict to the criteria by means of an extended analysis of the nature of the fiction movie. It is as if Perkins sees his evaluative criteria as immanent in the nature of the fiction film.

> In the fiction movie, reality becomes malleable but remains (or continues to seem) solid. The world is shaped by the filmmaker to reveal an order beyond chronology, in a system of time and space which is both natural and synthetic. The movie offers its reality in a sequence of privileged moments during which actions achieve a clarity and intensity seldom found in everyday life. Motive and gesture, action and reaction, cause and effect, are brought into a more immediate, dynamic, and revealing relationship. The filmmaker fashions a world more concentrated and more shaped than that of our usual experience.

> Movies are not distinguished from other forms of narrative by the fact that they isolate and mold aspects of experience in order to intensify our perception. But films are peculiar in performing this work primarily in the sphere of action and appearance rather than of reflection or debate.

> The storyteller's freedom is inhibited by his first two requirements: clarity and credibility. In movies, the most direct and concrete method of narration, these aims im-

pose a greater restraint than on any other medium. The audience has to know what is happening, of course, but it must be convinced by what it sees. The organization of image and sound must usually defer to these interests. The narrative picture, in most of its forms, submits to the twin criteria of order and credibility. *The movie itself creates these criteria whenever it proposes to be at the same time significant and convincing.* The impurity of the medium is consummated by a decision to project a world which is both reproduced and imagined, a creation and a copy. Committed to this impurity, the filmmaker is also committed to maintaining a balance between its elements. His aim is to organize the world to the point where it becomes most meaningful but to resist ordering it out of all resemblance to the real world which it tries to evoke. (*FAF*, 69–70, italics added)

Perkins sees the intrinsic function of narrative as the creation of a world of heightened significance, that is, a world more ordered, coherent, and meaningful than the everyday world of our experiences. Thus, the function of coherence making—which is associated with the creative potential of the film medium—becomes a measure of quality. Heightened coherence or heightened significance is the functional standard of quality in any narrative art. It is the very point of narrative art. But film must be differentiated from other narrative arts because it narrates by means means of recorded appearances. This places a restraint on the extent to which the filmmaker can impose or wrest meaning from recorded appearances. That is, by working with recorded appearances, the filmmaker commits to maintaining some semblance of the actual world as well as instilling an expectation of such resemblance in spectators. The primary goal of the narrative film—since it is the primary goal of any narrative—is to create or mold a fictional world of intensified significance. Working in the film medium, however, has its own special requirements. For recorded appearances—the result of the photographic/reproductive constituent of the medium—engender an expectation of verisimilitude. This entails a restraint on how significance can be created in the fiction film. The purpose of fiction film is not to produce verisimilitude, however; this is only a side-constraint. The purpose is to produce meaning—that is, co-herence. But the side-constraint must nevertheless also be re-spected: the film must be credible.[21]

The gist of Perkins's argument here seems to be: The nar-rative fiction filmmaker must reconcile cinema's potentially conflicting tendencies—copying and creating; the task of nar-rating entails that cinema's creative capacities be employed to achieve heightened coherence; at the same time, the task of narrating by means of recorded appearances entails that the realistic tendency enjoined by cinema's copying capacities must at least be respected; the filmmaker can respect the re-alistic tendency by keeping the film credible; therefore, the narrative fiction filmmaker must reconcile cinema's poten-tially conflicting tendencies by at least keeping the film cred-ible *and* by employing cinema's creative capacities to achieve heightened coherence. The credibility requirement will, of course, disallow certain coherence-making gambits of the sort discussed earlier. But within the bounds of credibility, the effective fiction filmmaker produces coherence.

21. In the above argument the term "heightened coherence" is ambiguous. It could signal that the film has more significance than a mere mechanical reproduction of the drama would have. Sometimes, however, when Per-kins speaks of the intensified meanings of narratives, he seems to have something different in mind; he seems to be contrasting narrative fictional events with everyday events, and it is the former that he finds more intense, more saturated with significance and more formed and shaped than the lat-ter. I will comment on this ambiguity at length in what is to come. Also, at times, Perkins seems to want the filmmaker not to produce added or heightened coherence but maximal coherence—that is, as much meaning/ significance as can be added to the film without violating the credibility criterion (*FAF*, 70). Nevertheless, I have not stated Perkins's argument in terms of maximal coherence. My reason for sticking with "heightened co-herence" is that when Perkins goes on to commend films, he does not dem-onstrate that they could not have had any more coherence than they do have (a rather awesome thing to try to prove). He shows only that they have more coherence—in terms of commentative saturation—than they would have had if the director had merely filmed the drama.

Perkins's entire argument might be summarized as follows:

1. Cinema is a hybrid medium with potentially conflicting tendencies.
2. In order to avert these conflicts, the narrative fiction film-maker can either (a) favor one tendency over its opposite or (b) reconcile the potentially conflicting tendencies.
3. The filmmaker—because of the nature of photographic narrative (which records creations)—cannot favor one tendency over its opposite.
4. Therefore, the filmmaker of narrative, photographic cinema must reconcile film's potentially conflicting tendencies.
5. The task of narrating entails that cinema's creative capacities be employed to achieve heightened coherence.
6. At the same time, the task of narrating by means of recorded appearances entails that the realistic tendency enjoined by cinema's copying capacity must at least be respected.
7. The filmmaker can (at least) respect cinema's realistic tendency by keeping the film credible.
8. Therefore, the narrative fiction filmmaker must reconcile cinema's potentially conflicting tendencies by (a) at least keeping the film credible and (b) employing cinema's creative capacities to achieve heightened coherence while respecting 8(a).[22]

22. This argument is stated in terms of obligations of the narrative fiction filmmaker. Undoubtedly some readers will be confused by this since I previously emphasized Perkins's assertion that his was a theory of criticism and not an attempt to impose obligations on the artist. But despite his claims to the contrary, he states the argument for his theory in terms of what the filmmaker must do: "Committed to this impurity [the mixture of copy and creation], the filmmaker is also committed to maintaining a balance between its elements" (*FAF*, 70). Thus, I see no alternative but to cast this argument in terms of what the filmmaker must do. If there is a confusion here, the confusion originates with Perkins.

Also, the conclusion of this argument sets forth two requirements for fiction filmmakers. In the chapter, "Form and Discipline," where the bulk of this argument is developed, the conclusion applies universally to all fiction filmmakers. In another part of the book, however, Perkins appears to

The first thing to note about this argument is that it establishes an imperative for creating a kind of heightened coherence that is far more general than the specific type of coherence that is operative throughout the analyses that Perkins offers. I have referred to the latter type of coherence as commentative saturation. It is the symbolic embellishment of an action, object, or element of cinematic presentation in such a way that it makes a comment on the drama while also performing some denotative function vis-à-vis the representation of the fictional world of the film. This is a very special kind of coherence. One could admit that narrative films are committed to producing "heightened coherence" without going on to claim that they must produce heightened coherence in the sense of commentative saturation. A case of commentative saturation may necessarily always be a case of heightened coherence. But to require heightened coherence of a filmmaker in no way entails that the filmmaker must traffic in commentative coherence. For example, narrative in and of itself implies heightened coherence but not commentative coherence. Thus, there is a logical gap between the criteria that Perkins established by his argument and the practical applications Perkins makes of those criteria in his examples.

One might respond that this is harmless enough, since "commentative saturation" seems to be at least one possible instantiation of the general concept of "heightened coherence," as that phrase is employed in the argument. But I am not sure that this move is so harmless. Consider step 5 in the argument: "The task of narrating entails that cinema's creative capacities be employed to achieve heightened coherence." What support does this premise have? Well, it is riding on the belief that the worlds of narrative fictions are, as a matter of fact, more shaped, more coherent, and more imbued with meaning than the world of ordinary experience. This is a function of narrative structure, full, as it is, of coincidences,

exempt certain directors of film comedies from the imperative to create commentarial coherence. I have commented on this anomaly in footnote 9.

correspondences, and condensations of space and time that allow one dramatically significant event to follow on the heels of its predecessor. Exposition succeeds as narrative by having this quality of heightened coherence, which might also be referred to in terms of an economy of intelligibility in the interrelationship of the actions that a plot comprises. Thus, narrating will entail a goal of heightened coherence. But this is heightened coherence as a function of narrative structure—something altogether independent of heightened coherence as a function of commentative saturation. Narrative coherence and commentative saturation may both be examples of some general concept of heightened coherence. But they are too distinct to be used intersubstitutively. Step 5 rings true only if we take its reference to heightened coherence to pertain to narrative structure. Parallel narration, for example, is a means of giving the cross-cut events heightened significance. The selection and arrangement of interrelated actions in a sequence that makes them stand out is the raison d'être of narrative and can be called a variety heightened significance. But commentative saturation is an independent variety of heightened significance. This can readily be seen by thinking of any well-told story that has no symbolic embellishment. A routine TV sit-com might be a case in point. Insofar as it has a narrative structure, it has heightened significance, especially in contrast to the mundane flow of events in most people's lives. But this type of heightened significance can be purchased without the sort of symbolic embellishments that Perkins prizes. In fact, if we read "heightened coherence" as referring to "commentative saturation," then step 5 in the argument is false. Narration may entail heightened coherence, but it does not entail symbolic embellishment. A film like *The Rise to Power of Louis XIV* is said to lack symbolic embellishment, but it certainly has the heightened coherence that narrative structure engenders.

Thus, if step 5 is read as extending generally to narrative structure, then the argument does not ultimately support the practice of assigning merit to films on the basis of commentative saturation. On the other hand, if heightened coherence in step 5 is read as extending to commentative saturation or as referring specifically to commentative saturation, then the premise is false and the argument stalls. In either case, the argument fails to do what Perkins wants it to. Stated bluntly, the reason for this is that Perkins wants to support the employment of one artistic strategy—commentative saturation—on the grounds that it is immanent in or entailed by the nature of narrative. But symbolic embellishment is, in point of fact, optional when it comes to narration. The commitment to narration, therefore, does not necessitate commitment to heightened coherence of this sort. Indeed, erecting heightened coherence of this sort as a criterion of value for fiction films may prejudice the case of filmmakers of a realist (rather than expressive realist) bent, who attempt to tell stories while eschewing symbolism altogether.[23]

Another way to launch a similar objection is to say that in the overall context of *Film as Film*, the use of "heightened coherence" is equivocating. The argument is banked on the idea of coherence as it pertains to narrative structure as such, but once the imperative of coherence is established, Perkins switches its application to the very different phenomenon of commentative saturation (or, as he calls it, cinematic elaboration), which is a special kind of symbolism rather than an expositional structure.

Undoubtedly, Perkins's proliferation of dichotomies—reproduction/magic, copy/creation, objective/subjective, recording/illusion, documentary/fiction, real world/imagination, real appearances/dramatic illusion, and so on—contrives a situation that is ripe for equivocation since it is easy to confuse these homologies between very different things as purported identities. Perkins also aligns meaning, significance, and coherence on the creative side of these contrasts. Thus, he moves from dramatic illusion to narrative to meaning to coherence and then presumes that the kind of coherence he's talking about incorporates commentative saturation. Unfortunately, it does not; commentative saturation is neither iden-

23. This is discussed at greater length in the next section.

tical to—as Perkins, at times, seems to think—nor is it entailed by dramatic, fictional narrative. But, in any case, no
matter how Perkins arrived at this obfuscation, the attempt to
ground his criterion of coherence on narration as such, rests
on an equivocation—either directly in step 5 or indirectly in
the attempt to read the fruits of step 8 as endorsing commentative saturation.

The line of argument embodied in steps 3, 6, and 7 also
seems suspect. Step 3 says that because fiction films record
creations, the narrative filmmaker must respect both the realist tendency and the creationist tendency. Step 6 says respect
for the realist tendency is a minimal requirement. Step 7 holds
that credibility is the means of meeting this minimal requirement. The best way to see the problem here is to approach
these steps in reverse order. Starting with step 7, we immediately wonder why credibility—construed as consistency—
should be the means by which the filmmaker meets a requirement for realism, where the requirement for realism is rooted
in the photographic aspect of the medium. What does photographic verisimilitude have to do with the consistency of
the fictional world of the film and the demand that there be
no unmotivated authorial comments? It is true that in certain
contexts photographic verisimilitude may be called "realistic." But it is less certain that mere narrative consistency
amounts to realism—a novel like *Voyage to Arcturus* is consistent on its own terms but not realistic. Nor is the absence of
authorial intrusion a mark of realism—Thackeray's *Vanity
Fair* is realistic. But even if in film these features of narration
were realistic, "realistic" in this argument would only be an
ambiguous middle term in a fallacious argument. For the
"realism" of photography and the putative "realism" of the
narrative style Perkins calls credible are independent concepts. One can make credible stories without photographic
verisimilitude—Weber and Watson's *Fall of the House of
Usher*—and incredible stories with photographic verisimilitude—*Blood of a Poet*. Perkins knows this, of course, but
nevertheless he strains after some connection between photographic verisimilitude and credibility. But I can see no log-

ical connection between the two at all. Nor can I find some less demanding sort of "fit" or "association" between them, save that most cinematographic narratives probably have been credible in the way Perkins requires. But this need not be the result of any conceptual relation between photographic verisimilitude and narrative credibility, but only a function of the fact that credible narration was the most pervasive style of narrating when filmmakers started using photography to tell stories. Why narrative credibility should be the filmmaker's way of satisfying film's purported commitment to photographic verisimilitude is unexplained. One would have thought that if the narrative photographic film were in fact wedded to verisimilitude, this would involve no greater requirement than that the imagery all be of a nondistorted, nonabstract, recognizable, mimetically realist sort. That is, the realism of photography, as that is pertinent to cinema (that is, if it is pertinent), is a matter that pertains to images. Each cinematic image is realistic or it is not. So why does Perkins relate photographic mimesis to the concept of credibility, which, as he develops it, is an attribute of stories (and the *combination* of images).

If we look at steps 3 and 6, we can see that Perkins has a way of defining photographic narration that tends to assimilate the storytelling feature of fiction films under the photographic dimension. He has an idea of narrative films as *recording* creations, by which he means recording fictions, or that films narrate by recording appearances. In these formulations, the idea of recording—which is associated with realism—is part and parcel of film narrating. To film-narrate is to record, copy, or photograph fictions. Note that when we speak of recording fictions, we are speaking in terms of records of something of larger proportions than individual images. Moreover, if recording is somehow an element of film narrating, it may seem plausible to demand that such records be credible against some standard of reality.

Does the notion of film narrating as recording fictions bridge the gap between the verisimilitude of images and the credibility of stories? I think not. For it is inappropriate to say that films record fictions. Films might be described as presenting or constructing or representing fictions, but films do not record fiction, if by "record" we mean factually reproduce. The reasoning here is simple; there is nothing to factually reproduce when it comes to fictions. Filmmakers record events, actors, and objects that come to stand for fictional events, characters, and objects. But filmmakers can't photograph fictions; it's ontologically impossible. At best, they might be said to photograph performances of fictions. Nor, by the way, is fiction narrating a matter of recording appearances—filmmakers photograph things, people, and events, not the appearances thereof, and they narrate fictions by assembling moving photographs in certain ordered sequences. The *moving photograph* is probably an essential ingredient in narrative photographic fiction filmmaking. But it is not clear that *recording* is such an ingredient, where we are not trivially treating "recording" as a cognate of "photographing." I wish to draw a distinction between photography, as a way of producing an image, and recording, as a purpose for making a photographic image, namely to document a person, place, thing, or event for posterity. With this distinction in mind, we might claim that narrative fiction films are not essentially involved in recording but rather, in fabricating images by means of photography to supply the materials for fictions. I think it makes sense to say that though the process of photography in a fiction film may incidentally involve the recording of Gregory Peck at age forty, the photographic image was not taken for precisely this purpose but as a way of creating an image to be used in a fiction. Thus, against Perkins's tendency to see film narrating and photographic recording as intertwined, they must be separated. But once the concept of recording is detached from that of film narrating, the temptation to see the narrative as committed to realist fidelity falls away.

Indeed, if the concept of recording can be cleaved from the concept of fiction film narrating, then it seems that the whole basis for Perkins's realist constraints on film narrative disappears. Realism is taken by Perkins as a gauge of success in recording, where recording is taken as an essential part of fiction film narrating. But if recording is not an essential part of the film narrating process, then realism is not a necessary gauge of the narrative's success. This is not to say that realism cannot be an element of value in a narrative fiction film, but only that it need not be. Stating this objection in terms of the way Perkins's argument has been outlined, we can say that step 3 is false. That is, since recording is not an essential element of the photographic narrative fiction film, there is no reason why the narrative fiction filmmaker must respect the realist tendency of the medium. The filmmaker could favor the creationist tendency instead. Where the word "record" is used as a synonym for "photograph" it will be contradictory to say that fiction films deal in moving photographs but not records. My point rests on claiming that there is a sense of "record" that is not equivalent to "photograph" and that it is this sense, which is connected to realism as its measure of achievement, that Perkins's argument rests on. I draw this distinction in terms of identifying a photographic/cinemato-graphic image as one generated by a specifiable technology, whereas a record is an image made for the purpose of show-ing how things were in the past. Photography in the service of fiction does not have this purpose as its essential point, even if it incidentally records the past. Thus, it does not fol-low that photographic fictions have realism as any index of their value.

Though Perkins continually rails at classical theorists for their attempt to found aesthetic theories of film on analyses of the *telos* of this or that technical constituent of the medium, Perkins himself has a tendency in this direction. He derives the filmmaker's commitment to realism from cinema's capac-ity to record, and he extrapolates from the use of film to re-cord *images* a requirement that a narrative film must be en-tirely constrained by respect for the realist tendency purportedly inherent in the image-making process. Perkins does not, like Kuleshov or Kracauer, say that entire films must be constructed so that the properties of their favored, basic cinematic constituents determine the use of every other constituent element in the film. But Perkins is like Kracauer in claiming that a structural aspect of film stories can be inferred from the photographic aspect of the medium. A similar, though more complicated point, can be made about Perkins's case for the demands of the creationist side of the medium. As Perkins's argument advances, he attempts to ground the creationist demand for coherence in the nature of narrative. But in the earlier stages of the argument, Perkins traces the origins of the creationist tendency to various proto-cinematic toys that created the impression of motion and to magic lantern spectacles. The idea seems to be that if realism in film originates in the photographic constituent, then creationism derives from the motion-inducing constituents that correlate to the sequential organization of the filmstrip. Thus, Perkins at least attempts to associate the demands of creationism with technical constituents of the medium. He also tries to relate narration to these technical elements of the medium, rather than to photography, and he attempts to dramatize this point through the dichotomy of Méliès, the storyteller, illusionist, and heir to the magic lantern, versus the Lumières, the documentarians, gatherers of fact, and heirs of photography. There is something very confusing and I think mistaken in Perkins's multiplication of these oppositions. Obviously the Lumières were as much heirs as was Méliès to the proto-cinematic toys of motion since they made *moving* pictures. Also, moving from magic to illusion to Méliès to fiction to narrative to coherence in building the composite genealogy of the creationist involves a pretty long throw, for, among other things, narrative can be either fictional or nonfictional. But this gives rise to the possibility of documentary narratives, something that would straddle Perkins's neat columns of opposites, because narrative is supposed to be listed with creationism, whereas documentary goes with realism in the photography column. My intent here, however, is not so much to critically explore Perkins's homologies as to remind the reader of the degree to which Perkins rests his defense of coherence and credibility on their basis in the technical resources of the medium—exactly what he berates classical theorists for.

Another area in which it appears that Perkins is liable to be tarred by his own brush is his condemnation of classical film theorists for their quest for the "cinematic," for a defining property of film that could be used to mark off the proper avenues for the development of the medium. Yet what is Perkins's credibility and coherence formula but a means of gauging whether a film narrative is cinematic? Like Kracauer, Perkins has restricted his purview to one type of film—the fictional narrative—and, for that type of film, he has argued that the correct line of development is one that accords with the basic capacities of the medium. Unlike Kracauer and other classical theorists, Perkins has defined the basic capacities of the medium compositely. He has forged a compromise between realist and creationist theories. But this, it seems to me, is no different in principle than what the classical theorists did—at least according to Perkins's account. If there is a difference between Perkins and the classical theorists, it is a difference in detail. Where they gravitated toward hypostatizing one tendency of the medium as its essence, Perkins amalgamates two tendencies into an ordered set of conditions for evaluating film as film. Needless to say, the phrase "film *as* film" suspiciously recalls the idea of "the cinematic." Also, for all Perkins's talk of the hybrid nature of film, he really only seems concerned with two capacities of the medium. This is evident in his proliferation of extended sets of homologies that strive to capture a multitude of features of the medium under one paradigmatic dichotomy. As I have stressed, these homologies are often more confusing and confused than they are convincing. Why should narrative or the impression of movement, for example, be considered more a matter of reconstituting reality than a matter of cinematography? And what is the connection between the impression of movement and commentative saturation? The issue right now, however, is not the persuasiveness of Perkins's dichotomy, but rather the significance of his propensity to create a dichotomy at all. This dichotomy exposes his tendency not to believe his own claim that cinema is multifariously hybrid but to see the medium as characterized by two essential characteristics, which are, moreover, in potential conflict. But is a definition of cinema rooted in two essential characteristics different in kind from a definition rooted in a single essence? Perkins still conceives of a determinant characteristic of film. He differs from classical theorists in that his determinant characteristic is a complex of two tendencies held in tandem by a principle that assesses a film as a film, which is to say, I think, assesses it "cinematically." Indeed, this dual characteristic appears to originate purportedly in the nature of the medium.

What is at stake if Perkins in fact is engaged in the same approach to theory as classical theorists, is that Perkins's pretension to have discovered a new way of doing film theory collapses. Indeed, Perkins's theory of film does not look different in structure from previous film theories.[24] He begins by designating the type of cinema that he intends to analyze—the narrative fiction film that, it is said, records fictions. This allows him to focus on what he believes is the determinant characteristic of film (for the purposes of cinematographic narration). The determinant characteristic turns out to be the tension between the capacities to record and to reconstitute profilmic reality. Once Perkins establishes this tension as the determinant characteristic of film, he goes on to show how it can be exemplified by the various articulatory processes of the medium. This indicates that Perkins has not inaugurated a new kind of film theory, although he takes himself to be offering an alternative to and replacement for classical film theory. Of course, this only shows that Perkins has failed to develop the alternative line of film theory—film theory as metacriticism—that he advocates. In the next section I will take up the issue of whether metacriticism, envisioned as an alternative to classical film theory, is viable in principle.

Perkins's Criteria

So far I have examined the strength of the arguments for Perkins's credibility and coherence criteria for evaluating film. I have not, however, determined the applicability of these cri-

---

24. The structure of classical film theory is discussed in the Introduction.

teria in film criticism. In this section, I will examine each criterion individually and then both together in order to evaluate their adequacy. In considering the cogency of Perkins's formula, I will also deal with the question of whether there can be a metacriticism of film evaluation that is distinct from the metacriticism of art evaluation in general.

Credibility

Perkins holds that a narrative, photographic fiction film must have the property of credibility if it is to be considered a candidate for commendation. Credibility is a side-constraint on the filmmaker's imagination, limiting the latitude the filmmaker has in coherently shaping and investing meaning in a fictional world. Perkins refers to credibility as the filmmaker's discipline. That the film be credible is the demand that the film induce a certain psychological state, namely that the fictional world appear believable. Perkins claims that this is achieved by at least meeting the structural condition of being consistent. But consistent with what? Consistent with what we know of the world outside of movie theaters? Perkins rejects this alternative for obvious reasons. Too many films violate it. Correspondence with reality is, therefore, a useless criterion if our purpose is to isolate what good there is in films as we know them. Whole genres would have to be rejected by a correspondence criterion: musicals, for example—cities do not typically burst into song and dance when they awaken—not to mention science fiction and horror films. It is because of this systematic divergence from reality by many standard film genres that Perkins eschews a correspondence criterion. Instead, he explicates credibility as internal consistency. The film must present a consistent fictional world and its mode of presentation must be uniform—for example, if the film does not adopt a convention of authorial asides from the outset, then it should not suddenly indulge in one.

It is the credibility criterion that makes Perkins's theory film specific. I say this because the credibility criterion, unlike the coherence criterion, is said to follow from a basic feature of the medium, photography. As I noted earlier, however, there are some serious questions about whether one can infer a commitment to credibility, conceived of as consistency, from the photographic dimensions of film. Indeed, one could understand Perkins's motivation more clearly were he championing credibility, conceived of as correspondence, as his criterion. That is, one can see how it can be said that a photographic image corresponds to its model, and how this might lead one to argue that entire films should have the correspondence characteristic of their basic constituent elements, cinematographic shots. And one could make this proposal without committing a fallacy of composition by claiming that it is the correspondence of cinematographic images that sets up a psychological expectation of continued correspondence in the audience. Whether this is true is debatable, but it is at least comprehensible. But when the concept of credibility is changed from correspondence to consistency, the connection with photography becomes obscure.

For Perkins, a film runs afoul of the credibility criterion if after an hour of depicting colors naturalistically it switches to some sort of symbolic use of color. Let us imagine a film that goes from naturalistic Technicolor to a scene in black and white—perhaps to emphasize that the scene is a flashback, say to the thirties. Moreover, let us assume that this is the only flashback of this sort in the film. It is inconsistent with the style of the rest of the film and the change in the range of color values has no explanation in terms of the fictional world of the film. Therefore, it is incredible by Perkins's standard. But this incredibility does not have anything to do with the photographic element of the medium "being betrayed" or with the frustration of expectations engendered by the correspondence feature or recording capability of photography. For in the case we have just imagined, the photography, in the relevant sense, corresponds with its model—at least to the fullest extent any black and white film image has ever corresponded to its model. It merely differs from the rest of the film stock used in the movie. The credibility-as-consistency criterion neither follows from nor is immanent in photography. The criterion is logically disjunct from photography.

Nor is it clear that "credibility" is really the concept Perkins should be using to designate the property he has in mind. For if I understand the criterion properly, a film made up of *consistently* absurdist events—*Duck Soup, Million Dollar Legs, Never Give a Sucker an Even Break, The Fatal Glass of Beer*, among others—are all credible. But it seems to me that if this is the case, then Perkins's concept of credibility is purely stipulative. *Dr. Stangelove* is consistently satirical in its exaggerated caricatures of international events and world leaders, but it is hardly credible. Of course, one might respond by asking what harm is done if Perkins stipulates that credibility is gauged in terms of consistency. The harm, I think, is ambiguity of a sort that one often finds in Perkins's text. Most of the time you read *Film as Film* with some ordinary notion of credibility in mind. So when Perkins adduces a case like the bedpost in *Red Desert* you assume that the problem here is that it is an incredible apparition in some nonspecialized sense of "incredible." And this corresponds with the general weight that Perkins gives to the (albeit modified) claims that the realist tendency of the medium makes on filmmakers. But if internal consistency is really the issue, then certain of Perkins's examples become problematic. For instance, *Red Desert* opens with shots of an out-of-focus landscape to signal the mental imbalance of the central character. From the start of the film we are offered what are to be interpreted as distorted images of reality that stand for the character's distorted and distorting psychological condition. Thus, the reddening bedpost can be seen as consistent with the rest of the film. Also, when one recalls the color stylization of *Moulin Rouge*—a film that attempts to ape the palette of Toulous-Lautrec's paintings and illustrations!—one must wonder whether the green lighting in the scene Perkins cites is so abrasively inconsistent with the assertive color style of the rest of the film. Has Perkins unfortunately just offered us poor examples? I don't believe so. Rather, I think that the ordinary notion of credibility is what he actually has in mind when he works through his examples.

But when it comes to explicating the concept of credibility, he realizes that the ordinary concept of credibility would debar too many films—such as genre musicals—from the order of good films. Yet, when Perkins moves to the concept of consistency—which seems primarily a stylistic matter—he seems unaware that it will not warrant many of the judgments we would reach using our ordinary concept of what is credible.

Evidence that Perkins is involved in the aforesaid confusion includes his remarks on Godard's *Les Carabiniers*:

> The values I have claimed for *Rope*, say, or for *Johnny Guitar*, cannot be claimed, in terms of this study, for a picture like Godard's *Les Carabiniers*, where the fictional action attempts neither credibility nor the absorption of personal meaning into a dynamic pattern of action. The degree to which *Les Carabiniers* is to be valued will have to be argued in terms of other than those proposed here. (*FAF*, 190)

Coming from Perkins, this is a peculiar statement. For if credibility is really to be analyzed by the notion of consistency, then one would think that the consistent ciné-Brechtianism of Godard's ellipses and authorial asides would have satisfied Perkins's requirements. Surely Perkins has no way of supplying a principled procedure for accepting the anti-naturalistic conventions of stylistically consistent genre musicals while rejecting stylistically consistent exercises in ciné-Brechtianism. Nor can he deny that *Les Carabiniers* is a photographic narrative film. His uneasiness with *Les Carabiniers* indicates that—his own claims to the contrary—Perkins really means to be speaking of credibility and not consistency. But, of course, if credibility is really his criterion, then his criterion is woefully inadequate to the task of evaluating films. *Ivan the Terrible, Part I* is a great narrative film, and its use of an acting style derived from grand opera, though unusual for a film, is consistent and undoubtedly contributes to the uniform effect of the film—enhancing the momentousness and monumentality of the film's fictional world. But, strictly speaking, the film is not credible. The theatrical flourishes, blocking, and timing of the actors, as well as their strained, overly demonstrative postures are pure artifice—we wouldn't expect to find people gesticulating like that if we visited medieval Moscow in a time machine (though such characters might turn up if we set our dials for the nineteenth-century stage). Further examples of problem films for a simple credibility criterion are innumerable. The issue here is not that Perkins as a critic cannot attempt to erect credibility as an evaluative criterion. Rather, Perkins himself has said that he does not wish to erect a critical standard but only to discover the standard by which existing achievements in fiction film can be judged rationally to be good. This means that his criterion should be applicable to the classics of the fiction film. But, as the *Ivan the Terrible* case shows, ordinary credibility as an evaluative criterion is not up to the task.

Of course, Perkins might respond with "Do as I say, not as I do." That is, Perkins does not claim to be abiding by our ordinary concept of credibility but explicitly allies himself to the credibility-as-consistency criterion. Credibility-as-consistency, however, also fails to accommodate many of the achievements of narrative fiction film. Going by Perkins's examples, inconsistency is a matter of a film having an unexplained element or elements while all or most of the others are explainable within the fictional world of the film. But what of narrative films that purposively contain unexplained elements—blatant incongruities—to make the point, for example, that there are more things in heaven and earth than can be explained in even a fictional world?

What of the ship in the tree in *Aguirre: The Wrath of God*? Of course, Perkins might carp about this example on the grounds that my evidence is based on a plot element whereas his examples show that he is concerned with the inconsistent employment of formal elements—lighting, color, editing, and so forth. But this rejoinder is just a request for a different example—although we might note that plot inconsistency is not really very easy to separate from the kinds Perkins deals with in his examples of cinematic inconsistency. Yet, if an example of an inconsistent use of a formal element is what is called for, consider *The Discreet Charm of the Bourgeoisie*. Scenes are edited together in that film in a way that makes it difficult to distinguish the line between the real and the fantastic. This, of course, is one of the themes of the film. The film is a purposive mix of the explainable and the unexplainable, and the editing—with its lack of any conventional cues for the transition from the real to the fantastic—is a major element in setting out the theme. The film is as inconsistent as a film can be—but inconsistency is part of its point. It is nevertheless a great film, though this cannot be acknowledged by Perkins's criterion. Of course, it may be argued that *The Discreet Charm of the Bourgeoisie* is stylistically consistent despite its logical inconsistency—indeed it is stylistically consistent *because of* its logical inconsistency—but this sense of stylistic consistency divorced from logical consistency also seems divorced from any but an ad hoc notion of credibility.

The discrepancy between stylistic consistency and logical consistency is the most nettlesome problem with Perkins's criterion. Films like *The Discreet Charm of the Bourgeoisie* and *Duck Soup* may be logically inconsistent yet purposively or coherently constructed in ways that require this inconsistency, saliently posed, for their overall effect. Such films, therefore, will be stylistically consistent. But in Perkins's system this will entail that they are both credible and incredible. This seems to me to be an unacceptable consequence. Some, less timid than I, might be willing to accept this result, perhaps noting that a great work of art is one that can imbue what is factually incredible with a veneer of credibility. My point, however, was not merely that *The Discreet Charm of the Bourgeoisie* is incredible but that this sense of incredibility is in the forefront of the viewer's experience of the film. Thus, I am arguing that Perkins's ideas about consistency will produce cases where the films must be said simultaneously to engender both feelings of credibility and incredibility via exactly the same set of cinematic devices. Some may still be unmoved, arguing that the way the film is experienced as incredible and credible is noncontradictory. The relevant sense of credibility, they may argue, only pertains to the spectator's apprehension that the blatant inconsistencies are aimed at a coherently planned, aesthetically unified, purposively organized effect. That is, the relevant sense of credibility is not at odds with the fact that the effect aimed at is incredibility. But if this line is taken, why call the state in question credibility? Really, it is a matter of whether the film is aesthetically coherent or makes sense or both. But merely making sense is exactly the opposite of what Perkins has in mind, since he ostensively felt that sense alone—remember his attacks on creationists—is not enough in a film but must be constrained or disciplined by a contrasting commitment to credibility. To summarize Perkins's alternatives we can say that: (1) if his concept of credibility is our ordinary one, then it is inadequate to the task of evaluating film excellence as we know it; or (2) if his criterion is credibility-as-consistency, it is either confounded by cases like *The Discreet Charm of the Bourgeoisie* or, if it is not, then it relies on a notion of stylistic consistency that has little to do with credibility and would better be called coherence—the very category Perkins wants to contrast with credibility. My own suspicion is that Perkins would reject cases such as *Duck Soup* and *The Discreet Charm of the Bourgeoisie*. But then his criterion does not jibe with cases of acknowledged excellence in narrative filmmaking.

It may be that Perkins believes that consistency is an essential causal factor in engendering credibility. Any fictional world that is inconsistent, mixing explicable and inexplicable elements, he may hold, must be experienced as not credible. This is an empirical claim and I have no data to confute it. I can at least imagine, however, a realist filmmaker who might argue that many seeming inconsistencies—ones that are never explained or explainable in terms of the fictional world of the film—were included on the grounds that life is like that and that these inconsistencies in fact make the film more credible, that is, more lifelike. For example, think of a film where the fact that a native village has been invaded is a background detail, and where throughout the film the uniforms, weaponry, and even the language of the invaders change, without explanation, from scene to scene. I see no reason why this aesthetic strategy could not impart a realistic effect. Or, think of a realist film that strives for an authentic, rough-hewn, on-the-spot look by mixing all sorts of film stocks: sometimes the grain is visible, sometimes not; sometimes it is one brand of color film, sometimes another; and sometimes it is black and white. The filmmaker wants to convey the impression that the film has been patched together. Perhaps the film is set in a revolutionary period and the filmmaker imagines that any film made at such a time would have to have been thrown together—for at such moments there is no time for planning and polishing. Suppose this presupposition is not explained in the film. Might not this aesthetic strategy still garner the desired authenticity effect—its stylistic *in*consistency grounding its credibility?

When Perkins speaks of the conditions that make credibility possible, he really seems to have as a root requirement that a given effect should not be jarring in the context of the film it appears in. This is what the talk of consistency finally appears to amount to. On the one hand, this prompts us to ask why effects shouldn't be jarring, if the point they underscore is worth having exclamation marks tagged to it? On the other hand, I wonder whether an effect's jarringness can really be ascertained solely in terms of its consistency with the rest of the given film. For there are devices that are conventions across films; when they appear one and only one time in a given film they do not jar, because the spectator is familiar with them as generic conventions. Flooding a passionate scene with a red light, shooting a riot scene with a wobbly camera, shooting a supernatural scene with a wide-angle lens are some examples. If one of these conventions is employed once in an otherwise nondemonstrably stylized film, the audience need not be jarred by the divergence from the rest of the film, because the generic convention is a well-entrenched one. The spectator does not ask for an explanation derived from the film's story of why the world is red, wobbly, or suddenly distended in these cases. Perkins's idea that the credibility of formal elements hinges on the structure of the film in isolation ignores the fact that films often employ symbolic devices rooted in conventions that have become familiar by appearing across many films.[25]

Under the heading of credibility, Perkins tries to foreclose authorial intrusions into the fictional world of the narrative by invoking the idea of internal consistency. The fictional world is supposed to have its own internal integrity; this is not to be encroached upon by something external to it, like an author's direct comment or aside. Why this should be is not clear. If it is a matter of a jarring effect, then we can ask both (1) aren't jarring effects sometimes aesthetically functional? and (2) aren't many authorial comments—cutting to flying birds to signal freedom, or crashing waves to symbolize inner tumult—so conventional that they jar no one? Furthermore, the use of pictorial elements by the filmmaker does not seem to violate film's basis in photography. So if I flood a scene with red light to symbolize that it is a passionate scene, I am not doing anything more or less peculiar, photographically speaking, than if I shoot the scene with normal lighting.

In elaborating his argument against direct authorial comments, Perkins seems to be ignoring a general fact about how narrative films are often structured—namely, that there are certain moments when authorial comments are particularly appropriate even if the film is predominantly naturalistic. Conventionally, the beginnings and endings of films, as well as the beginnings and endings of scenes, are often mobilized as moments ripe for authorial comment. Comments at these points jar no one—if they are not clumsy—because the practice is familiar. Conversant spectators of films are not shocked by such conventions because, I submit, they do not take narrative films to be replicas of fictional worlds, but, rather, they know that narratives are complex structures of discourse in

25. Indeed, the tendency to treat an artwork in general and a film in particular atomistically is something that often recurs in the type of formalist critical approach Perkins advocates. "Stick to the text" may be thought, that is, to urge the bracketing of conventional and institutional features of artworks.

which direct address is a customary, unproblematic element. Audiences, that is, know that narratives can, in principle, indulge in direct address at any point, and especially at certain privileged junctures like beginnings and endings. And it is this general knowledge of narrative that enables the audience to unflappably accept authorial asides. Of course, I agree that an authorial comment could misfire. It could be overstated, pompous, unintelligible, or possess any of a range of negative attributes. But I do not believe that all of these can be summed up by or reduced to consistency à la Perkins. Likewise, if such authorial comments are jarring, it may be because they lack sufficient dramatic motivation or appear overly redundant or strained or are just plain nonsensical, rather than because they are inconsistent in Perkins's terms. That is, for example, an authorial comment at the end of a film, where such comments are often nested, may not jar because it is consistent with a cross-film convention. Nevertheless, the same comment may still be jarring because of its all-too-blatant obviousness.

To probe some of the difficulties that Perkins's criterion of internal consistency confronts when we consider conventions, let us recall Perkins's objection to *The Criminal*. The background lighting lowers to call attention to the speaker. Perkins complains that this effect is inconsistent with what we are led to expect from this fictional world—for example, we have not been told that there was an electrical failure. Thus, it is argued that this sort of assertive authorial intrusion jars. But is it so jarring? One first notes that this technique is rather like the related conventions of soft-focusing the background or pulling focus from foreground to background, or vice versa. But who ever asks for weather reports from the fictional world to account for these apparent atmospheric changes? One fears that the analogy between variable focusing and variable lighting within a given scene may force Perkins's theory to reject all of the myriad films that employ soft focus and raking focus. Of course, we need not base our argument on this analogy, for the comparable lighting strategy that Perkins decries can also be found in films other than *The*

Criminal, and the device has some pretensions, I think, to being thought of as a convention. And because it is a convention it does not strike me, at least, as jarring. Nor am I persuaded that it is correct to describe it as inconsistent with the fictional world it presents (rather than simply represents) to us. For such a charge entails that every cinematic convention of presenting material should have a naturalistic explanation in terms of the film's fictional world. But this principle is nothing short of absurd. How are fade-outs to be naturalistically explained?

One film that employs a lighting schema comparable to *The Criminal* is Edgar Ulmer's *Detour*. The difference between the scenes from these two films may be that in *Detour* the scene in question comes right at the beginning. When we see this scene in *Detour*, we do not know what the rest of the movie will be like, so the scene cannot strike us initially as inconsistent—for all we know the whole film will be abstractly lit. Also, the scene is not jarring when we first see it because (1) the lighting schema is precedented (for example, *Secrets of a Soul*), (2) equivalent directorial conventions of emphasis are well precedented (for example, irising-in), and (3) the device seems well motivated in the film as an instance of imitative form where the blanking out of the inessential in the scene is a correlative of the character's intense preoccupation. Furthermore, coming at the beginning of the film, the scene seems to be justifiable as a very effective means of plunging the spectator immediately into a story of extreme, unrelenting emotional anxiety. Starting the film off at such a high pitch of psychological intensity sets us up for the despairing tone to follow, even though the abstractionist lighting schema of the opening scenes does not occur outside the framing story.

Since the film neither initially jars nor initially seems inconsistent, the question is whether we must criticize the scene retrospectively, the way Perkins lambasts the comparable scene in *The Criminal*. I don't think we can describe the scene as retrospectively jarring. Either it is jarring when it appears or it is not jarring at all. Is it inconsistent, retrospectively,

234

with the rest of the film?[26] It is inconsistent if that means that the lighting style is never so authorially intrusive again. It is not inconsistent, however, with the tendency toward authorial intrusiveness of the genre of *film noir*, to which *Detour* belongs. Nor is it inconsistent with the tone of the film as a whole, even if it has no explanation in terms of the fictional world of the film. The scene is both aesthetically functional and conventional. The former especially seems to justify the scene. The fact that the lighting has no explanation in the fictional world seems niggling in comparison. And indeed, the fact that the lighting schema is conventional would imply that it really has no need of an explanation in terms of the physical structure of the fictional world. Obviously, the fact that the scene comes at a conventionally privileged moment in the narrative makes its assertive stylization more acceptable than it would be had it come unexpectedly and clumsily in the middle of another scene with different qualities. The general points to be derived from the *Detour* example, however, are that authorial intrusions insofar as they are conventional, do not require explanations in terms of the film's fictional world and are even commendable if they are aesthetically functional. Appearing at certain conventionally privileged moments in a narrative may enhance an intrusive device's acceptability, but if the device is functional and/or consonant with the tone of the rest of the film, it can probably appear anywhere in a film. The conventionality of authorial intrusiveness short-circuits Perkins's explanation-from-the-fictional world arguments. Whatever force is left to Perkins's notion of the inconsistency of the film's address, it has less weight than the question of the aesthetic utility of the device in its filmic context. Perkins's demand for the consistency of address adds up, practically speaking, to the requirement that the authorship of a film be consistently invisible. But the conventionality and potential functionality of authorial intrusiveness are overriding factors that show that Perkins's affection for consistent au-

26. Sophistically we could argue, perhaps, that if there is a problem with *Detour*, it is not with this scene but with the rest of the film, which, because it does not follow up the initial style, is inconsistent with the opening scene. This line, however, would rub Perkins's closet naturalism the wrong way.

thorial invisibility is a preference for a certain style of story-telling, not a standard that all narrative films must abide by. No one would set up consistent invisible authorship as a standard to be met by all novels. Nor should it be made a standard for all narrative films. It should be obvious that consistent invisible narration no more follows from the nature of photography than it does from the nature of the typewriter.

Coherence

According to Perkins, if a film is credible, it is a candidate for commendation. But credibility in itself is not commendatory, it is rather a condition that must be met before a film receives any positive evaluation. That a film is good and the degree to which it is good hinge on how coherent it is. Perkins's examples of goodness in films depend upon the isolation of certain symbolic structures that I have labeled commentative saturations. A film is good if it evinces commentative saturations. A film is good in proportion to the amount of commentative saturations it contains. Most of the commentative saturations Perkins discusses are short-term in the sense that they appear in discrete scenes. This sort of symbolization can be developed on a larger scale, however. That is, it can be extended throughout an entire film. Perkins analyzes the film *Psycho* in terms of a system of symbolic upward and downward movements that is sustained through a multitude of images beginning with the windshield wipers in the flight sequence and extending to the last shot in the film (*FAF*, 107–115). Presumably, the elaborateness of this symbolic structure is a key reason that Perkins believes that *Psycho* is a major film.

The first objection to be made against a coherence criterion of cinematic goodness is that the standard excludes the possibility of certain aesthetic programs. A filmmaker may wish to fashion a fiction in which there is no symbolism whatsoever. Such a filmmaker might denounce symbolism as decorative excrescence. The result of such a project might be a film that is credible but contains no overt symbolism. Such a film cannot be good according to Perkins's criterion. Previously I allied Perkins with a tendency that I called expressive realism. The tendency I am imagining now could be called sheer realism. The point to be made is that Perkins's coherence criterion begs the question in the rivalry between expressive realists and sheer realists. Sheer realism simply cannot be good according to Perkins's criterion. Someone might respond to this by saying that this worry doesn't amount to much because sheer realism is impossible. One cannot drain a narrative film of every bit of symbolism. Filmmakers will always, if inadvertently, make some added, symbolic comment on their fictional worlds in the way they shoot it, frame it, construct it, and block it. I am not sure this is true. Nor am I sure that the *symptoms* we find of filmmakers' attitudes to matters in their fictional worlds are appropriately termed coherences or meanings of the film rather than indexes of something outside the film. Still, there is another issue, namely, that with works of sheer realism it may be the degree to which a film lacks symbolism—even if it does not erase symbolism entirely—that is the measure of its achievement. Perkins has supplied us with no reason to believe that the absence of the type of coherence he enjoys might not be the measure of cinematic goodness for certain kinds of narrative films. One might respond to this by saying that since Perkins is concerned with films as they are, my objection is beside the point because there are no films of sheer realism. But is this true? Rossellini's Medici cycle, along with a number of his other TV films, and perhaps *Toni, Jeanne Dielman,* and certain neorealist films may in fact be examples. As well, even if no one has ever made a perfect example of a sheer realist film, the program of narrative sheer realism has been proclaimed by filmmakers on more than one occasion—one thinks of Zavattini's idea that the ideal neorealist film would depict ninety minutes of a day in the life of an ordinary man. That sounds like sheer realism. Yet such a project would not win merit by Perkins's standard. Perhaps Perkins would say that Zavattini's proposal sounds more like a documentary film, not a fiction. But it is easy to imagine—given the history of film aesthetics—that a filmmaker might attempt to make a symbolically unadorned fiction of ninety minutes of an ordinary person's life. But such a film would never get a positive rating by Perkins's criterion, or at best would get a very low rating—ironically, given Perkins's self-avowed preference for standards that are immanent in the type of films in question—if only because the film fell short of its own ideal and let a little symbolism slip in.

By dealing with coherence solely in terms of commentative saturation, Perkins also ignores the value of certain forms of coherence that are not of the nature of comments or of symbolic elaborations on the themes, characters, and dramas set forth in the plot. Specifically, coherence, as Perkins outlines it, ignores that one source of coherence-value in the film may be the plot itself. That is, we may wish to commend a film for the structure or organization of its plot. "Magnificent plotting" and "suspenseful" are common forms of praise. But it is hard to file these under the type of coherence that Perkins consistently emphasizes in his examples. Perkins only seems to consider plot structure under the rubric of credibility. But since films do not appear to gain merit for being credible, Perkins cannot use this category to commend plotting. Perkins favors, it seems, a kind of image density as the relevant form of coherence in film. That is, he applauds a director's ingenuity in meeting the constraints of realism while at the same time constructing imagery, visual and/or aural, that underlines the ongoing drama. In this sense, the image is dense because it not only denotes and/or presents an action, object, or event in the fictional world, but also at the same time uses the same material to launch a comment about the drama.

In discussing the unity of a film, we can draw a distinction between at least two species of film coherence. We might speak of its coherence over time, the intelligibility of its linear organization. This would be analogous to the developmental structure of a piece of music or a musical form, for example, the sonata allegro. We might dub this, "horizontal coherence." On the other hand, a film might be said to be coherent in virtue of the unity or harmony or integration within one or more of its parts. This would refer to integration above and beyond what the story calls for to tell the spectator what is happening. The trampled hat in *Johnny Guitar* is an example of this. Let us call this, "vertical coherence"—the production of *added levels* of meaning by integrating elements of decor, cinematic presentation, blocking, and the like in a way that yields an added comment upon the story. Most often, vertical coherence is not continuous throughout a film—a symbolic comment is made in one scene and then another is added a few scenes later. Horizontal coherence is generally a property that applies continuously throughout a film that has it. A film can be vertically coherent or have examples of vertical coherence in it and not be horizontally coherent, and vice versa. Perkins's examples are all of the nature of vertical coherence. He does not give us the means to praise fiction films because of their standard horizontal coherence. He does not say how we are to assess the special positive qualities of a given plot. This is yet another ironic failure for Perkins, since he criticizes classical theorists for their obliviousness to narrative form (*FAF*, 24).[27] Nevertheless, Perkins does seem to situate value in the manipulation of aural and visual elements—elements of *mise-en-scène* and of film form—as the only type of coherence he cares about. In this, he appears to ignore plotting in and of itself as a source of value in a film. This is peculiar for a theorist who wishes to isolate the loci of value in films *as we know them*. Many admirable action films—*The Guns of Navarone* for example—will have high values on the horizontal coherence scale but no (or negligible) points on the vertical coherence scale. Perhaps his preference for the vertical scale with its emphasis on *mise-en-scène* and film forms is further evidence of a "cinematic" bias in Perkins.

It might be thought that Perkins's credibility criterion acknowledges narrative structure. If a narrative is inconsistent it will be bad. This, however, misses the thrust of the preced-

27. Whether Perkins's charge here is fair is another matter. Certainly it does not apply to Pudovkin or to Kracauer (who attempted to extend his analysis of the medium to a prescriptive analysis of narrative structure).

ing discussion. Perkins does have a way to deliver negative evaluations of some plots—he can call inconsistent ones bad, although we must remember that he has no way to call boring or redundant ones bad. Yet, and here is the crucial point, Perkins has no means—he provides us with no examples—to commend a film because of the virtues of its plotting. This, it seems to me, is a startling lacuna for a theory of the narrative fiction film as we know it, especially a theory dedicated to telling us what is good in it.

Another problem with the coherence criterion is that Perkins appears to have overlooked the fact that there are many ways in which the types of cinematic elaborations or comments that he prizes can backfire. He seems to believe that as long as a film remains credible, any added, integrated symbolic comment will count as a positive value in the film. But this is clearly false. One film he praises is *Bigger than Life*. He singles out an element of set decor to warrant this commendation. There are travel posters in the background of various shots, and Perkins interprets these as symbols of the central character's desire for escape. In the same film, however, there is another scene in which the central character—driven mad by "wonder drugs"—slams his bathroom cabinet closed. The mirror on it breaks and we are treated to a fractured image of the character—the broken glass standing for the character's "shattered self." I have seen this film with several different audiences, and when this image comes on screen I have heard many spectators greet it with laughter. When I have asked students why they giggled, they have said because it's tacky, cliched, overstated, or pompous. Perkins promotes coherence-constrained-by-credibility as the criterion for goodness in film. But this example shows that there are cases—innumerable in films as we know them—where the kind of symbolism Perkins champions is in fact bad. Such commentative symbols can be gauche, overblown, obvious, strained, unintelligible, distractingly oxymoronic, outlandish,[28] and so on.

28. For another example of this in a film Perkins likes, consider the case of *Carmen Jones*. At the end of one scene a piece of fruit is thrown at a zodiacal chart. This is supposed to communicate ill-fated destiny. It is credible as a

Within Perkins's system we have no way of grounding these negative judgments.

This argument against Perkins's coherence criterion may sound like the argument that Perkins made against montage, specifically with reference to *Triumph of the Will*. In reviewing that case, I exonerated the montagists from Perkins's charges. It may now seem inconsistent that I am attacking Perkins in a way that I don't allow him to attack montagists. But the cases are different. I pointed out that the montagists were not offering theories meant to ground critical evaluations. Perkins, on the other hand, is. And in this respect—that Perkins proffers a criterion of coherence unqualified by constraints other than credibility such that the types of coherent comments he endorses can go wrong—his criterion is incomplete.

One theme that can be summarized from the previous objections is that Perkins's coherence criterion is not rich enough—not rich enough to cover all the excellence that may be found in narrative fiction film and not rich enough or refined enough to exclude bad examples of coherence in fiction film. Perkins expects his coherence criterion to do all the work of assigning goodness to film. But surely there are many ways that narrative fiction films can be good that are not reducible to Perkins's conception of coherence. They may have certain qualities—gracefulness, soberness, sleekness, awesomeness, and the like—to a very intense degree without being distinguished by the types of commentative force that Perkins enjoys. Yet, it may be that the intensity of a given quality is the very reason that we consider the film a good one. *Port of Shadows* and *Man Escaped* come to mind here. Also, Perkins has no way to assess the merit of a film where this is due to various forms of complexity. For example, though Perkins would agree that *Rules of the Game* is a good film, his criterion does not allow us to count among the film's many virtues its rather large cast of diverse central characters deployed in an elaborate, interweaving, multitextured dramatic development. The dramatic complexity of *Rules of the*

gesture in the scene. In some respects the audience understands what it means. But they still cackle because it is such an oxymoronic combination of details to make the point it is meant to.

Game should be listed as one of the film's major merits. But I
see no way that this can be acknowledged under the criterion
of coherence as Perkins construes it.

   This objection can be stated more formally by contrasting
Perkins's criterion of coherence with Monroe Beardsley's
more pluralistic account of the reasons we can give for com-
mending a work of art. Beardsley holds that the reasons we
give for saying an artwork is good can be subsumed under
three canons: unity, complexity, and intensity.[29] Perkins's criterion, at best, can be seen as one, and only one, form of
unity. What of the merits a film may have in virtue of unity
other than (vertical) coherence and in virtue of intensity and
complexity? By relying on one kind of unity as the sole
ground of value in film, Perkins's theory is unduly and un-
realistically restricted. Nor does he give any argument why
only one type of unity should be considered the basis for attributing goodness to film. Yet without such an argument,
we have no reason to believe that films cannot be good in all
the general ways that other artworks can. Of course, in stating this argument I need not be committed to Beardsley's idea
that his three canons subsume *all* the reasons artworks can be
good. But if I leave Beardsley's framework and seek further
reasons for the goodness of artworks—like originality, which
is not subsumable straightforwardly under Beardsley's canons—then the situation only worsens for Perkins. The overall
point, however, remains the same. Coherence or the lack of
it—understood as a narrow criterion applying to the sort of
symbolism Perkins cherishes—is too impoverished to support all the rational evaluations made of narrative fiction films
as we know them.

Coherence and credibility together:
the prospects for cinematic metacriticism

Having examined Perkins's criteria, I have found that they are
not adequate as individual elements of his coordinated standard of evaluation for film. Each criterion individually appears

29. Beardsley, *Aesthetics: Problems in the Philosophy of Criticism*, 466.

to exclude, overlook, or ignore certain established avenues of accomplishment in the fiction film. Moreover, the credibility criterion seems ill-defined in a number of respects. Nor is Perkins's definition of it such that one is able to see the logical connection between credibility-as-consistency and the photographic constituent of the medium, despite the fact that Perkins's argument appears to assume such a connection. The coherence criterion, when seen as a preference for a certain variety of commentative symbolism, excludes several types of excellence in fiction filmmaking, while apparently accepting various functional but artistically dubious symbols as good. And, of course, the coherence criterion is given too much work to do in Perkins's system. It is the sole measure of goodness in films. But it does not track excellence in films that results from linear unity, complexity, intensity, originality, and so forth, but only assigns merit according to the incidence of one form of symbolism. Together, Perkins's two criteria fail because they both allow certain artistic flaws—like the mirror in *Bigger than Life*—to count as merits, and they also disregard certain dimensions of artistic accomplishment in film.

The failure of Perkins's synthetic theory—the name he gives to the credibility-coherence criterion—has a bearing on his attempt to shift film theory away from its traditional pursuits to a reconception of the discipline as the metacriticism *of film*. The failure of the credibility criterion—especially the logical gap between credibility-as-consistency and the photographic constituent of the medium—undercuts Perkins's claim that his standard is film specific. If credibility is not a cinema-specific metacritical category of value, then Perkins has no grounds for believing that his criteria in fact guide the truly medium-specific appreciation of film as film. That is, if Perkins is unable to establish the connection between credibility and photography, then we need not accept his claim to the discovery of criteria uniquely appropriate to film and no other medium. His criteria of value do not represent categories of a metacritical theory peculiarly suited to film. If there is to be a specifically cinematic discipline of metacriti-

cism or a metacriticism exclusively devoted to film evaluation, then it must produce at least one criterion of value that
convincingly pertains to film and film alone. Perkins has not
done this, insofar as credibility as he explicates it has no special ties with photography—indeed, credibility-as-consistency might be offered as a source of value in certain forms of
short-story telling. Credibility is not a necessary condition
for specifically cinematic value.

The arguments pitted against Perkins's coherence criterion
signal a special problem for the idea of a specifically cinematic
form of metacriticism. Coherence, we pointed out, was too
limited a category to canvass all the varieties of excellence in
film. One would have to recognize many other sources of
value in films—linear unity, complexity, intensity, originality, and the like—to ground film criticism comprehensively.
But as these criteria are added to coherence, one begins to ask
whether one is engaged in the metacriticism of film criticism
in particular or the metacriticism of art criticism in general?
That is, it seems the full range of abstractly described excel-
lences that artworks can have should be available for films to
have. But when one adds these criteria to Perkins's category
of coherence, one no longer has a theory of excellence in films
but a taxonomy of artistic excellence. We are no longer speaking of a metacriticism of film but of art. Thus, Perkins's proposal for a new kind of film theory transforms film theory
into a general theory of value in any art. When it comes to
evaluation, there does not seem to be a film-specific discipline
of cinema metacriticism. If Perkins had shown that at least
one criterion of value, like credibility, was an acceptably film-
specific criterion, or even if he had been able to show that his
kind of coherence was the only relevant factor in grading
goodness in film, he could claim to have shown that the theory of evaluative film criticism is different from that of the
other arts. But he fails in both directions. Moreover, the obvious need to add more criteria than Perkins's type of coherence in order to grade films indicates that the metacriticism of
film will exactly mirror the critical categories of art in general. On the basis of this, I conjecture that there is no cinema-

specific discipline of metacriticism—which is yet another reason that Perkins has failed to found a new way of doing film theory. Perkins has not discovered another mode of film theory; he is only asking film theorists to become sensitive to the metacriticism of art in general. At the very least this defeats his own stated goal of finding a way to evaluate film *as film*.

Before concluding, some comment on Perkins's formalism seems in order. The credibility-coherence criterion gauges the value of a film in terms of formal properties exclusively—it is not what the film says, but how it says it, that determines the film's value. Perkins supports this formalism with the following argument:

> If we are to claim an interest in film as film, our judgments must respect the framework within which judgment can sensibly operate, by presenting criteria which are capable of being most fully realized by medium and form.
>
> The weakness of much criticism is its insistence on imposing conventions which a movie is clearly not using and criteria which are not applicable to its form. Useful discussion of achievements within the popular cinema, in particular, has been obstructed by an insistence on the value of the films that are not made, and a corresponding insensitivity to the value of the actual product. Intelligent behavior, sophisticated dialogue, visual elegance, profound investigations of character, sociological accuracy or gestures of compassion are demanded from pictures which quite clearly propose to offer nothing of the sort.
>
> The most destructive version of the process is that in which the film is challenged to reveal instant meaning or to be "thought-provoking." (*FAF*, 188)

The thrust of Perkins's argument is that one should adjust one's criteria of goodness for a particular form solely in terms of the way the form is. The fiction film is not, as a matter of fact, produced to establish moral values, such as compassion or cognitive values, in the form of thought-provoking ideas or to make sociological or psychological investigations of characters. Therefore, these standards should not be brought to bear on fiction films. But there is good in these films, namely, successful cinematographic storytelling, which hinges on solving a formal problem: balancing the recording and creative powers of the medium so that the film carries added meaning while staying within the bounds of realism. Therefore, a formal standard like the credibility-coherence criterion is appropriate for film.

Though I am in many ways sympathetic to some of the aims that Perkins wants this argument to serve, I do not believe that it works. An immediate problem is the factual premise that states that fiction films do not offer the kinds of moral and intellectual values Perkins enumerates. Clearly this is not true of all fiction films. *Grand Illusion*—a film that would accumulate a high rating by Perkins's formula—offers profound insight into characters and acute sociological observation about European society and projects a moral viewpoint that is compassionate, humane, and democratic. If it is objected that this is not an example of popular cinema, we may not only challenge this retort but also point out that for Perkins's argument to really support his formalist criteria against competing intellectual and moral criteria, he must make his case cover the narrative fiction film in general—since that type of film is what he says his criteria are most appropriate to.

But even if *Grand Illusion* is *somehow* disqualified as an example, there are many more mass-distribution problem cases: for instance, *Citizen Kane* and *It's a Wonderful Life*. The former proposes psychological insight, while the latter unmistakably celebrates certain moral values. Nor can Perkins dodge these examples by saying that his factual premise is not a universal statement but only a summary of the general tendency of the fiction film form, especially in the popular cinema. For a great many mass-audience films do quite obviously have moral viewpoints as important if not major components: *The Gold Rush, Intolerance, Young Mr. Lincoln, E.T., Chariots of Fire*—the list could go on and on. Perhaps not all the explicitly espoused moral viewpoints found in fiction films are sophisticated or even acceptable. On the other hand, some are eminently defensible. But whether the moral views promoted by such fiction films are sophisticated or shallow is not the issue. The important point is that Perkins cannot deny that, as a matter of fact, fiction films quite often do propose things like compassion explicitly and that these films do appear to presume that their full appreciation includes appreciation of their moral perspective. Perkins is wrong to think that the type of formalism he favors can be based on the way fiction films present themselves, because many fiction films certainly do not appear to address audiences as if audiences were to evaluate them only against formal rather than, for example, moral criteria.

Nor can Perkins argue that although many films do propose things like moral values as part of what is good in them, since many other films do not do so, the fiction film cannot be said to have morality as a criterion of assessment. For if Perkins makes this move, he will cut the ground from beneath his own coherence criterion, since many fiction films, *Dick Tracy* serials for example, do not contain the sort of coherence that Perkins describes. Hence, if Perkins uses the preceding argument to say moral evaluation is inappropriate to the fiction film form, we may respond with an analogous argument that coherence is inappropriate to the form.

Of course, the general principle behind Perkins's argument—that a form should only be evaluated on its own terms, on the basis of the way the form is—is open to question. Above, I argued that Perkins is wrong about the way he characterizes the fiction film form. But suppose he is right. Wouldn't that only add fuel to the charges that detractors of film could raise? This is where the principle that forms are to be evaluated only on their own terms comes into play. But it can be challenged. Even if a form has its own internal system of evaluation, it may still be compared with other forms of the same general type. And, when Perkins's version of the fiction film, for example, is compared with fictional literature, a detractor of film may feel warranted in saying that the good in fiction film à la Perkins is not very good at all, indeed, that it is a paltry thing. Perkins's criterion, it might be charged, enables us to isolate only the best of a bad thing. The point here is that being good of a kind does not preclude evaluating the kind. And if the kind itself has a low or negative evaluation, it is not contradictory to hold that what is good of a kind is a bad thing.

Furthermore, in the case of the fiction film, it does seem that we should be able to ask Perkins why it has only formal good in it. That is, if we say that an example of a natural kind, a horse for instance, is good of its kind, we are generally satisfied that it is as good as it can be. We don't criticize horses because they are not eloquent but say they are good if they are fleet, powerful, and strong winded. But the case with an artificial kind, like fiction films, is different. We can't redesign the natural kind, the horse, so that it is eloquent, but we could—or, at least, it is in the realm of possibility for some people (for example, movie producers)—reconceive the fiction film so that it is not merely a vessel of formal value but of other value dimensions as well. If it were true that film had only formal value, that would seem to be a contingent and reversible fact. And if it is only a contingent, reversible fact, critics should be able legitimately to ask Perkins why fiction films can't be otherwise. Here Perkins will have to justify the lack of other than formal value in film. This cannot be done by saying that since films are made for a mass audience, they must find the lowest common denominator. At best this is an excuse. It overlooks the facts that (a) films could be directed at special audiences and (b) films not directed at the lowest common denominator have been successful. In any case, my major point is that Perkins cannot ground his formalism on a good-of-its-kind argument when the kind is man-made, because with artificial kinds we may ask why it is that the kind has only that much good in it. Applying this principle to Perkins's recommendation that we attend only to the formal goodness of films because that is the only type of goodness that films as we know them have, we can ask what possible justification there can be for this narrow compass of goodness to which the genre limits itself.

Formalism in film evaluation, such as Perkins's variety, does seem to gain some persuasiveness because it squares with certain of our intuitions. Many films, like works of art in other forms, seem clearly to have merit—to be ingeniously constructed, absorbing, exciting, moving, delightful, and the like—while not having a particularly uplifting moral point of view and without adding new or nuanced ideas to our culture. Perkins wants to defend the goodness of such films. Particularly, he wants to say that these films cannot be deprecated because they are not thought-provoking or morally inspiring. He does this by bracketing all questions of moral and intellectual value in film criticism. This maneuver also insures another goal, which also corresponds with our intuitions. No film can be called good simply because it conveys important values or ideas. That is, a formally ill-constructed film cannot be good because it is on the side of the angels. We might illustrate the results Perkins is searching for by briefly comparing the James Bond film *Moonraker* with Bergman's *Through a Glass Darkly*. *Moonraker*, we might say, is formally good. And it should not be criticized because it is mindless and amoral, if not downright immoral—it is certainly sexist. On the other hand, *Through a Glass Darkly* is a lumbering piece of cinema even though it propounds what many believe to be some very serious and important ideas. It should not be commended because of its intellectual values. It is thought-provoking in literally the worst way. When Perkins uses the term thought-provoking as an insult, he has in mind examples like this—examples where the film is inept but its ineptness is ignored by critics who overvalue it because they are fascinated by its ideas. Insofar as Perkins's formalism supplies us with a rationale for acknowledging that there can be good adventure films that are neither morally nor intellectually stirring, and that there can be ineptly made, pretentious idea-films that are bad, his formalism is tempting. Certainly the old studio wisecrack—if you want to send a message, call Western Union—reflects the sentiment that for a film to be good it must be more than simply "thought-provoking." And on the other hand, there are many examples of popular cinema—for example, *King Kong*—that have stood the test of time and have some claim to our regard as classics, that have little moral or intellectual insight to offer us. Perkins's formalism accounts for these facts.

There are some other intuitions about art, however, that formalism does not account for and that, in fact, it contradicts. We have spoken of formally good films with no ideas and formally inept films with high ideals and ideas. Formalism enables us to say that the former are good and the latter are bad. And this seems in accord with our intuitions. But there is at least another class of pertinent cases, namely, films that are formally good and also contain intellectual value and/ or morally valuable points of view. Formalism will say that such films are good, of course, because they are formally well made. But such films will receive no added points, so to speak, for the intellectual or moral contributions that they make to our culture. This, it seems, runs against the grain of our intuitions. That is, we might feel that the appropriate principle here is something like "If a film is formally well constructed, then it is good, and if it is also intellectually or morally excellent, then it is so much the better." Formalism, of course, denies the second half of this conjunction because the principle it enunciates to commend formal achievements in something like *Moonraker* while condemning the intellectual pretensions of *Through a Glass Darkly* operates by excluding consideration of all intellectual and moral values in film. This does not seem reconcilable with our intuitions.

Grand Illusion is a magnificently constructed film in both its images and its narrative development—it is a good film by any formal standards. And its insight into class and nationalism, as well as its compassion, are indispensable components of what makes it awe inspiring. Most people, *contra* formalism, would, I think, find it simply perverse to exclude the intellectual and moral achievements of *Grand Illusion* from an account of why it is good.

The formalist may respond to this with an attempted compromise, admitting that *Grand Illusion* is good formally, morally, and intellectually but adding that these are three independent types of goodness. That is, the film has several types of goodness in it, but only the formal achievements count in assessing *Grand Illusion* to be *good as film*. The formalist, thus, does not deny the moral and intellectual virtues of *Grand Illusion*. He agrees that we should honor them. We should just not consider them virtues that *Grand Illusion* has as film.

This compromise, however, may be difficult to implement. In a given film it may appear arbitrary and perhaps impossible to tease apart the formal, intellectual, and moral dimensions. For example, considering the last image of *Grand Illusion*, Stanley Cavell[30] comments that by pulling back for a long shot, Renoir is able to underline several of the themes of the film. By shooting the escapees from such a distance, Cavell notes, Renoir allows the white snow to dominate the screen. Our eyes search for the escapees. As we find them, we hear that they have reached safety in Switzerland. We look at the snow. Our eyes cannot find the dividing line between Switzerland and Germany. The snow emphasizes the undisrupted continuity of the natural terrain. The boundary between the two countries cannot be seen—it is effectively invisible. It might be said to be an "illusion." In a film about the illusions of nationalism, Renoir's formal choice in this last image—the extreme long shot of the snowy field—works with particular force to comment on and to sum up visually one of the points of the film. If Cavell's interpretation is persuasive—and I think it is—then this is certainly an exemplary case of the type of coherence that Perkins champions. But most spectators, including in this instance Cavell, believe that the ending of *Grand Illusion* is a good one not only because it is formally ingenious, but because it expresses a profound, morally significant truth—that matters of life and death often revolve around illusions. I do not think that such spectators will be readily convinced by the proposed compromise that the scene is good as film because of its formal solution to the problem of how to sum up the theme while being realistic,

30. Cavell, *The World Viewed*, enlarged ed. (Cambridge: Harvard University Press, 1979), 143–44.

and is *also* good as something else—humanistic political theory?—because of the truth it expresses.

The argument against the proposed compromise might run
as follows: in order to appreciate this scene formally—as well
as most of Perkins's examples—the spectator cannot ignore
the moral and intellectual themes of the film since the formal
coherence in this and many similar cases depends on reinforcing the theme of the work in question.[31] The formal ingenuity
employed in setting out the work can only be recognized by
spectators who, because they in some sense recognize the
theme, are able to recognize the blocking, camera movement,
editing, decor, framing, costume, camera angles, and so on
as economical or otherwise fitting reinforcements of the
theme. If such things as moral and intellectual themes are
often the conditions that make formal coherence both possible and intelligible, they cannot be ignored. This, of course,
will only lead formalists to answer that they are not committed to saying that the moral and intellectual dimension of the
work should be ignored, but only that assessments of the
value of the moral and intellectual themes—as opposed to the
mere recognition of them—can be made independently of assessments of the ingenuity, fitness, and economy of the formal arrangements. But in assessing the value of the formal
arrangement as reinforcing the theme it seems natural to ask
if the theme was worth reinforcing elaborately or even at all.
As long as we must be attentive in some cases to the theme,
in those cases it seems appropriate to make some assessment
of its value. Such an assessment would appear to include an
estimate of the worth of the theme as a justification (or deprecation) of the energy that was spent in the course of formal
invention.

It might be held that themes are inconsequential in making
cinematic evaluations because the themes can be seen as
merely pretexts for formal inventions.[32] But this seems to reverse the means/ends relationship in something like *Grand Il-*

31. A similar argument can be found in David Pole, "Morality and the
Assessment of Literature," *Philosophy* 37 (1962).
32. Russian formalists would be examples here.

lusion. It is plausible to hypothesize not that Renoir adopted an anti-war, anti-nationalism stance in *Grand Illusion* to motivate the formal choices of the last image, but rather that he chose that particular formal arrangement to reinforce the theme.

The anti-formalist might also hold that the effect of an image like that at the end of *Grand Illusion* is, inseparably, a function of both what it says and how it says it. That is, the thrill of this particular moment is an irreducible whole and should not be divided into values of various sorts. The value of the image is grounded in the experience it provokes, and that experience has a holistic character rather than a dualistic one involving a response to the film's message, on the one hand, and to the film as film, on the other. The formal arrangement and the meaning are so intermeshed here that it misrepresents the character of the effect to attempt to bifurcate the image into separate channels of value.

Formalism enables us to rationalize our positive judgments of certain films, like *Moonraker*, that are well made but intellectually and morally impoverished. Formalism also enables us to stand our ground when confronted by intellectually ambitious and morally uplifting films that are formally inane. That is, we can use formalism to reject well-intentioned or pretentiously intentioned but inept films. Formalism accomplishes this by making moral and intellectual value altogether irrelevant to film evaluation. But this, in turn, makes formalism insensitive to the special accomplishments of films that fuse formal excellence with other forms of excellence. It seems to offer a skewed picture of our experience of certain great moments of cinema like the last shot of *Grand Illusion*, or it asks us to reconceive these moments implausibly by reversing the means/ends structure of the event—regarding the theme as a merely convenient excuse for formal invention rather than vice versa.[33]

33. For a fuller account of formalism in relation to the criticism of the arts in general, see my "Formalism and Critical Evaluation" in *The Reasons of Art*, edited by Peter McCormick (Ottawa: University of Ottawa Press, 1985), 327–35.

Summary and Conclusions

Undoubtedly, V. F. Perkins would object to his inclusion in this book. For *Film as Film* presents itself as an alternative to and a replacement for classical film theory. It endeavors to shift the focus of film theory from questions of medium specificity—a mark of classical film theory—to a concern with the foundation of film criticism. Perkins wants to transform film theory into a species of metacriticism, specifically the metacriticism of film, that, in turn, eschews essentialism, notably of the mediumistic variety. Perkins narrows the compass of his attention to fiction film, and he attempts to erect a specifically filmic metacriticism upon the notion of a filmed fiction.

One purpose of this chapter has been to demonstrate that, appearances to the contrary, *Film as Film* is not really a departure from classical film theory. At root, Perkins's critical canons—most importantly credibility—are derived from medium-specificity considerations, as one might predict of a program dedicated to discerning evaluative criteria for film qua film. Admittedly, Perkins's componential view of the nature of the medium is more complicated than that of his predecessors; he sees the medium as having at least two (potentially conflictive) essential features. Though this is a more generous essentialism, essentialism it still is.

Perkins's mediumistic bent is evident in the ontological characterization of filmed fictions that he offers. These films are said to be *recordings* of fiction, where recording is thought of as connected to an essential constituent of film. I question this characterization not only for its essentialist bias, but also because it sounds metaphysically fishy to suppose one could record a fiction: it would probably be easier to see a dream walking.

Perkins's closest essentialism does enable him to construct critical standards that, in concert, would apply distinctly to film rather than to novels and operas and so on. The problem, however, is that Perkins's evaluative criteria are not comprehensive enough; they do not capture the extent of excellence and awfulness in the range of even the types of films Perkins intends to theorize about. To comprehend the dimensions of value Perkins's criteria exclude, I argue that one would have to abandon the search for a uniquely filmic metacriticism (a displaced version of the medium-specificity prejudice) and instead opt for a generalized metacritical investigation of art. That is, Perkins's presuppositions that there is a specifically filmic canon of critical criteria and that film theory can be reconstrued to be the metacriticism of film *as film*, are misguided. For if there is no specifically filmic form of metacriticism, it is not something film theory could be.

Like Bazin's and Arnheim's, Perkins's film theory appears to be an implicit defense of a particular style of filmmaking—in Perkins's case, expressive realism. Perhaps there are expressive realists in every period of filmmaking, and almost certainly in every period from roughly 1910 onward. This type of filmmaking flourished especially from the forties through the sixties and perhaps is returning again in the work of our presiding movie brats. Many of Perkins's examples come from American fiction films of the fifties and early sixties, and his theory is especially useful for disclosing overlooked loci of value in these works. Perkins's book might even be reconceived as a guide to the appreciation of films of this period. Some of the theoretical shortcomings of Perkins's work, like those of Arnheim's and Bazin's, can be recuperated as helpful recommendations about how their preferred styles of cinema are to be taken.

Having seen the tendency of classical film theory to function as covert critical advocacy, one may wonder whether there can actually be an area of enquiry called film theory. One may feel that the record shows that every attempt in this area will finally turn out to be the elaboration of some period-specific tastes and perhaps of even more eccentric ones.

Even if there may be a tendency in this direction in classical film theory, due to its emphasis on the essential nature of the medium rather than on the uses to which the medium is put, there seems to be no reason to think that all film theory must follow suit. Classical film theory tends toward the hypostatization of period-specific preferences by pursuing what might be called the Theory of Film, a series of observations coordinated by the type of structure outlined in the introduction of this book and deployed in succeeding chapters. Moreover, that type of theorizing is liable to (not guaranteed to) incline one toward identifying the determinant characteristic of film in terms of an essence, often mediumistically construed. As was suggested in this chapter, however, the enterprise of film theory need not be identified with the ambition of constructing the Theory of Film. Earlier, I suggested that the activity of film theory might construe film theorizing to be a matter of constructing theor*ies* about film—for example, theories of film suspense, of camera movement, of editing, of movie music, of the avant-garde, of the Art Cinema—rather than of constructing the Theory of Film. Such small-scale theories—such as a theory of the structure and function of the sight gag as it characteristically occurs in movies—need not invoke notions of the essence of film or the nature of the medium. And, more importantly, such a theory need not be a covert endorsement of one sort of filmmaking over others. Such piecemeal theorizing is still theorizing, as long as it is of sufficient generality, and is still *film* theory, as long as it is about some phenomenon relevant to cinema in any of its multiple dimensions.

Piecemeal theorizing need not be committed one way or another about whether there is, ultimately, a unified Theory of Film. Thus, pursuing film theory under the dispensation of piecemeal theorizing may be a useful heuristic device for avoiding elevating one's taste as theory.

It may appear that appending this advertisement for piecemeal theorizing at the end of a chapter about V. F. Perkins is unfair, since he announces that his theory is restricted to fiction film. Nevertheless, I hope that I have shown that medium-specificity biases creep into it. This shows that small-scale theories, as well, are not immune to mediumistic essentialism. I do still feel, however, that piecemeal theorizing about the multiple dimensions of film is less likely to invite essentialism than the project of the Theory of Film, for the latter project aims at the unification of the field, and essences are just the sort of theoretical gambits that are especially suited to that kind of work. On the other hand, even if Perkins veers toward essentialism, he, more than any other recent film theorist, has at least attempted to deal rigorously with the issue of film evaluation, an admittedly difficult but finally unavoidable feature of the film world.

Conclusion

The Question
of Essentialism

—

In this book I have been concerned with evaluating a series of arguments regarding the nature of film art, film expression, film representation, film realism, film criticism, filmed fiction, and so on. Although my primary interest has been in issues, I have arranged my topics in historical sequence. Rudolf Arnheim, the focus of Chapter One, is a representative of an early type of film theorizing—what I have called, generously, the silent-film paradigm. Proponents of this approach also include the Soviet montagists of the twenties. This line of silent-film theorizing emphasizes that film is not a mere record of reality but instead expressively manipulates it. In the chapter on Arnheim, I have paid special attention to his notion that film art arises only when filmmakers exploit medium-specific limitations in order to generate cinematic expression. Examining this proposition led me to the discussion of such general aesthetic questions as "What is the nature of the relation of a medium to an artform?" and "What is expression?"

André Bazin, the subject of Chapter Two, represents a reaction to, again generously, the silent-film paradigm. He is the major advocate of what can be referred to expansively as the sound-film paradigm. This perspective stresses the importance of the recording dimension of film and regards cinematography as the essential attribute of film. Adherents of the sound-film paradigm champion realism as the preferred style of film. In the chapter on Bazin, I have confronted the question of whether cinematic representation is a unique form of representation, and I have made an original proposal about the application of realism in aesthetic contexts.

Lastly, I have discussed V. F. Perkins. He is the most contemporary of the theorists that I canvass. He rejects both the silent-film paradigm and the sound-film paradigm and seeks to construct a new form of film theory that combines elements of the earlier paradigms. Perkins attempts to reject what he regards as the most ingrained tendency of previous film theory: a bias toward essentialism that attempts to deduce stylistic canons from the specific, identifying features of the film medium. In contrast, Perkins advocates that film theory become a species of metacriticism, setting forth general standards of evaluation for fiction films. For Perkins, this enterprise remains film theory, rather than the metacriticism of art in general, because Perkins believes that the evaluative standards that he produces derive from the specific peculiarities of filmed fictions. Needless to say, Perkins's reliance on the idea that *filmed* fiction has a special nature causes difficulties for his anti-essentialism. In that chapter, I was concerned with general questions of evaluation—such as the question of formalism—and with the specific issue of filmed fiction.

I have set out the theories of Arnheim, Bazin, and Perkins in a way that underlines that each successive theorist can be seen as responding to, answering, and refuting the earlier ones. Classical film theory has developed as a very coherently structured, historical dialogue where the dialectical moves and counter-moves stand out in sharp relief. By placing these theorists and the issues they raise within the evolving conversation in which they participated, what these theorists are saying as well as why they are saying it is clarified. A historical approach has the heuristic and expository value of showing what is at stake in these theoretical debates by revealing the presuppositions underlying the discourse. Historical exposition serves the purpose of focusing the issues. It is not undertaken here as simply an exploration in the history of ideas.

The bulk of this book has been preoccupied with the detailed contestation of the central tenets of Arnheim, Bazin, and Perkins. This enterprise has been joined because in these theorists one finds the expression of a great many of the prejudices and presuppositions that suffuse the theoretical and critical analysis of film. Admittedly, in the course of this work, the argumentation, at times, becomes intricately concerned with what may seem to be minute aspects of the debate. It may have appeared at times that the forest was missed not only for the sake of the trees but even for the sake of the leaves. So in concluding this book, it seems appropriate to end with a generalization about the kind of classical theory I have been examining at length.

Looking at Arnheim, Bazin, and Perkins in depth reveals something common to their approach. Each of these classical theorists, in different ways, is committed to the belief that certain features specific to the medium of film can be characterized theoretically so that the discussion of these medium-specific features can be parlayed into guidelines or principles of aesthetic decision making. Arnheim believes that cinema has certain medium-specific limitations that should serve as the basis for generating specifically cinematic expression. Bazin believes that cinematic/photographic representation is a distinct, unique mode of representation that, moreover, determines the proper direction of cinematic stylization—what I refer to as "spatial realism" throughout the text. Perkins believes that filmed narratives have special characteristics that, in turn, lead him to propose what he presents as a medium-specific mode of evaluating films. In their belief that certain specific features of the film medium should provide the basis for an aesthetic theory of film, Arnheim, Bazin, and Perkins evince the dominant tendency of film theory, at least as that area of study had crystallized before the sixties and the wide-scale prominence of semiotic and poststructural theorizing. Moreover, there is reason to believe that the shared approach common to this mode of theorizing is severely limited.

The classical tradition of film theory that Arnheim, Bazin, and Perkins exemplify emphasizes the nature of the medium as finally fundamental in our thinking about film. In this view, film art, film representation, filmed fiction, and film criticism each must be distinguished from its counterpart in other arts. Furthermore, these distinctions are based on medium-specific features. Different theorists in this tradition pick out different medium-specific features as central to our thinking about film. The high degree of disagreement about which set of these features should be relevant, should immediately alert us to the probable inadvisability of this way of thinking. For in this tradition of film theory, the explanatory buck stops when a claim about film can be connected to claims about some preferred feature "specific to the film medium." But we should want to know what principles direct the theorists to choose the very medium-specific features they stress in the formation of their theories of film. What I would claim we find as a common problem in the "specificity" approaches of Arnheim, Bazin, Perkins, and the classical tradition they exemplify, is their failure to appreciate that it is their prior commitments concerning the use, value, or role of cinema that lead them to focus upon the characteristics of ˉhe medium that have come to preoccupy them. In terms of the framework for reading film theory I set forth in the Introduction, I might make this point by saying that film theorists often do not pay enough attention to answering explicitly the question of the role, value, or use of film, especially in regard to the way that this question has a normative dimension. These theorists do not acknowledge the centrality of this normative dimension in their thinking and instead act as though they have discovered *the* medium-specific feature— the very fact—upon which our thinking about film should be based. But they forget that prior commitments have led them to select those features of the medium upon which they concentrate. Thus, this brand of film theory becomes mired in arguments about the *nature* of the medium when it may be more advisable to discuss the reasons and grounds underlying different *uses* of the medium.

A related way of making this point is to underscore that film—like photography and video—is a medium that was invented in human memory and that people self-consciously decided to use to make art, to make fiction, to make representations, and so on. These activities—artmaking, fiction making, representing—predated the existence of the film medium as well as (obviously) film art, film representation, filmed fiction, and so on. Film came to be modified, adapted, and developed to serve these already entrenched cultural uses or purposes most often, at least initially, through a process of imitation. Filmmakers imitated period-specific notions of art, as I stress in Chapter One. In regard to the question of representation, filmmakers most often do not emphasize the causal dimension of cinematographic representation—which would make physical portrayal the major form of cinematic representation—but rather, as I argue in Chapter Two, filmmakers embrace nominal portrayal (generally for the purposes of making fiction) as the dominant form of cinematic representation. And, as I point out in the section on Perkins's *Film as Film*, the idea that there is a uniquely cinematic form of fiction, distinct from other types of fiction, may well be incoherent, just as the notion that there is a special discipline of film criticism with a unique set of canons of evaluation is suspect.

Film art, film representation, film fiction, and film criticism develop under the aegis of pre-existing cultural enterprises: art, representation, fiction, and aesthetic criticism. The film world develops, at first and often thenceforth, through a process of emulating these pre-existing practices. The proponent of medium-specificity will, of course, add that film emulates these pre-existing practices on *its own terms*. But what is difficult to establish here is exactly what we are to identify as *film's terms* since film's potential only emerges by using cinema to achieve pre-existing aims.

In contradistinction to the type of classical theory practiced by Arnheim, Bazin, and Perkins, I believe we may learn much more about film by focusing not on some hypostatized medium-specific features but on the uses to which film is put. These will (as they have in the past) determine what aspects of the medium are selected for emphasis.

Throughout this book, we have seen that film theorists are least explicit about the reasons underlying their commitments concerning the role or use of film. More may be learned about film, however, if we spend more energy clarifying the various answers we wish to give to the question of its role or use than if we continue the quest for the central medium-specific features of cinema. That is, we may learn more about cinema by thinking about fiction than about *filmed* fiction and by thinking about representation rather than *cinematic* representation. "*Use* rather than *medium*" might be the slogan of our approach. If this is criticized by the charge that such a program is not film-specific, the answer, in one sense, is "of course." But the reason for this is that it is the use of the medium that historically gives the medium its shape and its significant features their pertinence.

In emphasizing the relatedness of film to larger cultural projects, I am not claiming that there are no differences between film and the other media in which those projects are pursued, but only that in comprehending film as art, as representation, as fiction, and so on, the conceptual frameworks of those institutionalized endeavors are more fundamental than questions of medium-specificity. Maintaining this line of approach puts me at odds with the classical tradition of film theory exemplified by Arnheim, Bazin, and Perkins. Of course, I cannot claim to be the only contemporary researcher who is disenchanted with this feature of classical film theory. In the seventies, the form of Marxist-psychoanalytic-semiotic film theory that became popular also often *appears* to criticize the classical film theorists' obsession with medium-specificity.[1] I have criticized the Marxist-psychoanalytic-semiotic alternative elsewhere;[2] and I am presently engaged in completing a book-length study of its failings.[3] In opposition to both that research program and the alternative provided by classical film theory, I am interested in continued research that involves directly addressing questions about the *uses* cinema serves—art, fiction, narrative, representation, nonfiction, and so on—at the level of abstraction found in philosophical aesthetics, to see how strongly defended, fully explicit, and reasoned clarifications of these concepts can be applied to the recurring issues of film theory. The present work has been propaedeutic to this larger project.

1. The qualification—"often appears to"—is added to the sentence above because despite their avowals of anti-essentialism, contemporary film theorists often endorse essentialist approaches. This is quite evident in the title essay of Christian Metz's *The Imaginary Signifier* (Bloomington: University of Indiana Press, 1981). For criticism of Metz's methodological essentialism, see my review of *The Imaginary Signifier* in the *Journal of Aesthetics and Art Criticism* 19 (Winter 1985), 211–16. Metzian methodological essentialism is also aped outright in John Ellis's *Visible Fictions* (London: Routledge and Kegan Paul, 1983).
2. See my "Address to the Heathen," *October*, no. 23 (Winter 1982), 89–163; and my "Reply to Heath," *October*, no. 27 (Winter 1983), 81–102.
3. Noël Carroll, *Mystifying Movies: Fads and Fallacies in Contemporary Film Theory* (New York: Columbia University Press, forthcoming).

Index

Library of Congress Cataloging-in-Publication Data

Carroll, Noël (Noël E.)
   Philosophical problems of classical film theory / Noël Carroll.
    p. cm.
  Includes index.
  ISBN 0–691–07321–x (alk. paper)
   1. Motion pictures—Philosophy. I. Title.
PN1995.C357 1988
791.43'01—dc 19   87–31155 CIP

Noël Carroll teaches philosophy at Wesleyan University.